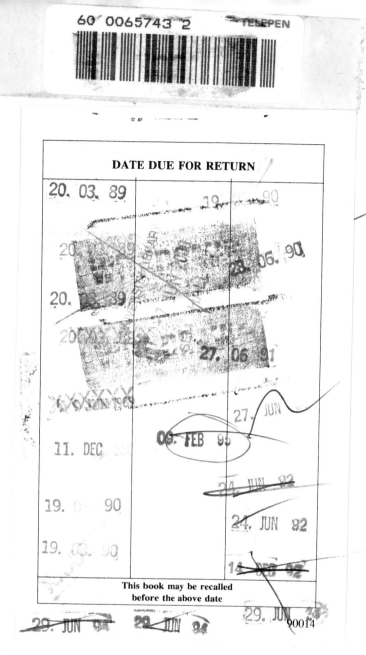

DATE DUE FOR RETURN

20. 03. 89	19. 90	
20. 89		23. 06. 90
20. 89		
20. 89	27. 06. 91	
XXXXXX		27. JUN
11. DEC	09. FEB 9	
19. 90	24. JUN 92	
19. 90	24. JUN 92	
		14. DEC 92

This book may be recalled
before the above date

SOCIAL PATTERNS
IN
CITIES

INSTITUTE OF BRITISH GEOGRAPHERS
SPECIAL PUBLICATION

No. 5 March 1973

LONDON
INSTITUTE OF BRITISH GEOGRAPHERS
1 KENSINGTON GORE SW7
1973

Printed in Great Britain by Alden & Mowbray Ltd
at the Alden Press, Oxford

Contents

iii

Preface

THE fifth volume in the Institute's series of *Special Publications* contains nine papers on an urban geographical theme, contributed by members of the Institute's Urban Study Group. The idea of such a collection of papers was put forward as long ago as 1969, and several members of the Study Group have been actively involved since then in encouraging potential authors and compiling the set of papers from which the present articles have been selected. The Editors are grateful to the compilers and to the necessarily anonymous referees who advised on the final selection.

C. EMBLETON, Hon. Editor
C. E. EVERARD, Hon. Assistant Editor

Foreword

B. T. ROBSON

Lecturer in Geography, University of Cambridge

URBAN geography in Britain was long dominated by an interest in morphology; in the layout of streets and road patterns, the evolution of the physical form of cities, the details of individual buildings. The great strengths of this tradition were its sensitivity to the variety and uniqueness of towns and its emphasis on a historical, or evolutionary, approach. It had, at the same time, inevitable dangers: it tended to divert attention away from more functional aspects of towns, from the ways in which they 'perform'; it also delayed the realization that towns are inhabited by people. The advent of a distinctly *social* urban geography has been very recent. Its eventual appearance awaited the re-discovery of the writings of the human ecologists of Chicago who had broached most, if not all, of the topics which have subsequently been tackled by urban social geographers: the spatial structure of residential populations, the distribution of social pathologies, and the segregation of social groups.

The theory underlying such interests has been but weakly developed; rather than theory, it would be true to say that there are various well-attested empirical generalizations which have formed the springboard of urban social geography. Most of these have been provided by factorial ecology which has been the meteoric growth node of the field. The ecology of cities in modern industrial societies suggests that urban populations are structured spatially along a small number of dimensions: occupation is one; stage in the family life-cycle is another. In addition to these two 'universal' dimensions, there are others which appear to be more specific: ethnic differentiation and differences in types of housing tenure, for example, may form important additional dimensions in particular cities or particular societies. There have also been suggestions that these various dimensions form regular and predictable aggregate spatial patterns—that occupational differences may be distributed in sectors radiating out from the central city, and that life-cycle differences may form concentric bands around the city centre with younger households being found in the more peripheral bands.

Other, rather primitive, generalizations have come from more historical studies. Cities have changed as technology and the structure of social and political power have altered over time: the relative attractions of central and peripheral locations have changed, as have the overall physical form of cities and the nature of segregation within them. Such changes have given rise to various evolutionary typologies—for example, 'pre-industrial', 'industrial', 'post-industrial'—which, if they have any meaning, are reflected in the different social structures of each category. Hand-in-hand with technological changes, new types of predominant social relationships have emerged: formal associations and interest groups have replaced the more all-embracing informal community groupings whose residues in Bethnal Green so delighted sociologists in the 1950s.

Such aggregate generalizations have provided valuable guidelines, but have suggested relatively little of the processes by which ecological patterns are produced, altered or maintained. It is partly in response to this need to understand processes that urban social geography can, at present, be seen as undergoing a phase of re-evaluation which might be seen as developing along three fronts: a change in scale from aggregate to individual; a widening of the areas and periods from which case studies are selected; and a more conscious incorporation of formal sociological concepts.

The change of scale in such work has introduced a new dimension to geographical studies which have hitherto been restricted essentially to aggregate analyses. The new emphasis on the individual can be seen in much of the work on behaviour and perception which, as yet, has added more jargon than insight to urban geography. The chief unresolved difficulty appears to be how one can make general statements from individual data without simply arriving back at the restrictive assumptions used to characterize aggregate behaviour; and also how one can isolate 'pure' behaviour from revealed behaviour which is so constrained by the unique set of opportunities open to an individual. One avenue which does appear to offer considerable potential in throwing light on the structure of residential areas, however, is the study of mobility at the level of the individual household. Since the aggregate ecology of cities is the product of the innumerable moves of individual households each making locational decisions, the question arises as to whether the importance of occupation and stage in the family life-cycle at an aggregate level is the product of a parallel importance of income, status and space requirements for individual households making such locational decisions. The eventual location of different types of households must be the product of the intersection of housing supply and demand: the decisions of builders and developers to provide housing of a specific type at a particular location; the pattern of housing vacancies; the evaluation of these housing opportunities by individual households; and the decision by the household to move to one or other of the potential locations or to remain in its original location. Only by tying together the aggregate patterns of social ecology and the characteristics of such residential mobility can one hope to translate the findings of factorial ecology into more meaningful understanding of the processes which underlie them.

The second approach to testing and reformulating ideas in urban social geography has been the widening of its field of coverage. By studying areas outside the ambit of the western industrial society, the universality of the generalizations has been questioned. The concept of 'culture', so important and yet so difficult to specify, has traditionally been seen as an intervening variable which distorts the 'normal' pattern of urban society. Yet who, having experienced Chicago, would claim that it provides a test of normality? As with the much earlier studies of Latin American cities which threw doubt on the generality of the ideas of the classical human ecologists, so the present studies of cities in culture areas outside Europe and North America are adding greatly to the awareness of the diversity of urban society, even though they have not yet led to convincing typologies of that variety. Similarly, the studies of urban social structure over time are eroding the neat historical typologies which have long been a convenient stock-in-trade of urban students. But, as the assumed distinctions between such categories as 'pre-industrial' and 'industrial' cities have become blurred, so are we learning more about the relationships between the structure of social, political and economic power on the one hand and the social and spatial structure of urban populations on the other.

The third avenue of approach has involved the more sensitive incorporation of sociological theory into the analysis of urban spatial structure. Much of the existing urban social geography has been underlain by only the crudest of social theory. The very interpretation of so central a concept as social class, for example, has left much to be desired; certainly the implicit assumption that one might throw light on social stratification by examining the spatial structure of occupational groups does less than full justice to the sophistication—or, at times, obfuscation—of sociological writing on social hierarchies. The aim in this more explicitly sociological urban geography is to tease out the relationship between social and spatial theory: while both are somewhat imprecisely specified, the argument—best exemplified in the work of the radical geographers of North America—is that there are aspects of the spatial location of social and physical phenomena within cities which can illuminate the life styles of, and the relationships between, social groups. Segregation of social groups is only one of many such connections; the provision of hospitals, schools and other elements of social welfare would be other equally tangible aspects. To what extent does the spatial patterning of such phenomena reinforce and to what extent is it predicated upon the existing structure of power and control within urban society?

The essays in this volume can be taken as representing some of these avenues of research. Three are concerned with factorial ecology: this is the tail, perhaps, of the meteor which, more than any other approach, has done so much to awaken geographical interest in the social structure of towns. A further essay looks at residential mobility, representing the natural extension of this concern into a more individual scale of study. Three are concerned with aspects of the segregation of various social groups and a fourth examines social networks. All represent that more conscious incorporation of social concepts which is needed to add cutting edge to any geographical analysis of social characteristics. Two are focused on cities in the developing world and a third turns to an English town in the nineteenth century, representing the extension of concern into areas and times outside the narrow lens of the mid-twentieth-century western world.

The thrust of these studies is more empirical than theoretical. If it has been a strength of British urban geography that its concern has been with the detail of individual towns, a phase of re-evaluation is an appropriate period in which to test that strength. If the ultimate goal is to develop general theory as a baseline for urban geography, it is from inductively-derived studies of individual towns that a stronger deductive theory might best emerge.

Religious residential segregation in Belfast in mid-1969: a multi-level analysis

M. A. POOLE

Lecturer in Geography, New University of Ulster, Coleraine

AND F. W. BOAL

Senior Lecturer in Geography, The Queen's University, Belfast

Revised MS received 30 August 1972

ABSTRACT. Religious residential segregation in Belfast has received prominent public attention because of its political significance amidst the recent disturbances in the city. Both the layman's perception of such segregation and existing academic research are, however, inadequate; the spatial dimensions of the city's religious composition, and their variation with the level of investigation, need to be systematically analysed.

The analysis, based on information on religious composition collected by the authors, could only proceed after five basic decisions had been made. These concerned (1) the choice of households as data elements; (2) the choice of the County Borough as the data set; (3) the choice of mid-1969 as the time period; (4) the choice of a binary division into Catholic and Protestant as the appropriate religious classification. Finally, it was decided to conduct the analysis at three levels of scale, namely, streets, tracts and a set of sectors and rings.

The sub-sets of data, at each level of scale, are classified according to their religious composition, and their frequency and spatial distributions are described. The pattern for Belfast as a whole is summarized at each scale by indices of relative dominance and of dissimilarity to measure respectively the degree of dominance and of segregation present. The intra-urban variation in the intensity of segregation is then analysed at the intra-tract level by means of indices of dissimilarity and at the inter-tract level by means of probabilistic share indices.

Finally, both the degree of segregation and the spatial pattern of the distribution of Catholics in Belfast are compared, using indices of centralization and map inspection, with corresponding findings for ethnic groups in cities elsewhere.

IN 1965 K. E. and A. F. Taeuber pointed out, in their analysis of negro residential segregation in the United States, that even the most casual observer could not fail to detect negro areas and white areas in almost all American cities with a significant negro population[1]; 2 years later, A. H. Pascal introduced his analysis of the same phenomenon by stating that his subject was a highly familiar one to newspaper readers as a result of its acute political relevance as a major component of the American race problem.[2]

Similarly, even the stranger visiting Belfast, though he might find it difficult to distinguish Catholic and Protestant people on the basis of visual appearance, would still, in many parts of the city, be able to recognize whether he were in a Catholic or a Protestant area. The nature of the local wall-slogans, for example, would represent an almost infallible guide at any time and, if the stranger's visit happened to occur during the weeks immediately preceding or following 12 July, he could hardly fail to notice either such street decorations as flags, bunting and painted kerbstones adorning extensive Protestant areas, or evidence of the commemorative parades and bonfires in these areas at this time of the

I

year.[3] The Catholic population, too, indulges in street decorations, bonfires and parades, especially to celebrate the Easter rising of 1916 and the Feast of the Assumption on 15 August. Moreover, since 1969, many of the boundaries between rival Catholic and Protestant areas have been clearly demarcated by the British army's 'peace line' barricades erected at potential flashpoints.[4]

The Belfast resident himself, of course, has an even keener awareness of the religious structure of the individual parts of his city, for, whereas the stranger's knowledge is likely to be based almost entirely on landscape manifestations, the local resident extensively supplements what he sees by what he hears and, indeed, by all the information he has accumulated from a multitude of sources throughout his years of living in this acutely religion-conscious city. The intense consciousness of the significance of the spatially varying religious structure of the city is indicated, for example, by the constant recurrence of allusions to this theme in Martin Waddell's novel on the 1969 crisis in Belfast.[5] Moreover, the profound consequences of the perception of religious structure on the behaviour of people has been stressed by F. W. Boal, who illustrated his point both by quoting from the autobiography of a local Protestant who rather flamboyantly emphasized his fear of going into and across Catholic territory, and also by presenting the results of movement analysis from a questionnaire survey which demonstrates forcibly the intense degree of segregation of activity between the two religious groups.[6]

Since 1968, the existence of residential segregation in Belfast, if not the precise detail of its spatial pattern, has become common knowledge to millions of people who not only do not live in the city, but who have not visited it and, indeed, will never do so. The reason, of course, is that the politico-sectarian problems of Northern Ireland have again erupted in the face not only of the British government but of every single resident of the province, in somewhat the same way as the American race problem did earlier in the 1960s. And, just as the world's mass media industry swooped in to give coverage to housing segregation in American cities and every other facet of this problem for as long as it was newsworthy, so the same industry has, since 1968, lavished considerable attention on the troubles in Northern Ireland and has frequently alluded, albeit in a necessarily over-simplified way, to the residential segregation of the two basic religious groups in the province, especially in Belfast.

The significance of residential segregation in the context of the politico-sectarian problems of Belfast stems not so much from allegations of unfair discrimination, either in the allocation of public housing or in the functioning of the private housing market, as from two other problems, one short term and the other more long term. First, the immediate problem of physical violence and conflict is, with the exception of bomb explosions and armed robberies, strongly concentrated in the highly segregated parts of the city: conflict between the two religious groups tends to take place at the boundaries where segregated Catholic and Protestant areas adjoin, and conflict between either religious group and the security forces usually occurs in the heartland of a segregated area occupied by the civilian group involved.[7] Secondly, the long-term task of attempting to achieve social integration between the two religious groups is clearly rendered extremely difficult by the lack of residential mixing which would provide at least one opportunity for people from the two sides of the religious fence to meet and interact in a non-violent way. Without such residential and social mixing, there is little contact between the two religious groups but a high level of contact within each group, thus consolidating each group's solidarity and conformity and accentuating the differences, both actual and perceived, between the two groups.[8]

These comments must not be interpreted as necessarily implying that the authors believe that a policy of residential mixing should immediately be implemented. There are enormous practical problems, resulting especially from the physical and psychological security which is provided, particularly at times of violent conflict, by living in an area occupied almost entirely by one's own religious group[9]; and it has been argued, too, that segregation is only a symptom, rather than a fundamental cause, of the conflict.[10] Moreover, it has even been suggested, in the context of ethnic problems in the United States and Britain, that a policy of 'ghetto enrichment' is preferable to one of attempted dispersal.[11] However, it is clear that there is some form of functional relationship between religious residential segregation and the politico-sectarian problems of Belfast, and this both explains the attention given by the mass media to the existence of such segregation since the recent troubles began and also underlines the importance of learning more about the degree and pattern of segregation as an aid both to understanding the politico-sectarian problem and to designing a public policy towards segregation.

It may perhaps be suggested, however, that enough is already known of the nature of religious residential segregation in Belfast, and the preceding paragraphs have indeed demonstrated that (1) visual observation in the city itself, (2) experience learned through living there, and (3) attention to the outpourings of the mass media have all combined to make knowledge of the existence of such segregation very widespread indeed. However, the quantity and quality of that knowledge varies across an extremely broad spectrum from individual to individual, depending especially on which of the three types mentioned is the dominant source of information; moreover, it is almost certainly true that, with the possible exception of some members of the security forces and a few activists in certain political parties who jealously guard their information, very few people have an accurate, detailed knowledge of the religious structure of substantial sections of the city beyond their own neighbourhood. What knowledge people do have of the city as a whole is at a very general level and is probably most accurate for those areas which are either very Catholic or very Protestant, partly because these are the areas which can be identified by visual observation and partly because it is these areas which have gained most notoriety as a result of sectarian conflict. Indeed, amidst all the discussion of segregated areas, it is easy to forget the fact that there are mixed areas in certain parts of the city. It is true that previous academic research has described the pattern of religious structure in the city as a whole, mostly using census information, but even the most recent of this research describes the situation as it existed over 20 years ago; and, in any case, these analyses, though pioneer work of outstanding quality, are insufficiently detailed or sophisticated for the needs of today.[12]

It is with the purpose of helping to provide a detailed, up-to-date and comprehensive picture of the religious structure of Belfast as a whole, including an indication of the location and character of mixed areas as well as of segregated areas, that this paper has been written. Its intention is to fill part of the general gap in knowledge which inhibits objective discussion of the social problems of Northern Ireland, though this dearth of information should soon be partly remedied by the work of many researchers who appear to have been attracted to the province by the recent troubles.[13] This statement of the general objective of the paper should be clarified by emphasizing at the outset that it is not intended, in the pages which follow, to explore, either theoretically or empirically, the causes of segregation.[14] This paper will therefore not attempt to make recommendations in relation to public policy towards segregation, for realistic proposals must await the outcome of research on its complex causes.

The objective of this paper is simply to describe cartographically and quantitatively the pattern of religious structure as part of the necessary prelude both to a subsequent analysis of process and to the eventual listing of policy recommendations. However, it is hoped that the systematic description of this pattern will, in turn, serve three further functions. It is designed, first, to provide empirical information which might contribute towards a better understanding of the politico-sectarian problems of Belfast; secondly, to contribute to the growing literature on urban residential structure in general and ethnic segregation in particular; and, thirdly, to serve a methodological purpose as an example of an approach to the analysis of residential segregation which combines elements from both geography and sociology, with special attention being paid both to the effects of spatial scale and to the use of a variety of indices of segregation.

CHARACTERISTICS OF THE DATA

The information on religious structure on which the analysis is based was not collected specifically for the purpose of examining residential religious segregation. Most of the information used was originally obtained in order to help analyse, in a report presented to the Scarman Tribunal of Inquiry, the movement of people displaced by the troubles of the summer of 1969.[15] As a result of not being designed specifically to analyse the city's segregation pattern, the data contain a few minor inadequacies, which will be discussed in this section of the paper. However, these inadequacies are considered slight and, in any case, the information is undoubtedly by far the best in existence for the analysis of the religious residential structure of the city. Not only is it the most up-to-date available, but it is also in a considerably more spatially detailed form than any that has ever been collected before for describing the entire city.

The statistic used as the basic expression of religious residential composition is the number of Catholic households in a particular area expressed as a percentage of all households in that area. The total number of households was obtained by counting the total number of separate residential addresses recorded in each street in the 1969 electoral list and by making adjustments, where necessary, to allow for subsequent demolition of old houses and construction of new property. The data on the number of Catholic households were much more difficult to obtain: they were eventually collected by compiling a complete list of streets in each Catholic parish in the city and asking the clergy in each parish to record the total number of Catholic families they knew to be resident in each street immediately before the refugee movements of August 1969.

In addition to these principal sources of information used in the paper, a further source was used to supply the data for that section of the paper which illustrates the effect of scale on the measurement of segregation in one small sample area in the city. For this analysis, data were required on the religious affiliation of individual households within the streets involved; such data were originally collected in order to help analyse, in another report presented to the Scarman Tribunal of Inquiry, the incidence of damage and destruction inflicted on residential property during the disturbances of August 1969.[16] This information was obtained from the local Catholic clergy in the areas concerned.

Only four slight notes of caution need be expressed here about the data. First, unlike population census material, the data do not apply to one specific day, because of the way they are continuously collected and updated by the curates and priests involved. Secondly, the count of Catholics was not made at precisely the same time as the count of the total number of households. Thirdly, the clergy have poor records in certain militantly Protestant districts where the Catholic clergy rarely if ever visit, but then it is highly unlikely that there are significant numbers of Catholics there anyway. Finally it should be noted that, while almost all the data refer to 1969, the clergy in two parishes, Holywood and Ligoniel, were not asked for data until 1971. It is considered, however, that little error is introduced by this anomaly, partly because only 4·2 per cent of the County Borough's households are located in these two parishes, and partly because there is reported to have been very little change in the religious structure of these parishes between 1969 and that period of 1971 to which the later data refer.

Five major decisions concerning the form and treatment of the religious data must now be discussed. These concern the choice of data elements, data sub-sets, the data set, the time period, and finally the appropriate religious classification. The data set relates to the area of study, a data element is the most disaggregated unit to which data may refer, and the data set is thus the entire group of data elements considered in a specific empirical problem. For spatial analysis, the data set is divided into sub-sets, each containing one or more data elements: the actual values used in the analysis are the values for these sub-sets.[17]

Choice of data elements

It has already been observed that the statistic used as the basic expression of religious residential composition is the number of Catholic households in a particular area expressed as a percentage of all households in that area. This contrasts with the earlier work of E. E. Evans and E. Jones on the religious residential structure of Belfast, for they calculated the percentage of the population which was Catholic.[18] In the terminology introduced above, therefore, this paper differs from the work of Evans and Jones in its choice of data element. Though the theoretical problem of whether to use individual people or individual households as the basic data element to identify religious affiliation was not considered in the publications of these earlier writers, they had, in practice, no choice anyway, for the population census, from which they drew their data, only presented information on the religious denomination of individual people. The only previous work on segregation in Belfast which has not used the population of individuals in the city as the data element was the earliest work of Jones, and it is perhaps significant that, for this analysis, he did not use the census: his data elements were the individual children attending public primary schools, and the information came from the schools themselves.[19]

The influence of the nature of the available census data on the choice of data element also appears to be strong in analyses of segregation in Great Britain, for it is possibly the presence of population data, and the almost complete absence of household data on ethnic characteristics in the British census which is responsible for such writers as R. J. Johnston and P. N. Jones using individual people as their basic data elements.[20] In the United States, segregation analyses have been undertaken using both people and households as the data elements, but once again the form of the available census data is at least one significant determinant of the nature of the analysis: thus, analyses using data for city blocks must use the household as the data element since ethnic population data are not available. Analyses using census tract data, however, have had the choice of using population or households as data elements though, in practice, they have generally chosen to use population. Taeuber and Taeuber have criticized this practice of using population, where a choice is available, because, they suggest, it is the household which is 'the fundamental residential unit', but, apart from this comment, the choice of data element is a subject that has largely been ignored in the literature on segregation.[21]

Since the data on which this paper on Belfast is based were specially collected by the authors, they chose what they considered to be the most appropriate data element, namely, the household, for it is the individual household which is the fundamental decision-making unit responsible for choosing where to live.[22] Since any spatial pattern of residential structure is essentially the outcome of decisions on residential location,[23] it follows that the household is the appropriate data element for analysing most aspects of residential structure, including segregation. This accords with the view of Taeuber and Taeuber.

Choice of data sub-sets

Details of religious denomination were requested and analysed in each successive population census carried out in Belfast from 1861 to 1961, but the smallest unit within the County Borough for which data were ever published was the individual ward.[24] These spatial units are much too large for particularly meaningful analysis of segregation as Evans fully admitted when he found himself compelled to use them in 1944.[25] E. Jones, too, expressed concern at the large size of the areas for which religious data were published by the census, pointing out that 'within such a large unit a considerable degree of segregation could be hidden entirely if a concentration of Catholics were split and included in two wards in which the overwhelming majority was Protestant'.[26] Jones, however, was able to undertake a much more detailed analysis than was possible from the published figures by using 1951 census data, specially obtained from the Registrar-General of Northern Ireland, for individual enumeration districts.[27] No published material of this spatially detailed type was made available, however, from the 1961 census, and no question on religious affiliation was even asked in the census in 1966.[28]

It was this complete absence of data on religious structure since 1961, and the total inadequacy of even the 1961 material as a result of the excessive coarseness of the spatial mesh used, that compelled the writers to collect their own data on the religious residential structure of the city. The decision on the size of the data sub-sets for which the material was to be collected was governed by two main factors. First, the areas specified had to be immediately meaningful, with clearly known boundaries, to the clergy providing the information; and, secondly, it was desirable to collect the raw data in as disaggregated a form as possible in order to permit maximum flexibility by allowing aggregation upwards to any of a wide variety of possible levels of generalization. It was decided that the street, or section of a street (where the street was a long one) satisfied both these criteria: any larger sub-set would neither have boundaries known to the clergy, nor would it be sufficiently small to allow enough flexibility for analysis at different scales.

Even smaller sub-sets, such as the individual household itself, would, of course, have satisfied these two criteria even better, and this, indeed, was the scale at which data were collected in the small sample areas suffering most damage to property during the 1969 disturbances.[29] However, it was considered that to request information at this level of

detail for the entire city would almost certainly have elicited a negative response from the clergy.

The total number of streets and street sections into which the city was divided for the purpose of obtaining information on religious composition was 3055, and there was an average of 38·0 households in each of these sub-sets. The degree of spatial detail embodied in these sub-sets is thus not only far greater than that in the fifteen wards, with their average of over 7700 households each in 1966, for which religious affiliation data are available in published form for 1961, but is also considerably in excess of that in the 231 enumeration districts, each with about 490 households on average, for which E. Jones obtained unpublished 1951 census data.[30]

Having established the characteristics of the data sub-sets for which information was collected, we can now consider the sub-sets used in the analysis. The choice of these is governed fundamentally by the fact that the empirical results of any spatial analysis are specific in scale: if the level of spatial aggregation is changed by altering the number and size of the sub-sets used, analysis of the same set of data is liable to yield quite different results. This is a familiar observation in the literature of other disciplines.[31]

The effect of scale on the measurement of residential segregation has received attention in the literature particularly since D. O. and M. S. Cowgill strongly criticized the use of census tracts as data sub-sets in earlier studies of racial segregation in the United States. They argued that city blocks were preferable to the larger census tracts because blocks were small enough to possess much greater homogeneity and thus have boundaries which approximated much more closely to the boundaries of areas of contrasting ethnic structure.[32]

Taeuber and Taeuber, however, after observing how the internal homogeneity of sub-sets can be increased by reducing their area stressed that such an effect is not necessarily an advantage, and that a small number of large sub-sets may be better for distinguishing the macro-features of patterns of segregation.[33] These critics unfortunately failed to carry the argument to its logical conclusion, for they still envisaged the problem as being one of choosing an appropriate size of sub-set for analysis. The full implication of their argument, however, is that comprehensive segregation analysis should be carried out at several scales. Such a conclusion is also supported by D. W. Harvey in the context of the general analysis of spatial point patterns.[34]

The investigation of the effect of scale on the measurement of residential segregation will be undertaken in two separate ways in this paper. First, the effects of spatial aggregation in a sample part of the city for which the authors have data on the religious affiliation of each individual household will be analysed. The sample area, Ardoyne, was initially covered with a 50 × 50 m grid; these grid squares were aggregated into 100 × 100 m squares and then into 200 × 200 m squares. This enabled the religious composition to be analysed at three distinct scales: the 50 × 50 m squares had an average of seventeen households each, the 100 × 100 m squares had an average of sixty-six each, and the 200 × 200 m squares had an average of 266 each. In addition, the results of this three-level analysis were compared with the result using the individual streets in this area as sub-sets, each of which had ninety-eight households.

The second way in which the effect of scale on segregation will be examined will be by using three strongly contrasting sizes of sub-set to analyse segregation in the city as a whole. The first of these three comprises the original 3055 streets and street-sections for which the data on religious composition were originally collected. The second group

B

comprises seventy-one areas which we shall refer to as 'tracts' and which are based on the
planning data units originally defined by Travers Morgan and Building Design Partnership, the planning consultants for Belfast. These seventy-one areas vary in size from 737
to 3124 households, but the average is 1638 households, which considerably exceeds the
average of thirty-eight for the 3055 streets. Our tracts are thus about the same size as the
American census tracts, with their average population of 3000–6000, whose use was
criticized by Cowgill and Cowgill, and our street sub-sets are even smaller than the city
blocks whose use Cowgill and Cowgill recommended and which have fewer than 100 households each on average.[35] Neither in the case of the streets nor the tracts were the boundaries
deliberately drawn in order either to minimize or maximize the internal religious homogeneity of the sub-sets: therefore, although Cowgill and Cowgill pointed out that, even
holding the size of sub-set constant, the measure of segregation would vary according to
how the boundaries were drawn in relation to the detailed religious structure, no such bias
should have crept into our measurement of segregation in Belfast.[36]

   The third group of data sub-sets used for the analysis of segregation in Belfast is a
set of nine sectors and six concentric rings into which the city has been divided. The sectors
have been introduced as sub-sets because, as was observed by J. S. Adams in a general
context and by both E. Jones and Boal in relation to Belfast specifically, families tend to
stay within the same sector of the city when they move house, thus perpetuating a pre-
existing level of segregation there and making each sector a separate and spatially continuous
residential sub-market.[37] It has been decided to use the rings, as well as the sectors, as
sub-sets for segregation analysis, because, just as sectoral differentiation is a normal feature
of a city's residential structure, so, too, is differentiation between rings. The basis of these
two types of differentiation is characteristically quite dissimilar, for social area analysis
has revealed that it is socio-economic rank which varies from sector to sector, but family
structure which varies between rings.[38] In addition to the specific sectors and rings, some
analysis is also included on the basis of the fifteen wards and the sixteen constituencies.
Many of the wards have identical or, at least, very similar boundaries to the constituencies,
and both are distinctly sectoral in shape.

   Ideally, the sectors themselves should perhaps be defined on the basis of the decision-
maker's perception of city structure, but, in the absence of this type of information, they
have been defined simply by regarding the main radial roads leading out of the city centre
as the central unifying axes of sectors, for it has been demonstrated that sectoral perception
probably results from the concentration of daily movement along these radial routes.[39]
The definition of the rings was made simply by repeating the assumption, made earlier
by Boal, that the City Hall occupies the central site of Belfast, and then designing rings
centred on City Hall.[40] Each ring had a width of 1 km, except for the innermost ring, whose
inner boundary was of irregular shape because it excluded the central business district
defined by Building Design Partnership.[41] Both the sectors and the rings varied considerably
in size, but the nine sectors had nearly 13 000 households each on average, and the six
rings had an average of over 19 000 each.

Choice of data set
The data which were specially collected to help analyse the 1969 residential displacement
problem and which are being used as the foundation for this paper suffer from the unfortunate deficiency that they are available for only about two-thirds of the population

of the Belfast urban area. Since almost all the areas deficient in data were outside the County Borough boundary, however, it has been decided to restrict the analysis in this paper to the single local authority administration unit, the County Borough of Belfast.

In this respect, the analysis presented is closely analogous to most of the research published on racial residential segregation in the United States, for the shortage of spatially detailed data on the racial structure of those parts of American metropolitan areas lying outside the 'central city' which forms the political unit at the heart of such areas precludes meaningful segregation analysis of these suburban belts. Taeuber and Taeuber, for example, in their countrywide analysis of racial residential segregation in American cities, limit most of their analysis to the central cities, and are able to perform only an unsatisfactorily incomplete analysis of metropolitan areas as a whole.[42]

Ignoring the suburban areas beyond a city boundary in this way seems, for the most part, quite unjustifiable theoretically since 'the political border of the city is seldom a meaningful barrier to the processes of growth and deterioration of urban neighbourhoods and accompanying population movements'.[43] Similarly, in relation to social area analysis, B. J. L. Berry and F. E. Horton argue that the appropriate unit is the urbanized area, together with the major commuting settlements beyond, rather than the politically defined central city, since it is the former which represents the combined housing and labour market for the metropolis.[44]

The relevant spatial unit should, in theory, be that segment of space which functions as both a relatively closed and highly integrated system in relation to the multitude of flows which characterize urban living. If the system is to be highly integrated throughout, this implies that the central city, if there is one, should have close links with the entire system. In the case of Belfast, therefore, one fairly simple criterion we can use to define the relevant system is to measure the links of the County Borough with each of the areas beyond and then to impose some arbitrary limit on the closeness of such links in order to delineate a discrete spatial unit from a series of gradually sloping surfaces.

Although the nature of the data prevented analysis of the religious structure pattern for the whole urban area in 1969 and limits such analysis to the County Borough alone, the authors believe that it is still extremely worthwhile to report on the County Borough situation. First, this political unit contains a high proportion of the urban area's population: the County Borough contained 398 000 people in 1966, which was 73 per cent of the 549 000 people defined by the Census of that year as living in the continuously built-up area.[45] Secondly, though the housing and labour markets of Belfast do extend quite considerably beyond the city boundary, a fairly high percentage both of the urban area's residential moves and of its work-trips takes place entirely within the County Borough itself. Thus 68 per cent of those people who work in Belfast County Borough also live there;[46] and 93 per cent of people usually resident within the city boundary in 1966 and who were alive at the 1961 census were also living within this boundary at that earlier census.[47]

Furthermore, the most important criticism that is levied at American analyses of negro segregation, namely, that they are limited to central cities, is not relevant to the Belfast situation. This is that negroes represent a much higher proportion of the central city population than they do of the population of the outer ring of the metropolitan area; any segregation analysis limited to the central city necessarily therefore ignores the segregation between the two sides of the city boundary.[48] In Belfast, on the other hand, the contrast between the County Borough and the remainder of the urban area is relatively slight: 25 per cent of the households within the County Borough are Catholic while, according to preliminary estimates, 17 per cent of those in the outer ring of the Urban Area beyond the city boundary are of the same denomination.[49] Thus this evidence, like that presented in the previous paragraph, makes it clear that, while it would have been desirable to have data for the entire urban area, it is still worthwhile to undertake analysis for the County Borough alone.

Choice of time period

The data collected by one of the authors in 1969 to analyse the movement of people displaced by the disturbances of the summer of that year portray the religious structure of Belfast as it existed immediately before these major disturbances commenced. Since the wave of refugee movement in 1969, there has been another major spate of residential displacement, and the same writer has assisted in the initial documentation of this displacement by the Northern Ireland Community Relations Commission.[50]

The period 1969–72 has seen segregation intensified at intervals by cataclysmic upheaval. In the context of this highly dynamic situation, the pattern of religious structure described and analysed in this paper represents the stage reached after several decades of relative calm and just before the political turmoil, which began in late 1968, became sufficiently intense to trigger off significant refugee movement. The value of such an analysis is that it demonstrates how much religious residential segregation existed in the city at the end of this long period of comparative calm and before the recent severe spasms of refugee movement began.

Choice of religious classification

It may be questioned how far the adoption of a simple binary classification of religion into Catholic and Protestant is justified, especially since the 1961 population census recorded 106 different religious denominations in Belfast.[51] Our dichotomy collapses these into only two groups, the Catholic group remaining the same as in the census definition, while the 'Protestant' group contains the other 105 denominations. These 105 denominations contained a total of almost 290 000 people in 1961, only 1500 of whom could be classified as non-Christian; this last group is thus numerically insignificant as a proportion of the total. Hence we are basically labelling all non-Catholic Christian groups in Belfast as Protestant, a usage noted by D. P. Barritt and C. F. Carter when they stated that the word 'Protestant' in Northern Ireland is synonymous with 'non-Catholic'.[52]

In this respect, this paper departs from the practice of both Evans, who mapped separately the distribution of Catholics, Presbyterians and Church of Ireland members, and E. Jones who, in 1960, separately mapped each of these three groups and also Methodists and Jews.[53] Jones did, however, point out that the most sociologically relevant feature of religious composition in Belfast was the Catholic-Protestant dichotomy, because the religious differences between these two groups also represented a cultural contrast between indigenous and intrusive cultures.[54] Thus the dichotomous religious division implies differences between the members of the two groups which stem directly from religion itself, such as attitudes towards divorce, family planning, Sunday observance and patterns of school attendance; but the division also implies other cultural differences stemming from contrasting national and political orientations. This has been demonstrated in a recent survey in the province as a whole which showed that 76 per cent of Catholics considered

themselves to be Irish in terms of national identity, whereas 75 per cent of Protestants
regarded themselves as being either British or Ulster.[55] The division in terms of national
identity extends directly into the political field, in that most Catholics support political
parties and candidates who favour a united Ireland, while most Protestants vote for parties
demanding the continuation of the present constitutional link between Northern Ireland
and Great Britain.[56]

The existence of these cultural differences between the two basic religious groups
allows us to apply two rather different sociological models to the Belfast situation. The
first model treats the Catholics as a minority group and implies a dichotomy between
Catholics and the remainder of the population. A minority group in this context is a sub-
group within a culture which is distinguishable from the dominant group in power by
virtue of differences in physical appearance, language, customs or cultural patterns.
Such a sub-group is regarded, or regard themselves, as inherently different from the
dominant group which controls power; and the members of such a group therefore with-
draw from, or are consciously or unconsciously excluded from, full participation in the
life of the dominant culture.[57] Though the Catholics in Northern Ireland obviously form
such a minority group, it should also be pointed out that the Protestants, in one sense, also
form a minority group or at least fear becoming one, and, indeed, many of the politico-
sectarian problems of the province stem from this fear. This is because many Protestants
are afraid of becoming a minority both in an all-Ireland state, if the whole island were
ever unified politically, and even in Northern Ireland itself if the growth of Catholic
population were sufficiently rapid.[58]

The second model generates a dichotomy that follows the same lines of division as the
first, but in this instance Catholics and Protestants each form a distinct ethnic group.
This term denotes a social group which, within a larger cultural and social system, claims
or is accorded a special status in terms of a complex of traits which it exhibits or is believed
to exhibit.[59] The Catholic-Protestant dichotomy in Northern Ireland, which assumes
considerable homogeneity within the groups and sharp differences between the groups,
can thus be regarded as an ethnic dichotomy and lends itself to the application of this
model as much as to the use of the minority group model. Whichever model is used,
however, the simple binary classification into Catholic and Protestant appears to be fully
justified on sociological grounds.

CATHOLIC HOUSEHOLDS AS A PERCENTAGE OF ALL HOUSEHOLDS

The previously published research on the distribution, within Belfast, of the Catholic
population as a percentage of the total population differs from that reported in this paper
in some significant respects. Most of these have been alluded to already but there is one
other important point of difference. Evans and Jones[60] each present maps which allow
both segregated Protestant areas and mixed areas, as well as segregated Catholic areas, to
be located, but both writers are overwhelmingly concerned in their text with describing
those areas where each individual denomination was at its strongest, especially those
areas in which the percentage of Catholics was very high. Moreover, although Jones in
his 1956 and 1960 publications analysed the variation in the degree of segregation from
one part of the city to another, he was concerned with studying the correlation between
segregation and socio-economic status rather than describing the actual pattern formed by
the distribution of mixed and segregated areas.

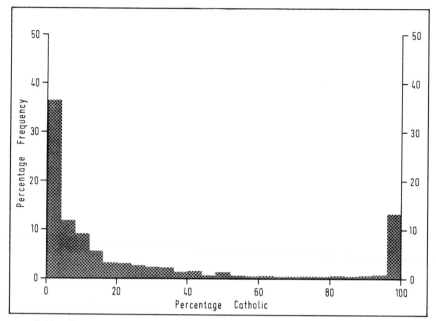

FIGURE 1. Belfast County Borough: the frequency distribution of streets classified on the basis of religious composition

In this paper, on the other hand, we discuss not only those specific areas which are almost exclusively Catholic, but also those which are almost exclusively Protestant and those displaying varying degrees of mixing. Indeed, in such a highly segregated city, it is perhaps the well-mixed areas which are the real anomaly rather than either type of segregated area. Moreover, if it should be agreed that residential desegregation is a desirable social goal, the nature of these mixed areas might be very significant in providing evidence concerning the viability of such a goal and the ways in which it might be achieved.

Streets as data sub-sets

Since we are interested in the entire spectrum of religious composition, the most useful initial step is to discover the relative frequency of occurrence of each segment of the spectrum. Figure 1 illustrates the frequency distribution of the 3055 streets which are used as the most detailed sub-sets for this analysis. The streets are classified into twenty-five cells according to the percentage of their households which were Catholic in 1969, and it is the percentage of all streets falling into each frequency-cell which is plotted.

The resulting frequency distribution is clearly bimodal, with the peaks being located at the two extremes. In fact, 36 per cent of streets are 0–3 per cent Catholic, and 13 per cent are 97–100 per cent Catholic: thus in virtually one-half of the city's streets, 97 per cent or more of the households are of the same religion. An examination of the remainder of the distribution shows that its overall shape is that of an asymmetrical basin, for there are many more streets predominantly Protestant with a significant Catholic minority than there are streets predominantly Catholic with a significant Protestant minority.

The asymmetrical shape is further confirmed by Table I, which shows the percentage

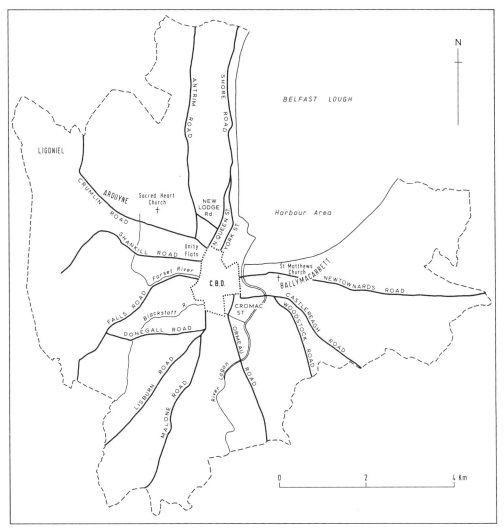

FIGURE 2. Belfast County Borough: locations mentioned in text

of households living in streets classified into seven frequency-cells. This Table demon-strates that the dominant environmental type in Belfast is the street which is o–9 per cent Catholic: no less than 53 per cent of the city's households live in streets of this type. In addition, about 13 per cent of the households live in each of three other types: those streets which are 10–19 per cent Catholic, those which are 20–39 per cent Catholic, and those which are 91–100 per cent Catholic. None of the three other street types distinguished has as much as 5 per cent of the city's households: streets which are between 40 and 90 per cent Catholic are thus very rare. Table I shows that two-thirds of Belfast's households live in streets in which 91 per cent or more of the households are of the same religion. However, the asymmetrical shape of the distribution means that segregated living is significantly more common for Protestants than for Catholics. Thus no less than 69 per

TABLE I

Number and percentage of households in streets classified by religious composition

Percentage Catholic by street	Total number of households	Number of Catholic households	Number of Protestant households	Percentage of total households	Percentage of Catholic households	Percentage of Protestant households
0–9	62 029	1724	60 305	53·3	6·0	68·8
10–19	15 172	2045	13 127	13·0	7·1	15·0
20–39	14 878	4134	10 744	12·8	14·4	12·2
40–60	4831	2302	2529	4·1	8·0	2·9
61–80	2453	1707	746	2·1	6·0	0·8
81–90	887	755	132	0·8	2·6	0·1
91–100	16 072	15 958	114	13·8	55·7	0·1
Total	116 322	28 625	87 697	100·0	100·0	100·0

cent of Protestants live in streets which are 91 per cent or more Protestant, and only 1 per cent live in streets which are less than 40 per cent Protestant; on the other hand, only the comparatively small figure of 56 per cent of Catholics live in streets which are 91 per cent or more Catholic, while as many as 28 per cent live in streets which are less than 40 per cent Catholic.

It is now necessary to describe the spatial distribution of each street type. Figure 3 illustrates the distribution pattern of those streets which are 91–100 per cent Catholic and demonstrates the way in which they are concentrated into certain limited sections of the city. In fact, no less than 99 per cent of those households belonging to such heavily Catholic streets live in just six areas, each of which is a continuous segment of uninter-rupted space consisting entirely of streets in this one category of religious composition.

By far the largest of these six areas is the Falls which contains more than 11 000 households, constituting 70 per cent of the total of over 16 000 households in the city living in streets that are so heavily Catholic. The Falls is visible on the map as the sector extending first westwards and then south-westwards from the western edge of the Central Business District (CBD). The 'blank' areas in this sector consist of non-residential land. The second largest dominantly Catholic area is much smaller; this is Ardoyne in the north-west of the city, with 11 per cent of the total number of households living in streets that are 91–100 per cent Catholic. In addition, 8 per cent of the total are in St Patrick's, the area just north of the CBD, stretching from Unity Flats along North Queen Street to the New Lodge Road; 4 per cent are adjacent to St Matthew's church in Ballymacarrett on the eastern bank of the River Lagan just to the east of the CBD; 4 per cent are on either side of Cromac Street in the Markets area just to the south of the CBD, and 2 per cent are adjacent to the Sacred Heart Church just east of Ardoyne.

Thus there emerges a pattern of one large Catholic area supplemented by five others which, though equally dominantly Catholic, are much smaller in size. These six areas were all identified by Jones in his 1952 paper as being predominantly Catholic, though the detailed boundaries he drew round them are significantly different.[61] They are also similar to the areas that he mapped, in 1956 and 1960, as having Catholic percentages above the upper octile (87·9 per cent) of the frequency distribution of his enumeration districts, except that Ballymacarrett was excluded.[62] However, they differ quite markedly from the principal Catholic areas identified earlier by Evans because the wards he had to use as data sub-sets were so large that he simply suggested the existence of a very heavily Catholic Falls sector and of a fairly strongly Catholic central area.[63] The 1969 analysis thus confirms this earlier research in observing that Catholic households are quite heavily concentrated into certain limited parts of the city, especially the Falls, but it should also be emphasized that as many as 44 per cent of Catholic households in Belfast are found outside streets that are 91–100 per cent Catholic. This confirms the need to study the spatial distribution of these other street-types.

Figure 4 maps the distribution of those streets at the other end of the spectrum: it shows those streets that are only 0–9 per cent Catholic. Inevitably they extend over large parts of the County Borough since Table I shows that no less than 53 per cent of the city's households were in streets of this type. However, there are four notable concentrations of such streets. The largest is in east Belfast, which contains 42 per cent of the city's households living in streets that are 0–9 per cent Catholic; and the second largest, containing another 29 per cent, is in the north-west of the city in a sector which, in the inner part, lies in a fairly narrow belt on either side of the Shankill Road but which then fans out to cover most of the outer part of north-west Belfast. The third concentration is a sector extending south-south-west from the CBD, principally around the Donegall Road, the Lisburn Road and the Malone Road and containing 18 per cent of the city's households in streets of this type: and the fourth, containing only a further 8 per cent, extends, again in sector form, northwards from the CBD along the Shore Road. Altogether, 97 per cent of those households in the city located in streets which are 0–9 per cent Catholic are found in these four concentrations, but it should be pointed out that these four areas are not continuous areas containing only this kind of street. On page 14 we defined the dominantly Catholic areas as continuous sheets of space containing only streets which were 91–100 per cent Catholic, but no attempt has been made to define continuously dominant Protestant areas in so rigorous a manner.

Finally, there are the five types of street listed in Table I which are not quite so strongly dominated by one of the two groups. The two most common of these five street types are those which are 10–19 per cent Catholic and those which are 20–39 per cent Catholic; their pattern of distribution is rather similar, for both types are concentrated in the middle and outer parts of the northern and southern sectors of the city. However, streets which are 10–19 per cent Catholic are approximately equally divided between the two sectors, whereas streets that are 20–39 per cent Catholic are rather more common in the north than in the south.

Streets which are 40–60 per cent Catholic and streets which are 61–80 per cent Catholic also have similar patterns of distribution, for both are concentrated in the northern and southern sectors of the city, especially the northern sector; they differ principally in that the southern fringe of the Falls sector also has a significant number of streets that are 61–80 per cent Catholic. It should be noted that those streets which are 40–60 per cent and 61–80 per cent Catholic are similar to those that are 10–19 per cent and 20–40 per cent Catholic since all four are found principally in the northern and southern parts of the city. However, there are two important differences: first, streets which are 40–80 per cent Catholic are not excluded from the inner parts of these sectors as is the case of streets that are 10–39 per cent Catholic; in fact, streets that are 40–80 per cent Catholic are more common in the inner parts of these sectors than in the outer parts. Secondly, the streets that are 40–80 per cent Catholic are concentrated into quite narrow sectors along the Antrim

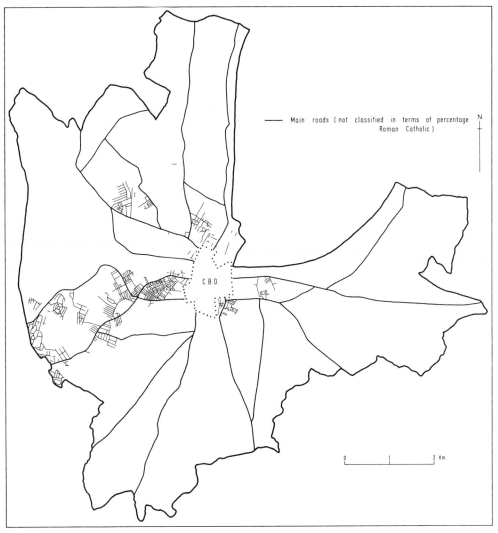

FIGURE 3. Streets in Belfast County Borough which were between 90·5 per cent and 100·0 per cent Catholic
in mid-1969

Road in the north, and along the Ormeau Road in the south, whereas those streets which
are 10–39 per cent Catholic are concentrated into much broader sectors in both the north
and the south including other radial routes additional to the Antrim and Ormeau Roads.

The final street type, those which are 81–90 per cent Catholic, is concentrated
principally just north of the CBD with a second concentration just south of the CBD.
Thus, though the distribution of these streets is rather different from the four types just
discussed, there is one remarkably similar feature: this is the concentration in the northern
and southern sectors. Thus all five street types which are at least fairly well-mixed in religious composition are located primarily in the northern and southern sectors of the city,
especially the northern one, though there is a tendency for the more strongly Catholic

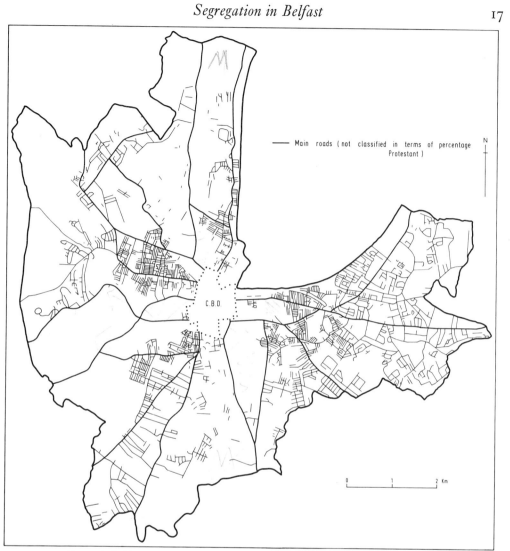

FIGURE 4. Streets in Belfast County Borough which were between 0·0 per cent and 9·5 per cent Catholic in mid-1969

of these street types to be located closer to the city centre within these sectors and, indeed, in more narrowly-defined corridors rather than in broad wedges. The fact that the more strongly Catholic of these street types are found closer to the city centre can be related to the fact that there are almost exclusively Catholic areas at, or close to, the inner tip of these sectors and that, as distance from these areas increases, the street becomes successively less Catholic in composition. Though these differences among the five street types which are at least fairly well-mixed should be borne in mind, the most outstanding feature of their distribution is their similarity by virtue of their concentration into the northern and southern sectors and, in this respect, they contrast strongly with the distribution both of those streets that are 91–100 per cent Catholic, with their concentration in the western

TABLE II

Frequency distribution of tracts classified by religious composition and number and percentage of households in tracts thus classified

Percentage Catholic by tract	Number of tracts	Total number of households	Percentage of total households	Corresponding percentage for street data
0–9	31	50 678	43·6	53·3
10–19	9	11 704	10·1	13·0
20–39	17	29 128	25·0	12·8
40–60	5	9679	8·3	4·1
61–80	3	5024	4·3	2·1
81–90	2	4425	3·8	0·8
91–100	4	5684	4·9	13·8
Total	71	116 322	100·0	100·0

sector and in pockets on the edge of the CBD, and of those streets which are 0–9 per cent Catholic, with their concentration especially into the eastern and north-western sectors.

Tracts as data sub-sets

The scale of analysis will now be enlarged by using the seventy-one tracts as sub-sets. Table II illustrates the overall frequency distribution of these tracts along a percentage Catholic scale that employs the same seven cells that appeared in Table I. In addition to the actual frequency distribution of the seventy-one tracts, Table II also shows the number and percentage of all households in each of the seven types of tract classified on the basis of religious composition. In addition, to facilitate comparison with the corresponding results obtained by the use of streets instead of tracts, the Table also contains a statement of the percentages of the households in each of the seven street types, similarly classified.

A comparison of these two sets of percentages shows that the principal effect of increasing the scale, by aggregating the streets into the larger tracts and using them as sub-sets, is that the frequency distribution of households is narrower: sub-sets which are 0–9 per cent, 10–19 per cent and 91–100 per cent Catholic are less common when tracts are used instead of streets, and all religious composition cells between 20 per cent and 90 per cent Catholic are better represented. A subsidiary effect of this is that the former markedly bimodal feature of the distribution, with peaks in the 0–9 per cent and 91–100 per cent cells, disappears, for, though the pronounced peak in the 0–9 per cent cell remains, the peak at the highly Catholic end of the spectrum is missing at tract level. The result of this disappearance is that, when the number of Catholic households as a percentage of all households is mapped at this scale, as in Figure 5, it is difficult to identify the almost exclusively Catholic areas illustrated in Figure 3, even though they consist of continuous belts of streets all in the 91–100 per cent Catholic category. Only the heart of the middle and outer parts of the large Falls area, together with the small pocket of the Markets, remain on this map as areas 91–100 per cent Catholic. This is because, on the whole, only the Falls area is large enough for entire tracts to be contained within it: even its narrow inner end and its northern and southern edges lie in tracts that straddle the boundary of the extreme Catholic area, as defined at street level, and hence lie in tracts

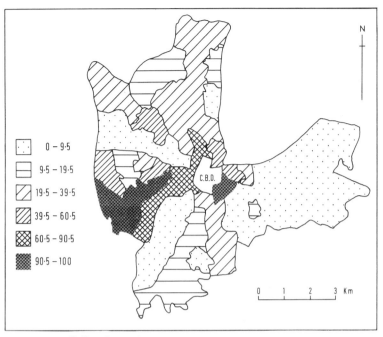

FIGURE 5. Belfast County Borough: percentage Catholic by tracts, mid-1969

whose overall percentage Catholic is much lower. Similarly, the smaller Catholic pockets, with the exception of the Markets, all lie in tracts that also include large areas that are not highly Catholic and that, in many cases, in fact, are highly Protestant. Only the tracts containing the Markets happens to be drawn so as to include virtually nothing but the almost exclusively Catholic area itself. Thus the narrow inner end of the Falls and its southern edge are identified on Figure 5 as being in tracts that are 61–90 per cent Catholic, as is the St Patrick's area; most of the northern edge of the Falls, together with the Ardoyne and Ballymacarrett areas are in tracts that are only 40–60 per cent Catholic, and the tiny Sacred Heart area is, in fact, in a tract that is only 20–39 per cent Catholic. In fact, all the tracts shown on Figure 5 as being 40 per cent or more Catholic are tracts which contain at least part of an area consisting of nothing but streets that are 91–100 per cent Catholic.

On the other hand, it is clear that, in the case of the most dominant street type, the 0–9 per cent Catholic cell, the areas where it is most common are faithfully reflected in Figure 5, for they are also the areas where tracts which are 0–9 per cent Catholic are found. This is because there are so many of these highly Protestant streets in virtually continuous belts that many tracts are made up almost entirely of such streets. The other street types, however, rarely have exclusive occupation of large enough segments of space for almost entire tracts to be made up of a single street type.

Thus the overall proportion of households which are Catholic in a tract is often simply an average figure based on a mixture of street types within the tract. This cannot be very misleading if the frequency distribution of streets, classified by religious composition, within a tract is reasonably normal, but if the distribution is markedly non-normal, especially if it is distinctly bimodal, then great care must be taken in interpreting the results

TABLE III

Catholic households as a percentage of all households: variation by ring and by sector

	Ring 1	Ring 2	Ring 3	Ring 4	Ring 5	Ring 6	Σ
Sector 1	—	89·7	1·9	5·2	4·1	3·3	7·3
Sector 2	94·1	11·2	7·2	3.1	—	—	9·3
Sector 3	42·2	25·4	23·3	24·4	—	—	28·2
Sector 4	24·8	9·9	7·8	9·0	9·9	—	10·2
Sector 5	0·4	5·5	6·2	6·5	5·4	—	4·6
Sector 6	86·6	84·6	82·3	68·7	—	—	80.1
Sector 7	24·7	4·5	23·0	30·0	13·0	47·8	16·3
Sector 8	87·6	66·0	34·8	26·5	15·3	31·5	34·3
Sector 9	88·5	24·4	5·3	10·5	14·6	26·5	19·2
CBD	53·4	—	—	—	—	—	53·4
Σ	40·8	27·4	23·0	25·1	10·8	17·4	24·6

Note: The sectors are identified by name in Figure 6.

of analysis at the tract level. Even such a situation need not be misleading as long as care is taken in interpretation, for the overall percentage Catholic figure for the tract as a whole is completely accurate and represents the relative frequency of Catholic households at that particular scale: however, it clearly should not be assumed that such a Catholic percentage is found uniformly within the tract, for the distribution of Catholic households within the tract is an entirely different problem at a very different scale, and the overall average Catholic percentage at the tract level provides no information about the distribution of Catholic households at any other scales.

Sectors and rings as data sub-sets

Finally we will study the spatial structure of religious distribution at a higher level of generalization, that of the rings and sectors into which the city has been divided. It has been evident from the preceding discussion, that at the street and tract levels there are certain general differences both between sectors and between rings in terms of percentage Catholic. These observations will now be analysed. The final column of Table III illustrates the variation between sectors. Clearly the Falls is by far the most heavily Catholic sector, with 80 per cent of its households Catholic, while the Queen's Bridge and Albert Bridge sectors, which adjoin each other in the east, and the Malone Road and Lisburn Road sectors, which adjoin each other in the south-west, emerge as the least Catholic, since the number of Catholic households in all four is 10 per cent or less of the total number of households. The next least Catholic sectors, the Crumlin-Shankill Road and Shore Road sectors, with 16 per cent and 19 per cent respectively of their households Catholic, are both in the north, well away from the four most non-Catholic sectors, but do not adjoin; and the two fairly Catholic sectors, with 28 per cent and 34 per cent of their households Catholic, are in the north and south, well away not only from each other but also from the heavily Catholic Falls. Thus a pattern emerges in which there are strong differences between sectors in the percentage of their households which are Catholic, and in which adjacent sectors often, though by no means always, have strongly contrasting overall percentages.

The bottom row of Table III shows the number of Catholic households as a percentage of all households for each of the six 1 km rings represented within the County Borough. In this case, the sequence appears to be much less random, for there appears to be a general tendency for the percentage Catholic to fall outwards from the city centre though, rather than there being a regular decline, there appears to be an inner belt consisting of the first ring, a middle belt consisting of the second, third and fourth rings, and an outer belt comprising the fifth and sixth rings. It should also be emphasized that the rings do not contrast with each other in the percentage of their households which are Catholic as markedly as do the sectors; thus the coefficient of variation is 91·7 for the sectors, but only 42·1 for the rings. This difference is partly the result of there being fewer rings than sectors, but this is by no means the entire explanation. Clearly the pattern of religious distribution is primarily sectoral rather than concentric.

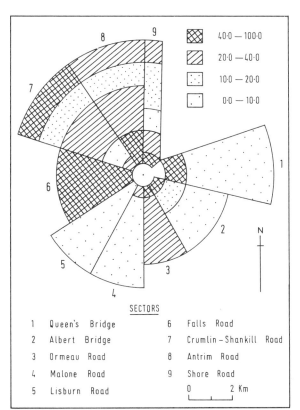

FIGURE 6. Belfast County Borough: percentage Catholic by sectors and rings, mid-1969

Figure 6 presents the values for the ring/sector cells in schematic map form, and this, together with the complete matrix of data in Table III, illustrates the marked regularity of the spatial pattern. There are four features which should be emphasized. First, those cells which are more than 40 per cent Catholic are, with only one exception, all found either in the Falls sector or in the inner two rings. Indeed, they are nearly all found either in the Falls or in the innermost ring, for only two of the sectors are so Catholic in their second ring; in one case, the heavily Catholic area spills over from the first ring into the second while, in the other case, the innermost ring is non-residential; thus the second ring, which is over 40 per cent Catholic, is, in fact, the innermost residential ring. The only exception is the Ligoniel area in the extreme north-west. Secondly, those cells, less than 10 per cent of whose households are Catholic, are strongly concentrated with only two exceptions in the eastern sectors (Queen's Bridge and Albert Bridge) and in the two south-western sectors (Lisburn Road and Malone Road), though in only one case (that of the Lisburn Road) is the sector so Protestant even in the innermost ring. Thirdly, both the cells which are 10–20 per cent Catholic and those which are 20–40 per cent Catholic are found entirely either in the north and north-west or in the south-east. Fourthly, the pattern of variation, ring by ring, within sectors is fairly consistent: in five of the nine sectors, the percentage Catholic is remarkably uniform, usually after dropping suddenly from the level in the innermost population ring, while in two sectors it falls all the way outwards towards the city boundary. That leaves only two rather anomalous sectors: in the Shore Road sector, the percentage Catholic rises consistently towards the periphery after initially dropping from the level in the innermost ring, while in the Crumlin-Shankill Road sector the pattern can only be described as wholly irregular.

THE RESIDENTIAL SEGREGATION OF CATHOLICS AND PROTESTANTS
The concept of residential segregation and alternatives to it

The preceding discussion of the pattern of spatial variation of the number of Catholic households as a percentage of all households has shown that this percentage varies considerably, thus indicating the probable existence of significant residential segregation. This section of the paper provides precise measurements of the degree of segregation both within Belfast as a whole and also within different parts of the city.

It is essential, however, to be completely clear about the concept of residential segregation that is to be employed. The customary academic definition of the concept is that a particular minority or ethnic group would be completely unsegregated if its members were distributed uniformly relative to the remainder of the population. Any deviation from such uniformity represents a situation characterized by segregation, and the greater the deviation the greater the degree of segregation.[64] This concept of segregation implies an inverse which, following P. Marcuse, will be referred to as 'residential mixing' rather than 'residential integration' because the latter is defined as implying that there is significant social interaction between neighbours belonging to different ethnic groups in addition to the sharing of the same neighbourhood by the ethnic groups involved.[65] The situation where the minority or ethnic group is distributed uniformly relative to the total population is thus properly referred to as residential mixing.

Segregation and its inverse, mixing, must be clearly distinguished from two other concepts. The first regards complete residential mixing as occurring when two ethnic groups are found in equal numbers in a particular area. It may be hypothesized that this is a particularly important concept to people themselves, for it seems likely that the fact that an ethnic group is found in the same proportion in a particular neighbourhood as in the city as a whole is of little perceptual relevance to the residents, especially since they are probably unaware of the overall proportion in the city as a whole, as P. A. Compton and Boal suggest.[66] What probably matters to the residents is which ethnic group is in the majority and by how much. This suggestion is not being made to imply that the definition of segregation as deviation from a uniform distribution constitutes an unimportant concept; instead, it is being proposed that the concept that complete mixing is found when there is equality of numbers of two ethnic groups is also a relevant notion in the context of the analysis of patterns of intra-urban ethnic distributions. However, in order to minimize semantic confusion, it would perhaps be better to restrict the segregation-mixing dichotomy to descriptions of uniform distributions and deviations from such uniformity, and to employ the terms 'dominance' and 'equality', albeit in a strictly numerical sense, as an analogous dichotomy for use in the context of describing deviation from the situation where each ethnic group is found in equal numbers in a particular area.

The second of the two concepts which are alternatives to the definition given of residential segregation and residential mixing is exemplified in the work of S. Sudman, N. M. Bradburn and G. Gockel, in which they defined racially integrated housing, not with reference to the racial composition of the entire group of residents in a neighbourhood at a particular cross-section through time, but in relation to the racial affiliation of the new residents moving into that neighbourhood during a particular period of time.[67] Such a concept is also implicit in the processual indices of segregation proposed by M. A. Beauchamp.[68] Unfortunately, the complete absence of adequate information on the religious composition of movers into different parts of Belfast makes it quite impossible to apply this essentially dynamic 'balanced-inflow' concept of integration in this paper, so analysis will be restricted to the other two concepts.

Little further analysis and comment, beyond what has already been included in the discussion of the number of Catholic households as a percentage of all households, is required on the concept of the dominance-equality dichotomy. Figure 1 and Table I contain, in a fairly generalized form, the necessary basic information at the detailed level of the individual street. If we arbitrarily define a high level of equality as existing when a street is 40–60 per cent Catholic, then only 4·7 per cent of all streets exhibit such a level of equality. Since, if all street types were equally common, streets that were 40–60 per cent Catholic would represent 21 per cent of the total, a relative dominance index of $(21-4·7)(100)/21 = 77·6$ may be derived. A lower, but possibly highly relevant, level of equality is that existing in streets that are 34–66 per cent Catholic, and since 7·3 per cent of Belfast streets are in this category, this implies a relative dominance index of 77·9. Finally, an index of 72·0 is derived if equality is re-defined as existing in streets that are 25–75 per cent Catholic, for 14·3 per cent of the city's streets are of this type. It has already been pointed out that, when the streets are replaced by larger data sub-sets, such as the seventy-one tracts, the frequency distribution is narrowed. This implies that a higher proportion of tracts than of streets is classified as containing approximately equal numbers of Catholics and Protestants and, therefore, the three new relative dominance indices, corresponding to the three calculated above, but based on data at the tract level, are 66·7, 65·8 and 50·2 respectively.

Clearly, even at tract level, let alone at street level, the dominance indices are high, thus emphasizing that relatively few streets in Belfast can be regarded as having approximately equal numbers of Catholics and Protestants: dominance of either one religious group or the other is the well-established norm. This follows from a combination of circumstances. On the one hand, the city as a whole is quite heavily dominated by Protestants, who form 75·4 per cent of all households; on the other hand, the distribution of the two religious groups relative to each other is not uniform. It is therefore appropriate that we now analyse the latter phenomenon which, it will be recalled, represents the concept of residential segregation.

The measurement of residential segregation in Belfast as a whole

The analysis of residential segregation will aim at two distinct objectives. The first attempts to measure the degree of segregation in the city as a whole, while the second attempts to measure the intensity of segregation in each part of the city, in order to illustrate the intra-urban variation in the level of segregation. The first of these objectives is one which is common in the sociological literature on residential segregation, but the second is a feature of segregation which has received little attention in the literature of any academic discipline.

The usual approach in the sociological analysis of the degree of segregation present

C

in a city as a whole is to employ a single index of segregation. This is devised after manipulation of data on the number both of minority group members and of the remainder of the population for each data sub-set within the city. In fact, no single index can fully embody all facets of a complex spatial pattern, but Taeuber and Taeuber, building on the earlier work of O. D. and B. Duncan, have demonstrated that the best single index, on both theoretical and practical grounds, is the dissimilarity index.[69] Moreover, partly because of the accepted superiority of this index, it has been applied quite widely to the analysis of residential segregation, so there exists an extensive set of findings with which comparison may be made. There are therefore great advantages in using the dissimilarity index for the measurement of residential segregation in Belfast.

No matter what index is used to measure segregation, the size of data sub-sets, as has already been observed, must be expected to affect the derived value of the index: specifically, the larger the sub-sets, the lower will be the level of segregation. Before calculating dissimilarity indices for Belfast as a whole, this effect of scale will be demonstrated with reference to the Ardoyne area in the north-west of the city. When this area is divided into eighty-five square sub-sets, each 50 × 50 m, the dissimilarity index is 84·8 but, when the same area is divided into only twenty-two sub-sets, measuring 100 × 100 m, the index falls to 81·6, and, finally, when these squares are further aggregated into 5·5 sub-sets, each 200 × 200 m, the index drops considerably to 71·4. Moreover, when the data on religious composition for this area are analysed at street level, the fact that the twelve street sub-sets are intermediate in size between the 100 × 100 and the 200 × 200 m grid-squares results in the emergence of a dissimilarity index, 79·0, which is also intermediate between the corresponding indices produced when these two sizes of grid-square are used.

This pronounced effect of scale is also found when dissimilarity indices are calculated for Belfast as a whole. Thus the index is only 56·9 when the seventy-one tracts are used as sub-sets but, when these are replaced by the 3055 streets, the index rises to as much as 70.9. On the other hand, if the scale level is enlarged by using the fifteen wards or sixteen constituencies as sub-sets, the dissimilarity index falls significantly: thus the index derived by using wards is 50·1, while that derived from using constituencies is 46·8. These values, however, are not much lower than the index obtained when the seventy-one tracts are used as sub-sets: the comparatively small difference resulting from this enlargement of scale follows from the fact that both the wards and the constituencies in Belfast, though especially the former, have a characteristically sectoral shape, and it has already been demonstrated that sectors are spatial units which, in relation to their size, have comparatively little internal variation in religious composition but differ markedly one from another. The validity of this explanation is demonstrated when dissimilarity indices are calculated using the nine sectors themselves as sub-sets and also, for comparison, using the six rings: the value derived from using sectors is 47·4, which is similar to the values using the wards and constituencies, but the index drops to a mere 10·7 when the six rings are used. This particularly large difference between the index based on sectors and that based on rings results not only from the rather smaller number and larger size of the rings, but also from the much greater heterogeneity within each individual ring.

Since the absolute value of any single dissimilarity index is of rather doubtful meaning, such indices are only really useful for comparative purposes. The religious segregation indices for Belfast presented so far have already been compared with each other to illustrate

TABLE IV

Actual and expected number and percentage of households in streets classified by religious composition

Percentage Catholic by street	Actual number of households	Expected number of households	Actual percentage of households	Expected percentage of households
0–9	62 029	2354	53·3	2·0
10–19	15 172	19 872	13·0	17·1
20–39	14 878	91 153	12·8	78·4
40–60	4831	2839	4·1	2·4
61–80	2453	83	2·1	0·1
81–90	837	2	0·8	—
91–100	16 072	19	13·8	—
Total	116 322	116 322	100·0	100·0

the effect of varying the size of data sub-sets, and it is proposed to defer any comparisons of dissimilarity indices between Belfast and other cities until the concluding section of the paper, which attempts to place our findings on religious distributions in Belfast in the context of intra-urban ethnic patterns elsewhere. However, one other form of comparison which is possible, and which was made in their analysis of negro segregation in American cities by Taeuber and Taeuber, is to relate the empirically derived values for the index to the values which would result from a random distribution of the two religious groups, relative to each other, within the city.[70] It need hardly be stressed that, if the distribution of the groups was purely the result of a random process, a completely uniform distribution of Catholics relative to the total population would be extremely unlikely: some segregation must therefore occur even if the process involved was purely random.

Taeuber and Taeuber tackled the problem of discovering precisely how much segregation would result from the operation of a random process in two distinct ways, one using a simulation approach and the other applying the binomial probability distribution. It is the second of these methods which has been applied to the Belfast data, though with two modifications. First, the suggestion of Taeuber and Taeuber that this method requires all sub-sets to be equal in size is rejected because, as E. C. Pielou points out, the only problem in applying the binomial distribution to sub-sets of varying size is that the procedure is complex. This follows from the fact that frequency distributions of the variable being studied must be generated for each size of sub-set found in reality, and these distributions must then be summed, after being weighted to take account of the relative frequency of the sizes of sub-set, thus deriving the overall required frequency distribution of the variable involved.[71] Secondly, since 31 per cent of the streets used as data sub-sets in Belfast had fewer than twenty households, the normal approximation to the binomial distribution, as used by Taeuber and Taeuber, was regarded as inadequate, and the binomial itself was employed.

The result of applying this procedure is illustrated in Table IV, which shows both the actual number and percentage of households in streets classified by religious composition, and the corresponding number and percentage produced from the aggregation of the binomial distributions which would represent the expectancy were the generating process purely random. Visual comparison is sufficient to emphasize the considerable differences between the actual and expected distributions, and this is confirmed by an extraordinarily high chi-square value of over 15 million! With six degrees of freedom, this chi-square value far exceeds the mere 39 which is the critical value even at the 99·9999 per cent probability level, thus stressing the fact that our empirically discovered level of religious residential segregation at street level in Belfast far exceeds that which would be generated randomly.[72]

Moreover, the dissimilarity index which indicates the level of segregation present in the street-by-street distribution of Catholic households relative to Protestant households that results from the random generation is only 11·8. Interestingly, this is similar both to the value of 13·0 which Taeuber and Taeuber found to be yielded by simulation, and to the value of 14·4 which they found to be generated by the normal approximation to the binomial distribution when in both cases they were using city blocks, as sub-sets, approximately equal in size to the Belfast streets. More important, our randomly generated value of 11·8 is well below the 70·9 which has been found in reality to exist in Belfast, thus strongly confirming once more that Belfast's level of religious residential segregation far exceeds the level that would be expected simply from the operation of a random process.

The variation of residential segregation within Belfast

Sociologists have characteristically derived ethnic segregation indices for entire cities in order to compare the segregation levels of different cities or to compare the degree of segregation exhibited by different ethnic groups within whole cities or to study changing levels of segregation through time in entire cities. As Jones has pointed out,[73] the segregation indices described and used in the sociological literature have not been applied to individual parts of cities in order to study spatial variation in the degree of segregation within cities. The only exceptions to this have been the spatially unsophisticated comparisons made between the level of segregation within cities which form political units at the centre of urban areas and the level found within the suburban periphery which forms the remainder of the urban area.[74]

Whatever the explanation for this general neglect of the study of intra-urban variation in segregation, this is a subject which cannot validly be ignored in Belfast. Two indices of intra-urban segregation will be used for this analysis. The first is the dissimilarity index which has already been applied to the city as a whole, but which, this time, will be used to measure segregation between the streets within each tract separately: it thus measures the deviation from intra-tract uniformity of the distribution of Catholic households relative to Protestant households. Hence the basic data sub-sets used are streets, and the data set is the individual tract, instead of the city as a whole; however, when the separate dissimilarity indices for each tract are then compared with each other, the tracts become data subsets at this second stage of the analysis, and the entire city again becomes the data set.

Figure 7 illustrates the spatial pattern revealed by mapping the dissimilarity indices for the tracts. It is clear that all tracts with indices above the upper quartile are, with the exception of one in Ballymacarrett, located in a broad sector in west Belfast, aligned along the Falls, Shankill and Crumlin Roads. Rather lesser levels of intra-tract segregation, though still above the median, are found in the inner parts of the city and in much of the east. Those tracts below the median, on the other hand, are found in the remainder of the east but particularly in the north and the south, though not in the innermost parts

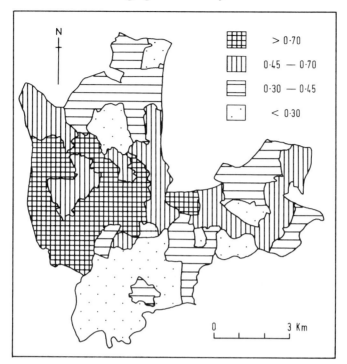

FIGURE 7. Belfast County Borough: tracts classified into quartiles on the basis of the dissimilarity index

of these sectors. The lowest indices of all, below the lower quartile, are concentrated principally in the south, along the Lisburn, Molone and Ormeau Roads.

The dissimilarity indices mapped in Figure 7 show the deviation from uniformity of the street-by-street distribution, within each tract, of those Catholic households that the tract contains relative to the remainder of the population. There is another aspect, however, to the segregation level of a tract, for, as J. W. Leasure and D. H. Stern point out, a data sub-set's share of the total number of minority group households in a city, relative to its share of all households there, is just as much a measure of its segregation as is the dispersion of that share within the sub-set.[75] Leasure and Stern applied this share-concept of segregation to eight data sub-sets in the Los Angeles metropolitan area. Taeuber and Taeuber used the concept simply to contrast two complementary sub-sets, the central city and the suburban periphery, of a metropolitan area.[76] All these writers ignored, however, the earlier work of Jones, who had devised a segregation index based on the share-concept and had applied it to the 231 enumeration districts of Belfast to study religious residential segregation.[77]

None of these segregation indices based on the share-concept will be applied, however, to the Belfast problem. Instead, we shall apply an index which is based on the binomial distribution, and which measures the probability that the deviation between (a) the number of Catholic households in a particular area and (b) the number that area would have if its share of the city's Catholic households were the same as its share of all house-

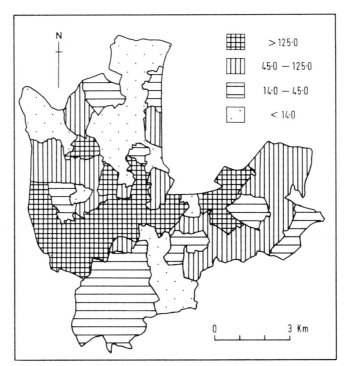

FIGURE 8. Belfast County Borough: tracts classified into quartiles on the basis of the probabilistic share index

holds in the city, could have occurred by chance. Because of these attributes, it is termed the 'probabilistic share index', and it is used to contrast the relative share found in each of the seventy-one tracts: it thus measures the segregation existing at a markedly higher level of generalization than that recorded by the dissimilarity indices. The construction of the probabilistic share index and its merits and demerits, and indeed the relative value of all the segregation indices referred to in this paper, have been discussed in detail elsewhere,[78] so it suffices to observe that the index takes a value of zero if there is no segregation, in the share-concept sense, in a particular area, and that there is no theoretical maximum to the value of the index.

The binomially-derived probabilistic share index of residential segregation is mapped in Figure 8. Once again, as in Figure 7, the most segregated tracts are concentrated in the west though, in the case of the share index, the sector is a much narrower one on either side of the Falls Road. Close observation of the tracts above the upper quartile on Figure 8 reveals that a rather high proportion of them (eleven out of eighteen, in fact) are strongly Catholic, including, in addition to the Falls sector, much of the central part of the city and also Ardoyne. The reason for this is that, for sub-sets as large as the seventy-one tracts, the binomial distribution is virtually normal in shape, and thus an exclusively Catholic area is much more improbable as a random deviation from the city average of 24·6 per cent Catholic than is an exclusively Protestant area. In fact, an entirely Protestant

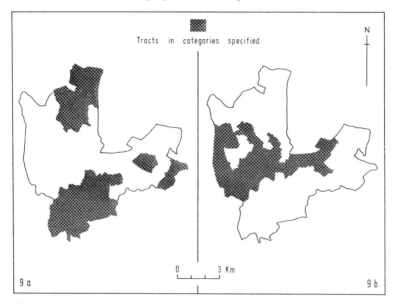

FIGURE 9.(a) Belfast County Borough: tracts below the median value of both the dissimilarity index and the probabilistic share index; (b) Belfast County Borough: tracts above the upper quartile value of either the dissimilarity index or the probabilistic share index

tract is only as improbable as a tract which is about 50 per cent Catholic. The seven Protestant-dominated tracts which do have a probabilistic share index above the upper quartile either adjoin the heavily Catholic Falls sector, in the Shankill Road area to the north and the Donegall Road area to the south, or are in a pocket in east Belfast. Most of the remainder of the eastern and western segments of the city are least above the median for this index, leaving the north and south almost entirely below the median. Within both the north and the south there is spatial differentiation, however, for the Antrim Road and Ormeau Road sectors contain almost all tracts below the lower quartile.

The salient features of Figures 7 and 8 are reproduced in the two parts of Figure 9. The first of these, Figure 9a, shows those tracts which are below the median for both segregation indices. In these tracts, therefore, the number of Catholic households as a percentage of all households does not deviate very much from the city average of 24·6 per cent, thus yielding a comparatively low probabilistic share index, and the Catholic households which are in these tracts are distributed fairly uniformly relative to the Pro-testant households. Thus, at both the inter-tract and intra-tract scale levels, there is only a moderate degree of religious residential segregation in these tracts; and the map makes it clear that their distribution within the city is quite simple, with a strong concentration into the middle and outer parts of broad sectors in the north and south, and with two small pockets in the outer part of east Belfast.

The area left blank on Figure 9a clearly shows those tracts, on the other hand, which are above the median on either one or both of the segregation indices and which are thus characterized by at least moderate segregation at one or both scale levels. Figure 9b takes this last aspect but uses the upper quartile as the critical level. Thus, in some of the tracts

indicated on Figure 9b, the number of Catholic households as a percentage of all households deviates widely from the city average of 24·6 per cent, while in others the number of
Catholic households is distributed far from uniformly relative to the Protestant households in these tracts; thirteen of the twenty-three tracts on this map, however, are above
the upper quartile on both indices. It is clear from Figure 9b that the distribution of these
tracts which are highly segregated at one or both scale levels is very simple in form:
they are concentrated throughout most of a broad western sector and in the inner part of
east Belfast.

RELIGIOUS RESIDENTIAL SEGREGATION IN BELFAST IN THE CONTEXT
OF ETHNIC RESIDENTIAL SEGREGATION ELSEWHERE

This paper is essentially a study of the residential segregation of ethnic groups in a single
city, Belfast. However, the authors believe that the significance of many of the Belfast
findings is more easily appreciated if they are evaluated in the context of ethnic residential
segregation elsewhere. This is not possible in relation to all aspects of our study because
some facets of it have not been replicated in research elsewhere, but, where analogous
empirical work has been published, we now compare our Belfast findings with corresponding results from other cities. Specifically, there are two main areas of research covered in
the Belfast study which have been sufficiently investigated in other cities to yield comparable
results: the first is concerned with the degree of ethnic segregation in entire cities, and the
second with the pattern of distribution of ethnic minorities within cities. Both these areas
of research have been investigated most extensively in the United States.

Comparison of the degree of segregation within entire cities

Comparison of the overall degree of residential segregation between Belfast and other
cities can only be meaningful where certain specific requirements are satisfied in the
analyses for these other cities. First, the measure of segregation must be the dissimilarity
index; secondly, the data sub-sets must be approximately similar in scale to the sub-sets
used in one of the Belfast analyses; thirdly, the studies of segregation in cities elsewhere
must be reasonably contemporaneous with the 1969 Belfast results; and fourthly, the data
set must be restricted to the central city at the heart of an urban area.

The salient results of research on segregation elsewhere comparable with our Belfast
findings are presented in Table V. To facilitate comparison, the dissimilarity indices for
the other cities are classified according to the scale of the data sub-sets used, and each
is allocated to one of three columns on this basis: for comparison, the Belfast dissimilarity
index corresponding to each of these three scales is stated at the head of the appropriate
column.

The most comprehensive analysis is that of Taeuber and Taeuber who measured the
segregation of non-white from white households in 207 American cities.[79] They used city
blocks as data sub-sets for this analysis, and Table V shows that this is the only study
comparable in scale to that part of the Belfast study which used streets as sub-sets. Taeuber
and Taeuber found the median dissimilarity index to be 87·8, with an upper quartile of
91·7 and a lower quartile of 81·2. The Belfast street-level index of 70·9 is clearly well below
even the lower quartile of the American data; in fact, no less than 95 per cent of the American cities studied had indices higher than this Belfast value. Taeuber and Taeuber also

TABLE V

Comparison of dissimilarity indices for Belfast and selected other cities

Sub-sets	Average size of sub-set	City	Groups compared	Streets 38 households	Tracts 5600 persons	Wards 28000 persons
					Belfast	
					Belfast indices	
			Catholics—rest of population	70·9	56·9	50·1
Blocks	100 households	207 American cities[1]	Whites—non-whites: median / range	87·8 / 60·4–98·1		
Enumeration Districts	900 persons	San Fernando[2]	Creole—East Indian	27·0		
Enumeration Districts	900 persons	San Fernando[2]	Whites—3 other ethnic groups: median / range	59·2 / 57·6–59·5		
Tracts	3000–6000 persons	12 American cities[3]	Whites—non-whites: median / range		79·3 / 61·2–89·8	
Tracts	3000–6000 persons	New York[4]	Puerto Ricans—other whites		73·0	
Tracts	3000–6000 persons	San Antonio[4]	Spanish surname—other whites		63·6	
Tracts	3000–6000 persons	Los Angeles[4]	Spanish surname—other whites		57·4	
Tracts	3000–6000 persons	San Francisco[4]	Spanish surname—other whites		37·3	
Tracts	3000–6000 persons	Los Angeles[4]	Other non-white—non-Spanish white		60·5	
Tracts	3000–6000 persons	San Francisco[4]	Other non-white—all white		51·4	
Sector-Ring Cells	47000 persons	Chicago[5]	Native whites—10 European immigrant groups: median / range			31·5 / 16–44
Sector-Ring Cells	47000 persons	Chicago[5]	Native whites—Mexicans			54
Sector-Ring Cells	47000 persons	Chicago[5]	Native whites—Puerto Ricans			67
Wards	28000 persons	Poona[6]	Hindus—Muslims			45
Census divisions	8800 persons	Auckland[7]	Europeans—5 Polynesian groups: median / range		36·8 / 31·9–49·6	
Census divisions	8800 persons	Auckland[7]	European—Maoris		31·2	
Wards	29000 persons	Birmingham[8]	Coloured immigrants—rest			50
Wards	29000 persons	Birmingham[8]	West Indians—rest			55
Wards	29000 persons	Birmingham[8]	Indians and Pakistanis—rest			45
Wards	29000 persons	Birmingham[9]	Irish immigrants—rest			26·9

1. K. E. and A. F. Taeuber (1965), 32–4
2. C. G. Clarke (1971), 201–7
3. K. E. and A. F. Taeuber (1965), 61
4. K. E. and A. F. Taeuber (1965), 65–7
5. K. E. and A. F. Taeuber (1964), 376–7
6. S. K. Mehta (1969), 486
7. P. H. Curson (1970), 172
8. P. N. Jones (1967), 7
9. P. N. Jones (1967), 30

calculated dissimilarity indices for the segregation of white from non-white households in twelve United States cities using census tracts, comparable in size to the Belfast tracts, as data sub-sets: the result was a median index of 79·3, and, indeed, all twelve cities had indices higher than the corresponding Belfast value of 56·9.

In most American cities, almost all the non-white population consists of negroes, so the figures quoted in the preceding paragraph are virtually measures of negro residential segregation. However, in some cities, other non-white races (such as Japanese, Chinese and Filipinos) are numerically significant. Using census tract data, Taeuber and Taeuber show that the segregation of these other non-white races from the white population is at about the same level of intensity in Los Angeles and San Francisco as is that of Catholics and Protestants in Belfast. Similarly, the level of segregation in Belfast is about the same as that between the Spanish surname population and other whites in both San Antonio (Texas) and Los Angeles, though it is much higher than the segregation of this group in San Francisco. On the other hand, the Belfast index is considerably lower than the value indicating the segregation between Puerto Ricans and other whites in New York.

The only detailed residential segregation indices available for a wide range of white ethnic groups is based on data for a series of sector-ring cells in Chicago, which are most comparable in size to the Belfast wards.[80] Results are presented for the segregation between each of twelve white immigrant groups (both first and second generation) and the whites of native parentage, and it is clear that the only two groups exhibiting greater segregation than Catholics and Protestants in Belfast were the two non-European groups, the Puerto Ricans and the Mexicans.

The only comparable research on ethnic residential segregation outside the United States, whose results are available to the authors, is in studies of San Fernando (Trinidad) by C. G. Clarke, of Poona (India) by S. K. Mehta, of Auckland (New Zealand) by P. H. Curson, and of Birmingham (England) by P. N. Jones.[81] The results of Mehta and P. N. Jones must, because of the size of the data sub-sets used, be compared with the ward-level findings in Belfast, and the results of Curson are comparable to our tract-level findings, but the indices derived by Clarke relate to a scale level intermediate between our streets and our tracts. Clarke suggests that the most socially relevant ethnic distinction in San Fernando is that between creoles and East Indians, but the dissimilarity index for the segregation between these two groups is only 27·0, which is much lower than even the tract-level index in Belfast. It is true that the whites in San Fernando are as segregated from each of the major ethnic groups there as are Catholics and Protestants in Belfast, but the whites are not numerically important, representing only 3 per cent of the population. In Auckland, Curson measured the segregation between the European population and each of five Polynesian groups, and found that even the highest index was lower than the corresponding Belfast value; he discovered, moreover, that the Maoris were less segregated from the Europeans than even the least segregated of the Polynesian groups. The results of Mehta in Poona, when he analysed the segregation between the two religious groups, Muslims and Hindus, also demonstrated a dissimilarity index lower than the corresponding index of religious segregation in Belfast. In the analysis of ethnic residential segregation in Birmingham, P. N. Jones focused his attention on first-generation immigrants, classified according to birthplace. Coloured immigrants as a whole in Birmingham show precisely the same degree of segregation as Catholics in Belfast, though the principal coloured group, the West Indians, are rather more segregated, while the immigrants from the Indian subcontinent are rather less segregated, than Belfast Catholics. However, Irish immigrants into Birmingham are considerably less segregated from the remainder of the population there than are Catholics from Protestants in Belfast.

This discovery, that the well-publicized residential segregation which exists in Belfast is no greater in intensity than the degree to which the coloured immigrants in an English city are segregated from the white population there, is particularly significant in view of the frequency with which it is stated that ghettos do not exist in England.[82] Such statements are based only on data for wards and entire local authority areas, and it is true that, at these very high scale levels, no single data sub-set is predominantly coloured in population, for the highest percentage coloured in any local authority area in England in 1966 was only 7·4 per cent in the London Borough of Brent and the highest in any ward was only just over 30 per cent in Northcote ward in Ealing, also in London. But the absence of all-coloured districts at this scale level is more a result of the low overall percentage coloured in Britain (West Indian, Indian and Pakistani immigrants made up only 1·8 per cent of the population in 1966) than of the degree of residential segregation. This is confirmed by the fact that, in Belfast, where the minority ethnic group constitutes 24·6 per cent of the total number of households, 13·8 per cent of the population live in streets that are entirely, or almost entirely, Catholic. Yet the degree of residential segregation in Belfast has been demonstrated to be no greater than that in Birmingham. It should therefore be emphasized that, despite the protestations that there are no coloured ghettos in Britain and despite the publicity given to the existence of all-Catholic areas in Belfast, the degree of ethnic residential segregation found in Belfast is far from unique in the United Kingdom. Moreover, the preceding paragraphs have made it clear that, in a broader world context, many ethnic minorities, especially negroes in the United States, are as segregated, or even more segregated, than are Catholics in Belfast.

Comparison of the spatial pattern of segregation

It is considerably more difficult satisfactorily to compare the spatial distribution of ethnic minorities within different cities than it is to compare the degree of segregation of such minorities in different cities. This is because adequate quantitative and objective indices are available for measuring the degree of residential segregation, but it is much more difficult to avoid being subjective and imprecise when describing a spatial pattern.

This problem of achieving precise description can be partly overcome by the use of the index of centralization, as proposed by Duncan and Duncan in a study of intra-urban occupational distributions, though clearly such an index only measures one facet of a spatial pattern.[83] When applied to the distribution of Catholics, relative to Protestants, in Belfast, the centralization index is positive, indicating that Catholics are, on the whole, located rather closer to the centre of the city than are Protestants, but the index takes the comparatively low value of 14·6. Though this index has not been applied on so widespread a scale as the dissimilarity index, there is, nevertheless, some previously published material with which to compare the centralization index for Belfast.

Thus an American study of the centralization of the non-white population in twenty-three United States cities showed that their median index in 1950 was 42·3, and only one of these cities had a value lower than that quoted for Belfast.[84] Such a low figure in Belfast could indicate simply that there is a lower level of segregation there; however, though a significantly higher index, 22·2, is achieved by measuring the centralization within Belfast, not of all Catholic households but only of the 56 per cent of those households which are in streets that are 91–100 per cent Catholic, even this figure is lower than all but one of the American indices quoted by R. W. Redick. Thus, whether we examine the entire Catholic population in Belfast or only that section living in streets almost exclusively Catholic, we find that centralization does exist, but only to a moderate degree. The only other ethnic centralization index available for comparison is for Muslims in Poona, who have an index of − 16·2, indicating that they are rather less centralized than the majority Hindu population: clearly, though the direction of concentration is different, the degree is at the same low level as in Belfast.[85]

The low level of centralization of the Catholic population in Belfast is not entirely surprising, for it has already been demonstrated that the spatial distribution of this religious group within Belfast takes a sectoral rather than concentric form. However, the degree of concentration of a minority group into sectors is more difficult to compare between cities because, though an index of sector concentration has been applied for example, by R. J. Davies, it necessarily suffers from the deficiency that the definition of sectors is rather arbitrary, and there will be variation, from city to city, in the number of meaningful sectors.[86] In the absence both of satisfactorily objective measures of concentration into sectors and of comparable empirical results using such indices, the only way in which any aspect (other than centralization) of the spatial pattern of religious distribution in Belfast can be compared with intra-urban ethnic patterns elsewhere is by examining maps and by referring to verbal descriptions which are themselves based on the examination of maps.

The intrinsic subjectivity of such an approach is particularly unfortunate in view of the apparent variation in the form of ethnic spatial patterns, as is suggested by the maps of the distribution of the negro population both in ten American cities used as examples by Taeuber and Taeuber and in the four others similarly employed by R. L. Morrill.[87] This variation is stressed by H. M. Rose, who suggests that Chicago, Detroit, Cleveland and Milwaukee are examples of cities whose negro distribution is sectoral, while Pittsburgh and San Francisco, on the other hand, are cities with a series of separate clusters.[88] The inevitable subjectivity of generalizing about spatial patterns which are so complex and variable is illustrated by the difference of opinion between Rose and T. R. Anderson, for Rose disputes Anderson's suggestion that negroes are an exception to his generalization that growing population groups within cities expand sectorally rather than concentrically.[89]

Despite this evidence of conflicting opinion and diversity of pattern, certain common denominators in the distribution of negroes within American cities do exist. As Rose points out, the negro areas generally tend to radiate in one or more sectors, albeit often highly truncated, from a location near the edge of the central business district after having been initially located in slum areas at the inner tip of these sectors. Such an initial location was indicated by Anderson as characteristic of most ethnic groups, except that most of them did not subsequently expand beyond this area.

This characteristic pattern of an ethnic minority occupying the inner portion of one or more sectors of a city is also repeated outside the United States, as is demonstrated both cartographically in the *Atlas of London* and also in Johnston's verbal description of the residential pattern of minority groups in British and Australasian cities.[90] True, the spatial structure of the housing market in some cities does lead to exceptions, such as the tendency for the coloured immigrants in Birmingham (England) to occupy pockets in a middle concentric zone or the occupation of certain outer suburbs of Auckland (New Zealand) and Melbourne (Australia) by minority ethnic groups, but the general pattern of inner clusters and truncated sectors is remarkably persistent.

The principal concentrations of Catholics in Belfast conform closely to this generalization about the intra-urban spatial patterns of ethnic minorities, for the initial locations of four of the six almost exclusively Catholic areas in Belfast were in four separate pockets adjacent to the central business district, and one of them has subsequently grown outwards along a complete sector to the city boundary and beyond. The sectoral pattern said to be characteristic of social groups experiencing growth of population over a long period is the dominant pattern in Belfast where the Catholic population is both long-established and has been growing, as has the Protestant. Since, in addition, the two religious groups have remained culturally quite distinctive, the Belfast pattern is much more sectoral than most intra-urban ethnic patterns, with the exception of those American cities with long-established negro populations, because most ethnic groups fail to expand in population as a result of assimilation. Neither the American negro nor the Belfast Catholics become assimilated into the population as a whole, but have retained a highly distinctive identity through several generations.

Despite the dominance of sectorization in its spatial pattern, the Catholic population of Belfast, especially that portion of it living in almost exclusively Catholic areas, is also centralized in relation to the rest of the population. Again, this is to be expected, in a western city, of an ethnic group whose members are of lower rank in society than the remainder of the population, both directly because of their membership of an ethnic group deprived of community-wide power and influence and also indirectly because their occupation-structure makes them of lower-than-average socio-economic status.[91] In this respect, the Catholics of Belfast display a pattern similar to those of ethnic groups elsewhere, but most of these other groups, with the partial exception of the American negro, are recent immigrants who have not yet risen in status or been assimilated: it appears to be rare for an ethnic group to be of such persistently low status as the Belfast Catholics or for a group to remain centralized after so long a period of settlement in a city. The explanation for this anomaly must lie not only in the distinctive political and social environment of Northern Ireland but also in the absence of any recent immigrant group of low status to displace Catholics from central Belfast.

CONCLUSION

This attempt to compare the residential pattern of the religious minority in Belfast with intra-urban ethnic patterns elsewhere is inevitably impeded by insufficient knowledge of the relevant social processes operating in the city. Without such knowledge, it is impossible to provide an adequate explanation for the differences found in ethnic patterns and, indeed, even where two spatial patterns are identical, one cannot be sure that the same explanation applies to both. The comparisons of pattern which have been made in the final section of the paper are therefore, of necessity, superficial. Similarly, the comparisons of the degree of segregation of ethnic minorities in different cities throughout the world must be interpreted with care since, even if two ethnic minorities are equally segregated in two cities, a different set of factors may be responsible for determining the level of segregation in each city. Moreover, both types of comparison are considerably limited by the relatively small amount of comparable information available on either the degree of segregation or the form of the intra-urban spatial pattern of ethnic minorities. Nevertheless, it is believed that these comparisons are valuable in allowing the Belfast analysis to be perceived within the context of similar phenomena elsewhere.

The appreciation of the Belfast pattern could clearly be increased much more, however, if, first, more comprehensive information was available on the segregation and spatial pattern of ethnic minorities in other cities and if, secondly, more was known about the social structure of the cities involved and about the process of residential choice in each one. Comparison could then be made not only of the patterns themselves but also of the social processes operating to create, maintain and modify them. It is with the intention not only of examining the Belfast pattern itself, which is so relevant politically and socially, but also of contributing to this general body of knowledge on pattern and process that this paper has been written.

ACKNOWLEDGEMENTS

The authors gratefully acknowledge the assistance both of Father A. Macauley in obtaining basic data for the analysis and of Miss J. A. E. Orr for undertaking much of the analysis itself. They are grateful to the Queen's University of Belfast for a grant towards the cost of illustrations, and to S.S.R.C. for other financial support.

REFERENCES

1. K. E. TAEUBER and A. F. TAEUBER, *Negroes in cities: residential segregation and neighborhood change* (Chicago, 1965), 28

2. A. H. PASCAL, *The economics of housing segregation*, Rand Corporation Memorandum RM-5510-RC (Santa Monica, 1967), 1

3. F. W. BOAL, 'Territoriality on the Shankill-Falls divide, Belfast', *Irish Geogr.* 6, 1 (1969), 33–4, 41

4. F. W. BOAL, 'Segregation in west Belfast', *Area* 2 (1970 a), 45

5. M. WADDELL, *A little bit British: being the diary of an Ulsterman, August 1969* (1970)

6. F. W. BOAL, op. cit. (1969), 40–7; R. HARBINSON, *No surrender: an Ulster childhood* (1966), 16

7. M. C. DAY, M. A. POOLE and F. W. BOAL, 'The spatial distribution of disturbances in Belfast, 1969–71', paper read at the Conference of Irish Geographers in Coleraine, May 1971

8. F. W. BOAL, op. cit. (1969), 30–50; *Northern Ireland Community Relations Commission, First Annual Report* (1970), 5–6

9. A. BOYD, *Holy war in Belfast* (Tralee, County Kerry, 1969); *Northern Ireland Community Relations Commission Research Unit*, 'Flight: a report on population movement in Belfast during August 1971' (1971)

10. N. GIBSON, 'The northern problem: religious or economic or what?' *Community Forum* 1 (Spring 1971), 4

11. A. DOWNS, 'Alternative futures for the American ghetto', *Daedalus* 97 (1968), 1331–1378; S. CARMICHAEL and C. V. HAMILTON, *Black Power* (1968); F. F. PIVEN and R. A. CLOWARD, 'The case against urban desegregation', *Social Work* (January 1967), 12–21; N. DEAKIN and B. G. COHEN, 'Dispersal and choice: towards a strategy for ethnic minorities in Britain', *Environment Plann.* 2 (1970), 193–201

12. E. E. EVANS, 'Belfast: the site and the city', *Ulster J. Archaeol.*, 3rd Series, 7 (1944), 25–9; E. JONES, 'Belfast: a survey of the city' in E. JONES (ed.), *Belfast in its regional setting: a scientific survey* (1952), 209–11; E. JONES, 'The distribution and segregation of Roman Catholics in Belfast', *Sociol. Rev.* 4 (1956), 167–89; E. JONES, *A social geography of Belfast* (1960), 172–206

13. M. THOMAS, 'The Northern Ireland knowledge gap', *Fortnight* 3 (23 October 1970), 5–7; J. DARBY, 'Community relations: 2:research', *Fortnight* 13 (19 March 1971), 8–9

14. The authors are currently undertaking a study, sponsored by the Social Science Research Council, of religious residential segregation and residential decision making in Belfast. This should enable the causal aspects of segregation to be more fully elucidated.

15. M. A. POOLE and M. C. DAY, 'Residential displacement in Belfast in the summer of 1969', report presented in April 1971 to the Tribunal of Inquiry constituted to inquire into certain acts of violence which occurred in the months of March, April, July and August 1969 at various places in Northern Ireland; see also M. A. POOLE, 'Riot displacement in 1969', *Fortnight* 22 (6–31 August 1971), 9–11

16. F. W. BOAL and D. E. FIELD, 1) 'Analysis of damage to property', and 2) 'Analysis of damage and religious affiliations in damaged streets', reports presented in January 1970 to the Tribunal of Inquiry constituted to inquire into certain acts of violence . . .

17. M. A. POOLE, 'An analysis of rural electricity consumption patterns in the Republic of Ireland', unpubl. Ph.D. dissertation, Queen's University of Belfast (1968), 74–5

18. E. E. EVANS, op. cit., 25–9; E. JONES, op. cit. (1956); E. JONES, op. cit. (1960), 172–200

19. E. Jones, op. cit. (1952)

20. R. J. Johnston, 'Population movements and metropolitan expansion: London 1960–61', *Trans. Inst. Br. Geogr.* 46 (1969), 69–91; P. N. Jones, 'Some aspects of the changing distribution of coloured immigrants in Birmingham, 1961–66', *Trans. Inst. Br. Geogr.* 50 (1970), 199–219

21. K. E. and A. F. Taeuber, op. cit., 228–9

22. E. J. Kaiser and S. F. Weiss, 'Decision agent models of the residential development process: a review of recent research', *Traffic Q.* 23 (1969), 597–8, 621; L. A. Brown and E. G. Moore, 'The intra-urban migration process: a perspective', *Geogr. Annlr* 52 B (1970), 1; C. C. Roseman, 'Migration as a spatial and temporal process', *Ann. Ass. Am. Geogr.* 6 (1971), 591–2

23. J. W. Simmons, 'Changing residence in the city: a review of intra-urban mobility', *Geogrl Rev.* 58 (1968), 622, 649

24. E. Jones, op. cit. (1956), 171–5; E. Jones, op. cit. (1960), 175, 177, 191–5; *Government of Northern Ireland: General Register Office, Census of Population, 1961—Belfast County Borough* (1963), 33

25. E. E. Evans, op. cit., 25

26. E. Jones, op. cit. (1956), 175; E. Jones, op. cit. (1960), 177, 195

27. E. Jones, op. cit. (1956), 175–88; E. Jones, op. cit. (1960), 136, 177–206

28. *Government of Northern Ireland: General Register Office, Census of Population, 1966—General Report* (1968), IX

29. F. W. Boal and D. E. Field, op. cit.

30. *Government of Northern Ireland: General Register Office*, op. cit. (1968), 25; E. Jones, op. cit. (1958), 175; E. Jones, op. cit. (1960), 136; *Government of Northern Ireland; General Register Office, Census of Population, 1951—Belfast County Borough* (1953), 2

31. P. Greig-Smith, *Quantitative plant ecology* (1964), 56–7, 85–93, 105–11, 169; K. A. Kershaw, *Quantitative and dynamic ecology* (1964), 25–6, 30, 104–13; W. S. Robinson, 'Ecological correlations and the behavior of individuals', *Am. sociol. Rev.* 15 (1950), 351–7; O. D. Duncan, R. P. Cuzzort and B. Duncan, *Statistical geography: problems in analyzing areal data* (Glencoe, Illinois, 1961), 65–7, 109–11

32. D. O. Cowgill and M. S. Cowgill, 'An index of segregation based on block statistics', *Am. sociol. Rev.* 16 (1951), 826

33. K. E. and A. F. Taeuber, op. cit., 222–3

34. D. W. Harvey, 'Pattern, process and the scale problem in geographical research', *Trans. Inst. Br. Geogr.* 45 (1968), 71–8

35. K. E. and A. F. Taeuber, op. cit., 223, 226

36. D. O. and M. S. Cowgill, op. cit., 826; R. Travers Morgan and Partners and Belfast Corporation, 'Travel in Belfast' (1968), 151–2

37. J. S. Adams, 'Directional bias in intra-urban migration', *Econ. Geogr.* 45 (1969), 302–23; E. Jones, op. cit. (1960), 145–6; F. W. Boal, 'Social space in the Belfast Urban Area' in N. Stephens and R. E. Glasscock (eds.), *Irish geographical studies* (1970 b), 388–91

38. B. J. L. Berry, 'Internal structure of the city', *Law Contemp. Probl.* 30 (Winter 1965), 115–16

39. F. W. Boal, op. cit. (1969), 48–9

40. F. W. Boal, op. cit. (1970 b), 376

41. *Building Design Partnership*, 'Belfast central area' (1969), 20

42. K. E. and A. F. Taeuber, op. cit., 30, 55–62

43. Ibid., 30; W. Bell and E. M. Willis, ('The segregation of negroes in American cities', *Soc. econ. Stud.* 6 (1957), 62) make a similar point.

44. B. J. L. Berry and F. E. Horton, *Geographical perspectives on urban systems: with integrated readings* (Englewood Cliffs, New Jersey, 1970), 317

45. *Government of Northern Ireland: General Register Office*, op. cit. (1968), XXII-IV

46. Ibid., 165

47. Ibid., 57

48. K. E. and A. F. Taeuber, op. cit., 55–62; W. Bell and E. M. Willis, op. cit., 62; D. O. Cowgill, 'Segregation scores for metropolitan areas', *Am. sociol. Rev.* 27 (1962), 400–2

49. The County Borough percentage is based on the sources of data described earlier in the text, while that for the outer ring of the urban area is based partly on the same sources and partly on the following: *St MacNissi's College (Editorial Office), Catholic Directory, 1969: diocese of Down and Connor* (Garron Tower, Co. Antrim, 1969) 9–82; *Government of Northern Ireland: General Register Office*, op. cit. (1968), XXII; *Building Design Partnership, Belfast Urban Area Plan Volume 1* (1969), 25

50. *Northern Ireland Community Relations Commission Research Unit*, op. cit.

51. *Government of Northern Ireland: General Register Office*, op. cit. (1963)

52. D. P. Barritt and C. F. Carter, *The Northern Ireland problem: a study in group relations* (1962), 1

53. E. E. Evans, op. cit., 25–9; E. Jones, op. cit. (1960), 172–99

54. E. Jones, op. cit. (1960), 172

55. R. ROSE, *Governing without concensus: an Irish perspective* (1971), 208

56. Ibid., 218–37

57. P. VALIEN, 'Minority group' in J. GOULD and W. L. KOLB, *A dictionary of the social sciences* (1964), 433

58. P. A. COMPTON and F. W. BOAL, 'Aspects of the inter-community population balance in Northern Ireland', *Econ. soc. Rev.* 1,4 (1970), 455, 475–6; N. GIBSON, op. cit., 5

59. M. M TUMIN, 'Ethnic group' in J. GOULD and W. L. KOLB, op. cit., 243

60. E. E. EVANS, op. cit., 25–9; E. JONES, op. cit. (1952), 209–11; E. JONES, op. cit. (1956), 167–89; E. JONES, op. cit. (1960), 172–206

61. E. JONES, op. cit. (1952), 209–11

62. F. JONES, op. cit. (1956), 176–81; E. JONES, op. cit. (1960), 196–8

63. E. E. EVANS, op. cit., 25–9

64. K. E. and A. F. TAEUBER, op. cit., 205–7; F. W. BOAL, op. cit. (1969), 30

65. P. MARCUSE, 'Integration and the planner', *J. Am. Inst. Plann.* 35 (1969), 114

66. P. A. COMPTON and F. W. BOAL, op. cit., 460–1

67. S. SUDMAN, N. M. BRADBURN and G. GOCKEL, 'The extent and characteristics of racially integrated housing in the United States', *J. Business* 42 (1969), 51

68. M. A. BEAUCHAMP, 'Processual indices of segregation: some preliminary comments', *Behavioral Sci.* 11 (1966), 190–2

69. K. E. and A. F. TAEUBER, op. cit., 202–16; O. D. and B. DUNCAN ,'A methodological analysis of segregation indexes', *Am. sociol. Rev.* 20 (1955), 210–17

70. K. E. and A. F. TAEUBER, op. cit., 231–4

71. E. C. PIELOU, 'The distribution of diseased trees with respect to healthy ones in a patchily infected forest', *Biometrics* 19 (1963), 451–2; E. C. PIELOU, *An introduction to mathematical ecology* (1969), 181

72. S. K. KHAMIS, 'New tables of the chi-squared integral', *Bull. int. statist. Inst.* 40 (1964), 799–823

73. E. JONES, op. cit. (1956), 184; E. JONES, op. cit. (1960), 200

74. W. BELL and E. M. WILLIS, op. cit., 71–4; D. O. COWGILL, op. cit., 401; S. LIEBERSON, 'Suburbs and ethnic residential patterns', *Am. J. Sociol.* 67,6 (1962), 674–80; K. E. and A. F. TAEUBER, op. cit., 55–60; T. G. CLEMENCE, 'Residential segregation in the mid-sixties', *Demography* 4 (1967), 563; R. FARLEY, 'The changing distribution of negroes within metropolitan areas: the emergence of black suburbs', *Am. J. Sociol.* 75, 4 (1970), 513–17

75. J. W. LEASURE and D. H. STERN, 'A note on housing segregation indices' ,*Social Forces* 46 (1968), 406–7

76. K. E. and A. F. TAEUBER, op. cit., 58

77. E. JONES, op. cit. (1956), 183–8; E. JONES, op. cit. (1960), 199–204

78. M. A. POOLE and F. W. BOAL, 'Probabilistic indices for the measurement of residential segregation', Queen's University of Belfast, Department of Geography, Working Paper

79. K. E. and A. F. TAEUBER, op. cit., 32–4

80. K. E. and A. F. TAEUBER, 'The negro as an immigrant group: recent trends in racial and ethnic segregation in Chicago', *Am. J. Sociol.* 69, 4 (1964), 376–7

81. C. G. CLARKE, 'Residential segregation and intermarriage in San Fernando, Trinidad', *Geogrl Rev.* 61 (1971), 201–7; P. H. CURSON, 'Polynesians and residence in Auckland, New Zealand', *N. Z. Geogr.* 26 (1970), 172; P. N. JONES, 'The segregation of immigrant communities in the city of Birmingham, 1961', *Univ. of Hull, Dept. of Geography Occas. Pap.* 7 (1967), 7; S. K. MEHTA, 'Patterns of residence in Poona, India, by caste and religion: 1822–1965', *Demography* 6 (1969), 486

82. R. GLASS, *Newcomers: West Indians in London* (1960), 41; N. DEAKIN, *Colour, citizenship and British society* (1970), 61–3, 135–6; N. DEAKIN and B. G. COHEN, op. cit., 194–5; E. KRAUSZ, *Ethnic minorities in Britain* (1971), 41–2

83. O. D. and B. DUNCAN, 'Residential distribution and occupational stratification', *Am. J. Sociol.* 60, 5 (1955), 495, 499–500

84. R. W. REDICK, 'Population growth and distribution in central cities, 1940–1950', *Am. sociol. Rev.* 21 (1956), 41

85. S. K. MEHTA, op. cit., 488

86. R. J. DAVIES, 'Social distance and the distribution of occupational categories in Johannesburg and Pretoria', *S. Afr. geogr. J.* 46 (1964), 26–7, 34–7

87. K. E. and A. F. TAEUBER, op. cit. (1965), 256–75; R. L. MORRILL, 'The negro ghetto: problems and alternatives', *Geogrl Rev.* 55 (1965), 343

88. H. M. ROSE, 'Social processes in the city: race and urban residential choice', Association of American Geographers, Commission on College Geography, Resource Paper 6 (Washington, D.C. 1969), 9

89. Ibid., 7–9; T. R. ANDERSON, 'Social and economic factors affecting the location of residential neighborhoods', *Pap. Proc. reg. Sci. Ass.* 9 (1962), 168–9

90. E. JONES and D. J. SINCLAIR, *Atlas of London and the London region* (1968), sheets 31 and 32; R. J. JOHNSTON, *Urban residential patterns: an introductory review* (1971), 284–90

91. A. BOSERUP and C. IVERSEN, 'Rank analysis of a polarized community: a case study from Northern

Ireland', *Pap. Peace Res. Soc. (Int.)* 8 (1967), 60; R. ROSE, op. cit., 280

RÉSUMÉ. *Ségrégation par religions des habitants de Belfast, mi-1969 : une analyse à plusieurs rangées.* La ségrégation par religions des habitants de Belfast a attiré l'attention d'un large public par suite de son importance politique dans le cadre des troubles récents dans la ville. Cependant, l'insuffisance tant en perception de cette ségrégation par l'homme de la rue qu'en enquêtes scientifiques qui s'y rapportent fait ressortir le besoin d'une analyse systématique des dimensions spatiales de la composition de la ville pour ce qui concerne les religions et de leur variation selon le niveau d'échelle.

L'analyse, basée sur des renseignements sur la composition religieuse assemblés par les auteurs, ne pouvait avancer sans une considération de cinq problèmes principaux. Ceci a mené au choix de ménages comme éléments des données, de la région enfermée par les limites municipales comme ensemble des données, du milieu de 1969 comme période temporale et d'une division binaire en catholique et protestant comme classification religieuse convenable. Finalement, on a décidé de conduire l'analyse à trois niveaux d'échelle en employant des rues, des zones et un ensemble de secteurs et de cercles comme les trois mesures de sous-ensemble des données.

Les sous-ensembles des données, à chaque niveau d'échelle, sont classifiés selon leur composition religieuse, et fréquence et distribution spatiale sont décrites. Le modèle pour Belfast dans son ensemble est résumé à chaque niveau d'échelle par des indices relatifs de dominance et par des indices de dissemblance pour mesurer respectivement le degré de dominance et de ségrégation qui existe. La variation intra-urbaine dans l'intensité de la ségrégation est soumise ensuite à une analyse au niveau intrazonal en employant des indices de dissemblance et au niveau interzonal en employant des indices probabilistes de proportion.

Finalement, le degré de ségrégation ainsi que le modèle spatial de la distribution de catholiques à Belfast sont comparés au moyen des indices de centralisation et d'une inspection de cartes, avec les conclusions correspondantes pour des groupes ethniques dans d'autres grandes villes ailleurs.

ZUSAMMENFASSUNG. *Die konfessionelle Absonderung der Einwohner in Belfast Mitte 1969: eine Mehrstufen-Analyse.* Der konfessionellen Absonderung der Einwohner in Belfast ist, infolge ihrer politischen Bedeutung in den jüngsten Unruhen in dieser Stadt, seitens der Öffentlichkeit beachtliche Aufmerksamkeit zuteil geworden. Doch die Unzulänglichkeit, sowohl der Vorstellung des Nichtfachmannes von dieser Absonderung als auch der einschlägigen wissenschaftlichen Forschung, weist hin auf die dringende Notwendigkeit einer systematischen Analyse der räumlichen Ausdehnung de konfessionellen Zusammensetzung der Stadt und deren Variierung mit der Stufe des Massstabs.

Die Analyse, die sich auf von den Verfassern sesammelte Informationen gründet, konnte nur nach Prüfung von fünf Hauptproblemen in Angriff genommen werden. Das hatte zur Folge die Wahl der Haushalte als Dateneinheiten, der Stadt als Grafschaftsbezirk als Datengruppe, Mitte 1969 als Zeitabschnitt, und die Zweiteilung in Katholiken und Protestanten als passende konfessionelle Einteilung. Zuletzt wurde entschieden, die Analyse auf drei Massstabsstufen vorzunehmen, wobei die Strassen, die Zonen und eine Gruppe von Sektoren und Ringen als die drei Grössen der untergeordneten Datengruppe verwendet wurden.

Auf jeder Massstabsstufe wurden die untergeordneten Datengruppen nach konfessioneller Zusammensetzung eingeteilt, und ihre Häufigkeit und örtliche Verteilung beschrieben. Um den vorhandenen Grad des Vorherrschens b.z.w. der Absonderung zu messen, wird das Bild der Verteilung für ganz Belfast für jede Massstabsstufe mittels Indexe des relativen Vorherrschens und der Verschiedenheit zusammengefasst. Die innerstädtische Variierung der Intensität der Absonderung wird dann auf der Innenzonenstufe mittels der Verschiedenheitsindexe und auf der Zwischenzonenstufe mittels Indexe des Wahrscheinlichkeitsanteils analysiert.

Schliesslich wurde unter Verwendung von Zentralisationsindexen und durch Prüfung der Karten, sowohl der Absonderungsgrad als auch das Raumbild der Verteilung der Katholiken in Belfast mit entsprechenden Ergebnissen für ethnische Gruppen in anderorts gelegenen Städten verglichen.

D

FIG. 1. Grafschaftsbezirk Stadt Belfast: die Häufigkeitsverteilung der auf Grundlage der konfessionellen Zusammensetzung eingeteilten Strassen

FIG. 2. Grafschaftsbezirk Stadt Belfast: im Text erwähnte Orte

FIG. 3. Strassen im Grafschaftsbezirk Stadt Belfast, die Mitte 1969 ihrer Zusammensetzung nach zwischen 90,5 prozent und 100 prozent katholisch waren

FIG. 4. Strassen im Grafschaftsbezirk Stadt Belfast, die Mitte 1969 ihrer Zusammensetzung nach zwischen 0,0 prozent und 9,5 prozent katholisch waren

FIG. 5. Grafschaftsbezirk Stadt Belfast: Prozentsatz der Katholiken nach Zonen Mitte 1969

FIG. 6. Grafschaftsbezirk Stadt Belfast: Prozentsatz der Katholiken nach Sektoren und Ringen Mitte 1969

FIG. 7. Grafschaftsbezirk Stadt Belfast: auf Grundlage des Verschiedenheitsindexes nach Quartilen eingeteilte Zonen

FIG. 8. Grafschaftsbezirk Stadt Belfast: auf Grundlage des Indexes des Wahrscheinlichkeitsanteils nach Quartilen eingeteilte Zonen

FIG. 9.(a) Grafschaftsbezirk Stadt Belfast: Zonen, die unter dem Zentralwert sowohl des Verschiedenheitsindexes als auch des Indexes des Wahrscheinlichkeitsanteils liegen; (b) Grafschaftsbezirk Stadt Belfast: Zonen, die über dem oberen Quartilwert entweder des Verschiedenheitsindexes oder des Indexes des Wahrscheinlichkeitsanteils liegen

Social networks in urban society

JOHN CONNELL

Research Officer, Institute of Development Studies, University of Sussex

Revised MS received 12 May 1972

ABSTRACT. Urban studies have become increasingly complex with the introduction of concepts from the general field of urban sociology. One such concept, that of the 'urban village', is considered here; it is shown that superficial and imprecise use of the term to encompass such varied situations as localized working class, middle class and ethnic groups within urban areas has resulted in considerable confusion over the processes involved in urbanization. Social network analysis, originating in anthropological work, has a sufficient rigour to be used as a heuristic tool to analyse small-scale urban social systems and to examine the spatial constraints on socio-economic links. Limited geographical contributions in this field, especially through diagrammatic and cartographic representation of spatial links, enable socio-spatial groups within cities to be seen as hierarchically ordered. But the hierarchies cannot yet be carefully depicted because of the inadequate rigour of existing social network analysis.

THE rapid development of theory in urban geography has revealed the imprecision with which such terms as 'urban', 'urbanization' and 'urbanism' have been used. As in several of the social sciences, the everyday use of words that are also used to describe social facts has resulted in some confusion in the terminology; 'everyone knows what a city is except the expert' (H. Miner, 1967, p.3). This paper attempts to look at one such term, the 'urban village', considering its usage within a general field of urban change and, more specifically, to examine the use of social network analysis, a relatively new sociological technique, as a heuristic tool for the analysis of the spatial and social characteristics of towns and cities.

Social network is a term that anthropologists and sociologists have often used in the past, principally as a convenient metaphor or a suggestive analogy rather than one derived from theory. Despite attempts to introduce formal definitions to informal metaphors, network tends to retain a general image of something difficult to grasp, an impressionistic reference to complex pheonomena. Yet the rapidly increasing literature incorporating the notion of 'social network' in its analysis is strong evidence for the fertility of an idea introduced to social science by J. A. Barnes (1954). Numerous subsequent studies have followed this sort of orientation in attempting to analyse such diverse phenomena as family organization, social class, community organization and rural–urban migration. Despite the proliferation of material,[1] much of which is related to traditional geographical concerns of spatial variation, the complexity of social network analysis has so far severely restricted its transfer into geographical analysis.

The proliferation of network terms and definitions in less than two decades (E. Bott, 1971) within many empirical studies of varying emphases has produced severe problems of terminology and hence of comparability. Here, following Barnes (1969a), 'It seems . . . preferable to use the term "network" only when some kind of social field is intended, for there has been much confusion about ego–centric and socio–centric extracts from the total network. In my usage we can never speak of an ego–centric network'. However, the term network has become too well entrenched in the ego–centric sense to be abandoned;

there are therefore two levels at which social networks should be conceived, the network of a single individual and the series of networks that make up a particular social field.

The general use of the notion of 'network' subsumes and partly obscures important aspects of social relationships such as 'connectedness' (or density), intensity, status and role, while there is not yet an acceptable set of criteria which might be used to distinguish the characteristics of one type of network from another, so far partly because of the amount of fieldwork involved. Furthermore, J. C. Mitchell lists four morphological characteristics of networks (anchorage, reliability, density and range) and five interactional criteria (content, directedness, durability, intensity and frequency) all of which should be distinctive characteristics of individual networks. This represents an increase in sophistication compared with earlier recognition of networks that are 'closely knit' (many members having direct contact with each other) and 'loosely knit' (few members having direct contact). This complexity is a fundamental and significant difference from the primarily morphological networks studied by P. Haggett and R. J. Chorley (1969) and although the characteristics distinguished by them make comparison between networks difficult, the majority of these characteristics are inherently more easily measurable than those of social networks. Indeed, despite the existence of much general and mathematical theory concerned with social networks (Barnes, 1969b) it is significant that geographical method finds it possible simply to dismiss the field with a single reference to work published in 1934 (Haggett and Chorley, 1969) while M. Woldenburg and B. J. L. Berry (1967) compare networks drawn from economic and physical systems but do not extend this analysis to social systems. However, in Sweden, T. Hägerstrand (1968) has revived a concern for the analysis of individual time-budgets which may be studied in terms of linkages and systems. The environment is viewed as consisting of 'communication lines' (*kommunikationsleder*) and 'stations' (*stationer*), and the approach of subsequent workers in this field (J. Anderson, 1971; T. Carlstein, 1971) indicates emerging similarities with social network analysis. The criteria listed by Mitchell are indicative of the potential value of this new technique, when used rigorously, for the comprehension of both the spatial and social processes involved in social and organizational change in urban areas. Networks enable the sterile urban-rural division to be abandoned in favour of a more behavioural and sociological analysis of social organization and some integration of the multiplicity of bits of ethnography that have hitherto been the corpus of urban sociology.

A critical question concerns the nature of the inter-personal links, the characteristics of which are being measured. Mitchell's five interactional criteria pose problems of content, frequency and intensity which at this stage in the development of social network analysis are almost too rigorous to be operationally useful, yet more superficial examinations, without this analytical rigour, are indicative of particular insights. Fundamentally, for an analysis of social organization, the most important links may be those of friendship, but other possible kinds of links are economic, commercial, political and religious. Here, social links are taken to refer also to these other sorts of link.

Possibly the most interesting aspect of social network analysis within an urban context is the unusual case where a series of networks is finitely bounded within an urban area, that is, where there is a spatial boundary to a social field. However, the marginality of this case is reflected in the ultimate openness of any network; boundedness is, in practice, a question of diminished degree of openness, and the problems of boundary analysis have produced their own, largely anthropological, literature (Y. A. Cohen, 1969; F. Barth,

1969). The extent of the necessary fieldwork has precluded extending network analysis into the connectedness and degree of closure of social and/or spatial groups, and single groups have only exceptionally been the locus of network studies. G. A. Lundberg and M. Steele (1938) made a network analysis of friendship links in a Vermont village and found that the population of the village, which numbered approximately 1000, could be divided into seven major groups plus a fringe of isolated and semi-isolated individuals. Yet their analysis considered only friendship links rather than a wide range of potential social and economic relationships.

THE URBAN VILLAGE

The specific concern of this paper is to look, in the light of this kind of analysis, at a sup-posedly universal small-scale social system,[2] the urban village. Although it was not until 1962 that H. J. Gans (1962) first used the term 'urban village' when referring to Italians in Boston, many writers had earlier considered the unique position of rural or alien immigrants within an urban area. Gans did not define the term, and despite its wide use, the only apparent definition is that of R. L. Meier (1962, p. 311) in a speculative article on the plan-ning of Indian cities, where he conceives the urban village as 'a plac ewith fixed boundaries, speaking one mother tongue and holding to the same general set of customs. (A few villages could be constituted as mixtures of a wide variety of subcultural backgrounds, so that the in-migrant is granted some choice when he arrives.) This is a community that has some basis for co-operation independent of arbitrary authority asserted from the outside . . . The urban village was proposed as an environment that made possible a rapid adjustment to city life, while at the same time it provided a convenient basis for administration'. He saw the urban village as a sufficiently meaningful unit to be used as a basic structure for urban planning. For social network analysis, one can consider an urban village as a population group spatially restricted and existing in a part of the urban area, within which individual social networks are totally connected; the social system is bounded within the city. It is argued that, hitherto, much analysis of small communities or areas within large cities has been without a rigorous theoretical base and that the recognition of 'urban village' has been a result of wishful thinking, often combined with distant enchantment, resulting in the glamorization of the situation of often poor and deprived urban communi-ties. Although the working definition proposed will be seen to be too restrictive, it must be used as a theoretical basis.

The generality of Meier's definition of 'urban village' raises some problems. A parallel inherently is implied with rural villages and implicit, therefore, is the idea of a spatial relocation either of rural persons in an urban setting or of a village situation in an urban area.[3] This poses the initial problem of defining a village. A 'village' has always been so easily recognized subjectively that the simplicity of definitions has been assumed to the extent that accounts of village life and organization, especially in anthropology, proceed from the underlying assumption that what is studied is a village, but as a result of diverse assumptions of what is a village, studies of villages often contain little that is comparable. Various partial definitions of village may include references to some form of small-scale agricultural community, an internal social system, small size and remoteness (J. Connell, 1970b). Ultimately, the village is a cluster concept describing entities with family resem-blances. The most used criterion is that of 'community' possibly because it also is un-satisfactorily defined (G. A. Hillery, 1955) but is employed here in the sense of a group of people sharing common traditions and interests. Many villages, even in this loose sense, are not communities.

Of the two possible concepts of urban village, namely, the spatial relocation of a group of rural persons or the existence of a local social system within an urban area, the second is the one mainly relevant to the present English situation. Two types of urban village have been suggested. The first is the upper-middle class urban village of the Hampstead, Highgate and Dulwich type, while the second is the working class community, such as that held to exist in East London. (Working class and middle class must be used here in the loosest possible sense, as over-generalized categories, since lines of demarcation are imprecise and dependent on several varying and ambiguous criteria, such as power, prestige, style of life and economic achievement, and the secondary studies considered here use varying definitions.)

The middle class urban village

Description of areas such as Highgate as an urban village are based on a feeling that the community life there approximates to that of a working class community, but at a rather more esoteric and sophisticated level. Thus R. Firth, J. Hubert and A. Forge (1969) comment on the social heterogeneity of Highgate and suggest that this diversity 'seemed to allow it to have assumed a more integrated character, with the variety of occupations, class relationships and institutional allegiances providing a sort of functional complementarity and furthermore that this "village" atmosphere was more apparent in time of trouble.' The name 'village' is largely a legacy from a time prior to engulfment by urban expansion and is retained purely for connotations of status (J. Eyles, 1968) in local names. Various local names in London such as Hampstead, Golders Green or Camden Town, have significance locally as an expression of the occupations, education and social pretensions of the people who live there, or rather, the kind of people who are supposed to live there; hence 'the city is seen as something like an irregular lattice work from which a person's behaviour and appearance can be gauged, interpreted and reacted to, depending on the section to which he belongs' (G. Suttles, 1968).

This situation is paralleled in American examples such as Greenwich Village (E. T. Delaney, 1968) which, like the English examples, is morphologically distinct from the rest of the city, being independent of the grid-iron street system and focused on the green space of Washington Square. The area was unique to New York; the social composition of the population was extremely varied and there was no local social system that could encompass them all; thus the Village could not be regarded as a single community except in the minds of the residents who, just as in Highgate, could define their own individually acceptable boundaries (Delaney, 1968). As in the English case, its village status depended on its historical tradition, partially separate from the rest of the city.

The middle-class urban village is far from being a single social system. Its existence is entirely spatial and its boundaries are usually subjective and indeterminate; it is a product of status symbolism and is not an isolated urban community. The middle class are most likely to maintain communications with other members of spatially dispersed 'non-place communities' (M. Webber, 1964a). Social propinquity is here, at best, incidentally related to spatial propinquity, while the social networks of the middle class extend far beyond the residential locations and exclude many close at hand.

The working class urban village

The most often cited example is Bethnal Green. M. Young and P. Willmott (1957) write that Bethnal Green appears 'a community which has some sense of being one. There is a sense of community, that is a feeling of solidarity between people who occupy the common territory'. The factors that they stress as being of importance in community development are continuity of residence of both individuals and families (here reinforced by the tradition of descent from Huguenot stock), the local network of kinship and the local distribution of workplaces, clubs and shopping centres.

It is in R. Hoggart's (1957) generalized account of working class life in Leeds, notably in the inter-war years, that the subjective village emphasis is most apparent; parts of Hunslet 'are small worlds, each as homogeneous and well defined as a village . . . (the inhabitants) know it in infinite detail automatically slipping up a snicket here or through a shared lavatory block there; they know it as a group of tribal areas'. In Swansea too there appears to be little difference; 'except in a very general sense of external geographical reference, and in a few internal contexts connected with municipal administration and sport particularly, individual families do not live in Swansea, but rather in one of the many neighbourhoods or local communities *within* Swansea . . . All contain neighbourhoods within them, and the Chinese puzzle of neighbourhoods within neighbourhoods down to a single street, or side or end of a street, or turning or cul de sac or whatever' (C. Rosser and C. Harris, 1965). Localized social networks are most likely to develop in areas where the inhabitants feel they belong to the same social class and this appears to be strongest in 'long-established working class areas in which there is a dominant local industry or a relatively small number of traditional occupations' (Bott, 1957). Although propinquity initiates friendships, it is not of itself sufficient to create the intensive relationships that are the case within a homogeneous community. Nevertheless, Bott suggests that 'it is only amongst the working class that one is likely to find a combination of factors all operating together to produce a high degree of connectedness: concentration of people of same or similar occupations in the same local area, jobs and homes in the same local area; low population turnover and continuity of relationships; at least occasional opportunities for relations and friends to help one another to get jobs; little demand for physical mobility; little opportunity for social mobility'.

M. Stacey (1969) develops this argument into a series of propositions on the nature and origin of local social systems. The basis of this is in the form of three propositions. First, the minimum condition for the existence of a local social system is that the majority of the local population should have been present together in the locality for some period of time, probably at least 50–80 years. Secondly, the longer this period is, the more likely there is to be a local social system present, and thirdly, where the majority of the population have been born and bred in the locality, it is highly likely that there will be some sort of local social system present. Extensions of this are that the more institutions are present in a locality, the more likely it is that a local social system will develop and that, in a locality which is entirely residential, only sub-systems connected with family and with neighbourhood can develop. The addition of workplaces to the locality not only increases the number of available roles, but may allow a different kind of social system to develop. Local workplaces increase the probability that a localized social system will develop, by reducing the need for residents to move outside their spatial environs. Where this is not so, 'the job holder may have to leave the neighbourhood daily, but he follows a fixed transit course to his destination, and returns with little intercourse *en route*' (Webber, 1964b, p. 62).

Yet against these more traditional accounts of the working-class community, K. Coates and W. Silburh (1969), in the poorest part of Nottingham 'came to realise that these romantic ideals of plebeian community fit it rather ill', while J. H. Goldthorpe *et al.* (1969) argue that the three bases of traditional working class life, the network of kinship, the pattern of neighbouring and the collective actions and rituals of common solidarity, are disappearing so that the local and particularistic nature of working class life is immediately threatened. On these grounds alone it is scarcely possible for an urban village to exist in working class areas of Britain at the present day. In the past this might have been more probable when workplaces were smaller, nearer together and transport was less developed. There is little doubt that, although the traditional working class are different from other urbanites, small-scale economic and social links are insufficient to provide an operational local social system, or more specifically, an urban village.

At the present time, on cultural grounds and because of a changing economic organization, it would be difficult to recognize an urban village in this situation. Historically, a more distinct working-class culture and more localized workplaces would make this recognition simpler; yet even for the nineteenth century it is almost impossible to characterize a particular working-class community as a local system. Bethnal Green, for example, has always merged 'in so many different ways with other parts of London and industrial Britain' (P. Townsend, 1957) and there are also differences within Bethnal Green; 'Bethnal Green has many points of similarity with a village or rather with a whole series of overlapping and interlocking villages' (J. H. Robb, 1954). We have therefore an indication of a loose hierarchical organization of communities; it is hypothesized that this kind of system is universal if, in many cases, little more than incipient.

R. H. Morris and J. Mogey (1965, p. 146) recognized two types of residential group within working-class areas, the small group of ten to fifteen families, whose constituent ties may be primary, and the large residential group, whose physical unit is the street, containing sixty to a hundred families. These are the lowest levels in the hierarchy; above them various levels may be recognized, culminating in the city-region and the state. Yet the levels in the hierarchy are linked by different kinds of network. At the lowest level, social and domestic ties are critical; links between hierarchical levels are economic and political rather than social, and at a regional or national level of hierarchical integration, links are primarily political; at this level, personal networks tend also to be institutional networks.

The ethnic urban village

A kind of hierarchical organization has been observed in various ethnic immigrant communities within western cities. G. D. Suttles (1968) describes the organization of four ethnic groups in Addams, Chicago, where there is an ordered segmentation of two different kinds of socio-spatial unit, the 'gangland' and the residential area. In opposition to different kinds of external pressure, these units combine hierarchically. Indeed, a characteristic feature is the organization of the larger community into small-scale local groups based on the town, village or region or origin (Connell, 1970b). Unfortunately it has been the wider area within which all the different ethnic groups are located that has been referred to as the urban village; the West End of Boston was the area where 'European immigrants and more recently Negro and Puerto Rican ones try to adapt their non-urban institutions and cultures to the urban milieu. Thus it may be called an urban village. Often it is described in ethnic terms: Little Italy, the Ghetto or Black Belt' (Gans, 1962). Hence this urban village contained various other groups besides the Italians and, although it was possible for the Italians to form a local social system in the area, its cosmopolitan character meant that the area was not a local social system; ethnic groups only exceptionally combined together.

The basis of this ethnic localization is the need for a new migrant to join other migrants from his own cultural area before he can become independent of economic and social assistance, as for example in Sparkbrook, Birmingham, where 'the newcomer (lives) in a tight-knit community, perhaps one that is more tight-knit than any he knew in his village. But he is also launched into a larger society in which he has new rights and obligations as a citizen and in which, in time, he will be able to make his own way, emotionally dependent only upon his own immediate family' (J. Rex and R. Moore, 1967). Yet many immigrants do not arrive in western cities from villages or rural areas; the urban experience is not new. On the other hand, the possible middle-class and working-class urban villages discussed in the previous sections were the result of cultural differences continued over a long period; ethnic urban villages are a result of migration bringing different cultures into juxtaposition. There are no British examples of current rural-urban migration creating particular urban enclaves in the same way that still occurs in the United States G. Hyland, 1970).

Rarely, however, is it indicated exactly how concentrated these immigrant communities are or become; detailed census material tends to indicate that present-day immigrants are more widespread than popular connotations of 'immigrant ghettoes' would suggest. In established cities, rather than the rapidly-growing cities of the Third World, it is exceptional for an ethnic community to emerge as a socio-spatial unit, because of the necessity for a massive degree of residential change. What is remarkable is that in certain cases, this has almost occurred; after more than a decade of Jewish migration into Leeds, 90 per cent of the households in many of the streets in the heart of the immigrant area were Jewish (Connell, 1970a). Within this new ghetto the Jews formed smaller communities based on their town or region or origin; again, within the wider ethnic community a more localized community was present. Yet the Jewish ghetto of the last century was exceptional; for some time it remained almost completely encapsulated within the urban area. Often physically separated from the remainder of the city, the Jews were separate by language, religion, culture, and, more important, by occupation. The almost complete dominance of the home-based tailoring industry, where only a few organizers had contact with the rest of the city, meant that since the community was large, with its own shops, newspapers, schools and synagogues, the need for individuals to move outside their own social system into an alien system was almost non-existent. Few social or economic networks connected with the rest of the city, while the rapid decline in migration meant that the social organization of the ghetto was introspective rather than continually being replenished by cultural change from distant areas; it is an unusual case of urban involution. Because of its size and economic system, the hierarchical social organization was almost completely truncated at the ghetto boundaries; the late nineteenth-century Jewish ghetto in western Europe and north America may be the closest approximation we have to an urban village (Connell, 1972).

Yet insularity was not permanent; there are few cities that now have distinctive Jewish areas.

From the wide variations in contemporary urbanization in less developed countries there appear to be many alternative situations for migrants in urban areas. The standard situation is assumed to be 'detribalization', where rural immigrants from a particular ethnic group adapt to new social realities by adopting customs from other groups or by developing new customs shared with other groups, both as a process of modernization and as an adaptation to city life. Often urban associations help this transition to be made with a minimal amount of dislocation. New power and class structures and interest groups eventually cut across ethnic groups and, in time, ethnic bonds weaken.

Yet 'urbanization' is not the same as 'detribalization' and there are considerable difficulties in defining either process objectively (Connell, 1970b). Adoption of a new way of life is not necessarily unidirectional, towards the acquisition of urban mores and the abandonment of tribal customs, but is a product of a variety of circumstances. P. Mayer (1961) has outlined the organizational principles that may be involved generally for urban associations and are involved for the migration in South Africa of 'Red' Xhosa to East London; 'they appear to him (the 'Red' Xhosa migrant) in the form of two basic commandments: to keep up an unbroken nexus with the rural home and to abstain from unnecessary contact with non-Reds or participation in non-Red kinds of activity' (p. 90).

In Cairo, there are two immigrant groups, the cream who are numerically less significant but who have the drive and facility for assimilation into the city culture, and secondly, non-selective migrants who are drawn principally from the 'have-nots' of the village. With a lower capacity for assimilation, they tend to build for themselves within the city a replica of the culture they left behind (J. Abu-Lughod, 1961). One effect of this incapacity to be absorbed into any dominant urban cultural form is that the new urban residents reform their rural culture, which is often intensified. This particular situation is often referred to as 'retribalization' where an ethnic group adjusts to new realities by reorganizing its traditional customs or by developing new customs under traditional symbols, often using traditional norms and ideologies to enhance distinctiveness within the contemporary situation. This does not necessarily reflect the shortness of stay of the rural migrants in urban areas and in most of the cases where this situation has been recognized (Connell, 1970b), ethnic quarters have been established over more than one generation. In the case of the Hausa in Yoruba towns (A. Cohen, 1969), it is specifically those who intend to remain in the town who are most established in the social life of the Hausa quarter. In complete contrast, the Ankole in Kampala live in traditional Ankole huts for the duration of their stay in the city, which is rarely more than 2 years until they have enough money to pay bridewealth; their only contact with the city is for employment, and even the labour gangs in which they work consist almost entirely of Ankole or a related tribe. D. J. Parkin (1969) making apparently the only use of the term in Africa, describes this situation as an 'urban village'. Where the immigrants are thus unwilling to be assimilated or incapable of being assimilated, either through their own limitations or those of the host society, and especially where economic links with the remainder of the city are severely limited, the 'rural' or 'tribal' nature of the local community is likely to be intensified.

The distinction between 'detribalization' and 'retribalization' is primarily a function of the immigrant group rather than of the city itself. Kisangani (formerly Stanleyville) contains various ethnic groups with wide variations in rural-urban relations and with very different adaptations to the city (V. G. Pons, 1969). The Lokele are socially a relatively 'closed' group, in close contact with their villages and maintaining and developing a distinctively Lokele way of life; while the Babua rarely visit their villages and their way of life in town has relatively little cultural content; there is a sense in which their way of urban life is 'the Stanleyville way of life', developed by persons with little continuing participation in rural-tribal life. The Topoke, who unlike the other two groups are unskilled and have difficulty obtaining employment in the town, thus attach exceptional importance to their home villages as sources of security. Both the Lokele and Topoke are relatively 'closed' communities and the Babua more 'open'. The Lokele are highly involved in both town and country and their high rural and urban involvements tend to reinforce each other; for the Topoke, their high rural involvement results from incapacity to achieve urban involvement. In these cases there is no such thing as an urban village because of the dense social networks between urban and rural locations. Although the form of accommodation to the city is related to the characteristics of the migrant group rather than the city, the kind of social and economic organization within the city is important for fixing the different orientations of different groups. Where no single ethnic group dominates a city, as in Kisangani or in Medan, Sumatra (E. M. Bruner, 1961) there is no apparent urban or even national culture, and no directed cultural change with variable pressures on immigrants to discontinue tribal affiliations. There is therefore some evidence that, in situations where there are many ethnic groups, interpersonal relationships are more likely to be generated within the individual group than they would in situations where one ethnic group was overwhelmingly dominant. Furthermore, it is apparent that it is differential economic development rather than the persistence of cultural factors *per se* that leads to an emphasis on tribalism.

The city in both situations alters the ethnic situation, and in the latter case results in a reversion to a more rural or tribal norm. Hence A. L. Epstein (1967) redefines 'urbanization' as a process of movement and change. Its essence is that it creates the possibility of discontinuity with some pre-existing set of conditions; it is not therefore a unidimensional phenomenon. Nor is it unidirectional. Nevertheless, in the majority of cases, distinctions between detribalization and retribalization are not apparent; rural culture makes a contribution to the process of urbanization and influences the development of an urban culture. If the rural way of life is changed in the city, by what criteria is it possible to say that it is changing in an urban or a rural direction? What represents urbanism? Indeed, it becomes increasingly difficult to provide a simple answer; P. Wheatley (1970, p. 102) regards 'the concept of urbanism as compounded of a series of disparate sets of ideal-type institutions which have combined in different ways, in different cultures and at different times'. The nature of change in non-western cities clearly necessitates this amount of flexibility.

CONCLUSION

Although Meier's definition of the urban village is far from satisfactory, and was scarcely referring to a small-scale urban community, it is not possible to substitute a more useful definition. Sociological criteria such as 'small-scale', 'localized' and 'distinct' are not easily definable and yet are fundamental for a definition; their very number makes this even more difficult. At the same time the techniques involved in social network analysis have not yet given rise to adequate generalizations that would enable the term to be redefined. The precise use of social network analysis militates against an over-hasty desire to recognize communities and demands a scrupulous examination of linkages.

G. Sjoberg (1966) shows that ethnic enclaves within transitional cities perform at least three functions, the indoctrination of newcomers, the provision of a channel through which urban influences can pass to the villages with returning migrants and the maintenance of rural traditions. But it does appear that in some urban situations the first two functions are largely absent while the third is all-important; even so this maintenance and preservation of rural traditions is largely a conscious process and must therefore be a feature of urbanization. In the case of the Jewish ghetto, however, where the first two functions are most conspicuously absent, there are no rural traditions. Almost the entire Jewish migration was from the towns of East Europe. The density or connectedness of social relationships in a small area may be greatest at present in some urban situations in the Third World, especially where there has been rapid migration to the urban area, or in variants of this, such as historical Jewish or Italian migration. A high degree of connectedness in the network is largely discouraged in an urban environment, however, because separate agencies take charge of separate aspects of life there and ethnic associations tend to be concerned with ameliorating the process of integration.

A valuable new technique that may be used in social geography to consider such situations is social network analysis. In the context of the spatial organization of communities it may be possible at present largely to ignore the quality of the interactional criteria and to concentrate on the spatial location of the individuals within the networks. It may be enough at this stage to understand the locations of the individuals within a network, the nature and regularity of their relations (whether economic, social or other) and the connectedness of the ensuing bundle of individual networks. There has been almost no examination of the spatial location of individual networks; only one geographical study has mapped relationships (G. A. Hyland, 1970) although T. Caplow et al. (1964) and some of the contributors to Mitchell's collection of papers (Mitchell, 1969) give diagrammatic representations of spatial variations. Clearly the content of these spatial links remains critical and morphological networks alone are inadequate; social networks, by definition, are only marginally spatial.

Social network analysis is not a systematic theory of urban society but a series of techniques used to study urban social relations. The variable use of the techniques, in time and space, but more particularly in the character of the individual foci and the definitions of the key characteristics, has resulted in few conclusions, yet it is clear that the techniques provide more profitable insights into non-Western situations than attempts to transpose supposed terms of universal value such as 'urban', 'urbanism' and 'urbanization' from particular western to particular non-western situations. It is not possible to specify a universal urban social system as a distinctive form of human organization. The spatial structure of urban society, especially in less developed countries, demands that much current terminology be abandoned and that processes and links, especially in small communities, be reconsidered.

NOTES

1. The recent proliferation of material on urban social structure and related systems is phenomenal. The

following books and papers, listed in the References, contain fundamental bibliographies in this field: J. Anderson (1971), G. Beijer (1963), E. Bott (1971), A. Buttimer (1971), T. Carlstein (1971), J. Connell (1970b), G. Kushner (1970), R. A. Lobban (1970), W. Mangin (1970) and J. C. Mitchell (1969).

2. Social system is considered as a set of interacting persons or groups. The system includes a social structure of interrelated statuses and roles, and hence includes processes of change and interaction within the system.

3. A third definition is that of the village that is the apparent size of a town, such as the south Italian agro-towns (A. Blok, 1969), but this is an entirely different concept and is disregarded here. A fourth definition covers villages separate from urban areas but where the majority of the population work in urban areas and occupations. R. E. Pahl (1965) calls these 'metropolitan villages'. Some new villages, such as New Ash Green in Kent, are also of this kind. Finally there is also the 'industrial village' of nineteenth-century industrialism, occasionally with one factory monopolizing village employment (Pahl, 1970, p.20).

4. In general, 'ethnic' refers to 'races' or large groups of people classed according to common traits and customs. This may include racial, linguistic, religious or other cultural habits.

REFERENCES

ABU-LUGHOD, J. (1961) 'Migrant adjustment to city life: the Egyptian case', *Am. J. Sociol.* 67, 22–32
ANDERSON, J. (1971) 'Space-time budgets and activity studies in urban geography and planning', *Environment Plann.* 3, 353–68
BARNES, J. A. (1954) 'Class and committees in a Norwegian island parish', *Human Relations* 7, 39–58
BARNES, J. A. (1969a) 'Networks and political processes' in *Social networks in urban situations* (ed. J. C. MITCHELL)
BARNES, J.A. (1969b) 'Graph theory and social networks: a technical comment on connectedness and connectivity', *Sociology* 3, 215–32
BARTH, F. (1969) *Ethnic groups and boundaries*
BEIJER, G. (1963) *Rural migrants in an urban setting*
BLOK, A. (1969) 'South Italian agro-towns', *Comp. Stud. soc. Hist.* 11 (2), 121–35
BOTT, E. (1957) *Family and social network*
BOTT, E. (1971) *Family and social network* (2nd ed.)
BRUNER, E. M. (1961) 'Urbanization and ethnic identity in North Sumatra', *Am. Anthrop.* 63, 508–21
BUTTIMER, A. (1971) 'Sociology and planning', *Tn Plann. Rev.* 42, 145–80
CAPLOW, T., S. STRYKER and S. E. WALLACE (1964) *The urban ambience*
CARLSTEIN, T. (1971) 'Time allocation and the relevance of the spatial dimension', mimeo. Dept. of Geography, Lund University
COATES, K. and W. SILBURN (1970) *Poverty: the forgotten Englishman*
COHEN, A. (1969) *Customs and politics in Urban Africa*
COHEN, Y. (1969) 'Social boundary systems', *Curr. Anthrop.* 10, 103–26
CONNELL, J. (1970a) 'The gilded ghetto: Jewish suburbanization in Leeds', *Bloomsbury Geogr.* 3, 50–9
CONNELL, J. (1970b) 'Urban villages and social networks', (Dept. of Geography, University College London, Occas. Pap. No. 11
DELANEY, E. T. (1968) *New York's Greenwich Village*
EPSTEIN, A. L. (1967) 'Urbanization and social change in Africa', *Curr. Anthrop.* 8, 275–96
EYLES, J. (1968) 'The inhabitants' image of Highgate village (London)', Graduate School of Geography, London School of Economics, Discussion Pap. No. 15
FIRTH, R., J. HUBERT and A. FORGE (1969) *Families and their relatives*
GANS, H. J. (1962) *The urban villagers*
GOLDTHORPE, J. H., D. LOCKWOOD, F. BECHHOFER and J. PLATT (1969) *The affluent worker in the class structure*
HÄGERSTRAND, T. (1968) 'Methods and new techniques in current urban and regional research in Sweden', *Plan* 22, 3–11
HAGGETT, P. and R. J. CHORLEY (1969) *Network analysis in geography*
HILLERY, G. A. (1955) 'Definitions of community: areas of agreement', *Rural Sociol.* 20, 111–23
HOGGART, R. (1957) *The uses of literacy*
HYLAND, G. A. (1970) 'Social interaction and urban opportunity: the Appalachian immigrant in the Cincinnati central city', *Antipode* 2, 68–83
KUSHNER, G. (1971) 'The anthropology of complex societies' in *Biennial review of anthropology 1969* (ed. B. J. SIEGEL), 80–131
LOBBAN, R. A. (1970), 'The role of urban associations and social networks in the "Three Town" area of the Sudan and their relationship to urbanization', *Afr. urb. Notes*, 5, 37–45
LUNDBERG, G. A. and M. STEELE (1938) 'Social attraction patterns in a village', *Sociometry* 1, 375–419
MANGIN, W. (1970) *Peasants in cities*
MAYER, P. (1961) *Townsmen or tribesmen*
MEIER, R. L. (1962) 'Relations of technology to the design of very large cities' in *India's urban future* (ed. R. TURNER)

MINER, H. (1967) *The city in modern Africa*

MITCHELL, J. C. (1969) 'The concept and use of social networks' in *Social networks in urban situations* (ed. J. C. MITCHELL)

MORRIS, R. N. and J. MOGEY (1965) *The sociology of housing: studies at Berinsfield*

PAHL, R. E. (1965) *Urbs in Rure* (Geographical Monograph No. 2, London School of Economics)

PAHL, R. E. (1970) *Patterns of urban life*

PARKIN, D. J. (1969) 'Tribe as fact and fiction in an East African city' in *Tradition and transition in East Africa* (ed. P. H. GULLIVER)

PONS, V. G. (1969) *Stanleyville*

REX, J. and R. MOORE (1967) *Race, community and conflict. A study of Sparkbrook*

ROBB, J. H. (1954) *Working-class anti-semite*

ROSSER, C. and C. HARRIS (1965) *The family and social change*

SJOBERG, G. (1966) 'Cities in developing and industrial societies: a cross-cultural analysis' in *The study of urbanization* (ed. P. M. HAUSER and L. F. SCHMORE)

STACEY, M. (1969) 'The myth of community studies', *Br. J. Sociol.* 20, 134–47

SUTTLES, G. D. (1968) *The social order of the slum*

TOWNSEND, P. (1957) *The family life of old people*

WEBBER, M. (1964a) 'The urban place and the nonplace urban realm' in *Explorations into urban structure* (ed. M. WEBBER)

WEBBER, M. (1964b) 'Culture, territoriality and the elastic mile', *Pap. Proc. Reg. Sci. Ass.* 13, 59–69

WHEATLEY, P. (1970) Review of A. L. Mabogunje, 'Urbanization in Nigeria', *Econ. Geogr.* 46 (1969), 102–04

WOLDENBURG, M. J. and B. J. L. BERRY (1967) 'Rivers and central places; analogous systems', *J. reg. Sci.* 7, 129–39

YOUNG, M. and P. WILLMOTT (1957) *Family and kinship in East London*

RÉSUMÉ. *Les réseaux sociaux dans une société urbaine.* L'introduction de concepts tirés du domaine général de la sociologie urbaine dans les études d'urbanisme rend ces études de plus en plus complexes. Un de ces concepts, « le village urbain », est examiné dans cet exposé; on démontre que l'utilisation superficielle est vague de ce terme, en vu d'en globes des entités variées et localisées tels que classe ouvrière, classe moyenne et groups ethniques au sein des zones urbaines, a donné lieu à un degré de confusion considérable quand on examine les différents processus d'urbanisation. L'analyse du réseau social, au défait rélevant des études anthropologiques, comporte subisamment de ligeur pour être utilisé comme instrument heuristique dans l'analyse d'un système urbo-social à petite échelle et dans l'examen des contraintes spatiales imposées aux liens socio-économiques. L'apport limité de diagrammes dans ce champ d'études, en particulier de diagrammes centographiques et géographiques mettant une évidence sur les liens spatiaux, soulignant l'ordre hiérarchique qui régil les groupes socio-spatiaux au sein des villes. Mais cette hiérarchie ne peut-être fautement décrite à cause du manque de rigem suffisante dans l'analyse des réseaux sociaux dont on dispose.

ZUSAMMENFASSUNG. *Soziale Verbindungen in der städtischen Gesellschaft.* Mit der Einführung von Begriffen aus dem allgemeinen Gebiet der städtischen Soziologie wird das Stadium der Städte immer komplexer. Ein solcher Begriff, ,das Stadtdorf', wird hier untersucht. Es wird gezeigt, wie der oberflächliche und ungenaue Gebrauch dieses Wortes (z.B. für die Stadtteile, wo Arbeiterschaft, Bürgertum oder ethnische Gruppen wohnen) zu irreführenden Schlüssen über den Urbanisierungsprozess geführt haben. Die Analyse der sozialen Verbindungen, die aus der Anthropologie hervorgeht, ist dagegen genau genug, um als heuristisches Werkzeug für die Untersuchung kleinstädtischer Gesellschaftsysteme zu dienen. Sie erweist sich als besonders brauchbar in der Untersuchung des Verhältnisses von Raumordnung zu sozio-ökonomischen Verbindungen. Mit Hilfe von geographischen Mitteln, vor allem von Zeichnungen und Karten, können raumbedingte Gesellschaftsgruppen innerhalb der Stadt als heirarchisch geordnet gesehen werden. Dennoch können diese Heirarchien nicht mit völliger Genauigkeit aufgezeigt werden, da der gegenwärtige Stand der Verbindungsanalyse noch zu wünschen übrig lässt.

Pluralism and stratification in San Fernando, Trinidad

COLIN G. CLARKE

*Lecturer in the Department of Geography and Centre for Latin American Studies,
University of Liverpool*

Revised MS received 11 May 1972

ABSTRACT. The study uses the concept of social and cultural pluralism to examine social patterns in San Fernando, a complex urban community in Trinidad. Attention is directed to the town's racial and religious groups and to key institutions practised by them. Census data for race, religion, occupation, family and education are compared using correlation techniques and linkage analysis. Certain social and cultural patterns are discerned; some are related to 'stratification', others to 'pluralism'. Questionnaire data are then introduced to support the ecological evidence, and to explore certain values and attitudes held by the most important elements in the population. The results are discussed with reference to the plural hypothesis; and individual behaviour is compared with spatial patterns in the town.

THE role played by race and colour in Caribbean societies has been keenly debated by sociologists and anthropologists. Although there is general agreement that the larger islands are composed of hierarchically organized strata, some observers contend that these are based upon distinction of colour-class[1] or, in the case of Haiti, upon a system of colour-caste.[2] A different interpretation of Caribbean social structure has been offered by M. G. Smith[3] who stresses the importance of culture in defining social boundaries. Smith has refined and amplified the concept of the plural society first advanced by J. S. Furnivall.[4] Describing conditions in Burma and Java, Furnivall claimed that 'the first thing that strikes the visitor is the medley of peoples—European, Chinese, Indian and native. It is in the strictest sense a medley for they mix but do not combine. Each group holds by its own religion, its own culture and language, its own ideas and ways. As individuals they mix, but only in the market place in buying and selling. There is a plural society with different sections of the society living side by side but separately within the same political unit. ' . . . few recognize that in fact all members of all sections have material interests in common, but most see that on many points their material interests are opposed.'[5]

Smith[6] has suggested that only political units in which a minority section is dominant should be called plural societies, and has argued that these should be distinguished from others which simply possess pluralistic traits. According to Smith the islands of the Commonwealth Caribbean are characterized, at the very least, by social and cultural pluralism. The major social groupings are culturally distinct, and each is characterized by a specific combination of institutions. The principal institutional systems which are involved are family and kinship, education, religion, property, economy and recreation.[7] People who practise the same institutions and for whom they have the same values and implications form a cultural and social section in the society. Smith distinguishes between sections and classes. In his view social classes possess a common system of values and are 'differentiated culturally with respect to non–institutionalized behaviours such as etiquette, standards of living, associational habits, and value systems which may exist as alternatives on the basis of common values basic to the class continuum.'[8]

Cultural sections possess their own value systems. They may be ranked hierarchically or may occupy parallel positions in the social order. Moreover, each section may be internally stratified by social class. Smith clarifies his argument about cultural differences by citing the case of religion. He emphasizes that 'variants of Christianity share common basic forms of organization, ritual and belief',[9] but Christianity, Hinduism and Islam do not. He concludes that societies typified by the former kind of differentiation are culturally and socially heterogeneous; the latter socially and culturally plural. Smith admits that 'pluralism is a dimension',[10] and it is clear that the cultural differences that are critical in Jamaica are not the most important in Trinidad. Critics of Smith's model claim that it emphasizes cultural differences and neglects the importance of shared values.[11] Others contend that it lays insufficient stress upon those distinctions of race and colour[12] which were once so vital in the Caribbean in distinguishing between masters, slaves, freedmen and indentured labourers. Furthermore, another critic, referring to the problem of institutional analysis, has enquired at what point 'variations within one institutional sub-system become great enough to warrant our identification of two separate sub-systems'.[13]

Despite these criticisms the plural model is extremely useful when examining complex societies. It provides a system of institutional analysis which is both open-ended and independent of race; it facilitates the study of acculturation and places race in a broader perspective. Moreover, the model supplies an alternative to the premise adopted by most sociologists—that a common system of values is the *sine qua non* of stability in social systems and that without it societies cannot exist. L. A. Despres[14] has already explored the notion of the plural integration of cultural sections in Guyana while Smith[15] has demonstrated for the Commonwealth islands of the Caribbean in general, and Granada in particular, that when minority cultures are socially and politically dominant, consensus is replaced by force. This paper does not attempt to investigate these ideas thoroughly; nor is it concerned with Smith's more recent work on the jural, political and organizational aspects of pluralism.[16] The principal object is to use the ideas of social stratification and cultural pluralism as a means of analysing and understanding social and spatial patterns in a town in the highly complex island of Trinidad.

Differences of race, colour, status and culture are significant in Trinidad, and each factor defines important elements in the population. The principal feature of the social structure is the dichotomy between creole and East Indian. The term 'creole' has a particular meaning in Trinidad. It excludes the East Indian population, together with the small Syrian, Portuguese, Chinese and Carib minorities. Creoles may be white, brown, or black, and genotype correlates with socio-economic status. Stratification of the creole segment was established during slavery. Soon after emancipation in 1834, Indian indentured labourers were brought in to work on the sugar estates. This influx continued until 1917. Their descendants, known as East Indians, now make up almost 40 per cent of the island's population. The East Indians themselves are highly segmented and comprise Hindus, Moslems and Christians.

RACIAL AND RELIGIOUS GROUPS IN SAN FERNANDO

San Fernando is the second largest settlement in Trinidad and in 1960 recorded nearly

40 000 inhabitants. The community is split into a neat division in which creoles account for more than 70 per cent of the population and East Indians for just over one-quarter. The creole population comprises three major elements, whites (3 per cent of the town's inhabitants), negroes (47 per cent), and a mixed group (21 per cent). The mixed, or coloured, group is composed predominantly of mulattoes, though it also contains the off-spring of miscegenation between negroes or mulattoes on the one hand and Indians, Chinese, Syrians, Portuguese or Caribs on the other. Not only are the creoles numerically dominant in San Fernando; they are also proportionately more numerous in the town than in the island as a whole. Most of them are either Anglican or Roman Catholic, and San Fernando may, with some justification, be described as a creole and Catholic town. No member of the white population and only a few negroes and mulattoes are adherents of Hinduism or Islam; Hindus and Moslems are almost exclusively East Indian. The distinction between creole and East Indian is therefore reinforced by religious differences. Moreover, most of the East Indian converts are Presbyterian, and nearly all Presbyterians are East Indian.[17] Presbyterian East Indians comprise 8·5 per cent of the town's population and outnumber Hindus (7·6 per cent) and Moslems (5·8 per cent), though the converse is true for Trinidad as a whole.

The size of the Presbyterian population of the town is partly explained by the fact that Susamachar Church in San Fernando was established as the headquarters of the Canadian Mission during the second half of the nineteenth century. Proselytization proceeded at a rapid rate in San Fernando and on the surrounding sugar plantations where East Indians comprised the labour force. Conversion provided a major avenue for accul-turation and social mobility among the East Indians and contributed indirectly to their migration to the town. In recent years the economic prosperity of San Fernando has further stimulated urban growth and social change. In addition to its status as the industrial capital of Trinidad, the town is the major service centre for the southern part of the island, and its hinterland embraces sugar plantations, oilfields, and oil refineries.

SELECTION OF VARIABLES

The complex interrelationship between the racial characteristics and institutional com-position of the population of San Fernando may be examined by the statistical analysis of enumeration district data derived from the 1960 census. Eighteen variables have been set out in five groups which, with the exception of the racial category, are equivalent to the more important institutions specified by Smith (Table I). Little additional comment is required to justify the selection of the input for race and religion. Portuguese, Caribs and Syrians cannot be considered, since they do not appear in the enumeration district tabulations. The white population occurs in less than three-quarters of the census districts and, of necessity, has been omitted from this part of the study. But material does exist for the important East Indian and negro groups and for the Chinese and mixed populations. While the East Indians are divided between Hindus, Moslems and Christians (mostly Presbyterians), the majority of creoles are members of the orthodox Christian denomina-tions. However, a large minority of negroes supports a variety of sects and cults described in Table I as 'other Christians'.

The input of data for the family calls for additional comment. Anthropological research in the Commonwealth Caribbean has focused sharply on the household composition of lower class negroes.[18] Among this group, female household headship is quite common,

E

TABLE I
Variables used in correlation analysis

(a) *Race*
   % Negro
   % East Indian
   % Chinese
   % Mixed
(b) *Religion*
   % Denominational Christian
   % Other Christian
   % Presbyterian
   % Hindu
   % Moslem
(c) *Family*
   % Heads of household who are female
   % Females aged 15–44 in common-law unions
   % Females aged 15–44 visiting
   % Females aged 15–44 married
(d) *Education*
   % Population aged over 15 with secondary education or above
   % Population aged over 15 with less than standard 6 education
   % Population aged over 15 with standard 6 or 7 education
   % Population aged over 15 with no education
(e) *Occupation*
   % Males in labour force in non-manual occupations

Source : Trinidad and Tobago Population Census, 1960, vol. 1, Parts A and B. San Fernando comprises forty-five enumeration districts (district number forty-eight is omitted because it is a hospital). Two additional districts, Victoria Naparima ninety-two and ninety-three, are important suburbs and have been included in the analysis.

mating is usually initiated by a system of visiting, and the majority of births are illegitimate. As individuals proceed through the life-cycle there is a tendency for visiting to be replaced by consensual cohabitation or the common-law union. By the time they are forty most women have been legally married. However, none of these three methods of mating 'has an exclusive place within a series, nor within the individual life-cycle'.[19] In contrast, upper class whites practise orthodox monogamy and marry before they mate, and household headship is usually invested in males. People of mixed descent combine elements of both systems. East Indians lay great stress on early marriage and male headship. Hindu and Moslem fathers, in particular, still exert considerable influence over their children's choice of spouse. These various behavioural patterns are reflected in the variables which have been selected.

Until the late 1950s secondary education in Trinidad was the prerogative of the rich. Secondary schools were fee-paying, there were few scholarships, and only the most able East Indians and negroes won free places. Hindus and Moslems were particularly handicapped: Hindi or Urdu remained alternative languages to English. Girls were often kept at home until they married, and boys left the Christian mission schools in their early teens. Among the East Indians, the Presbyterians were a relatively privileged group and converts were encouraged to prolong their studies in the denomination's secondary schools in San Fernando. Despite the rapid modernization of the Hindu and Moslem groups after the Second World War, most of these factors still had a bearing on educational attainment

TABLE II

Matrix of Spearman rank correlation coefficients for the variables

Variables	Negro	East Indian	Chinese	Mixed	Denominational Christian	Other Christian	Presbyterian	Hindu	Moslem	Female Head	Female, Common law	Female Visiting	Female Married	Secondary School	Less than Standard 6	Standard 6 and 7	No education	Males in non-manual occupations
Negro	1·0	-0·67	-0·41	-0·25	0·62	0·41	-0·47	-0·46	-0·38	0·40	0·28	0·56	-0·34	-0·52	0·30	0·58	-0·35	-0·61
East Indian	-0·67	1·0	0·25	-0·09	-0·37	-0·16	-0·58	0·79	0·50	-0·26	0·05	-0·40	0·20	0·06	0·17	-0·51	0·65	0·16
Chinese	-0·41	0·25	1·0	0·41	-0·29	-0·19	0·24	-0·02	0·23	0·13	-0·15	-0·25	-0·10	0·43	-0·27	-0·17	-0·26	0·58
Mixed	-0·25	-0·09	0·41	1·0	-0·25	-0·15	0·15	-0·35	-0·04	0·26	-0·13	0·11	-0·29	0·42	-0·48	-0·33	-0·12	0·53
Denominational Christian	0·62	-0·37	-0·29	-0·25	1·0	-0·38	0·05	-0·39	-0·43	0·35	0·19	0·57	-0·17	-0·33	0·27	0·45	-0·12	-0·41
Other Christian	0·41	-0·16	-0·19	-0·15	-0·38	1·0	-0·06	-0·16	-0·09	0·10	0·32	0·22	-0·19	-0·48	0·25	0·46	-0·06	-0·43
Presbyterian	-0·47	-0·58	0·24	0·15	0·05	-0·06	1·0	0·26	0·09	-0·05	-0·13	-0·08	0·31	0·19	-0·06	-0·13	0·31	0·30
Hindu	-0·46	0·79	-0·02	-0·35	-0·39	-0·16	0·26	1·0	0·34	-0·43	-0·01	-0·49	0·29	-0·10	0·15	-0·54	0·67	-0·04
Moslem	-0·38	0·50	0·23	-0·04	-0·43	-0·09	0·09	0·34	1·0	-0·17	0·02	-0·36	0·05	-0·02	0·06	-0·21	0·26	-0·14
Female Heads	0·40	-0·26	0·13	0·26	0·35	0·10	-0·05	-0·43	-0·17	1·0	-0·01	0·46	-0·65	0·02	0·03	0·34	0·37	-0·09
Female, Common law	0·28	0·05	-0·15	-0·13	0·19	0·32	-0·13	-0·01	0·02	-0·01	1·0	0·23	-0·36	-0·44	0·71	0·06	0·37	-0·56
Female Visiting	0·56	-0·40	-0·25	0·11	0·57	0·22	-0·08	-0·49	-0·36	0·46	0·23	1·0	-0·29	-0·32	0·24	0·44	-0·10	-0·40
Female Married	-0·34	0·20	-0·10	-0·29	-0·17	-0·19	0·31	0·29	0·05	-0·65	-0·36	-0·29	1·0	0·14	-0·20	-0·12	0·14	0·24
Secondary school	-0·52	0·06	0·43	0·42	-0·33	-0·48	0·19	-0·10	-0·02	0·02	-0·44	-0·32	0·14	1·0	-0·74	-0·39	-0·33	0·88
Less than Standard 6	0·30	0·17	-0·27	-0·48	0·27	0·25	-0·06	0·15	0·06	0·03	0·71	0·24	-0·20	-0·74	1·0	0·13	0·49	-0·75
Standard 6 or 7	0·58	-0·51	-0·17	-0·33	0·45	0·46	-0·13	-0·54	-0·21	0·34	0·06	0·44	-0·12	-0·39	0·13	1·0	-0·40	-0·28
No education	-0·35	0·65	-0·26	-0·12	-0·12	-0·06	0·31	0·67	0·26	0·37	0·37	-0·10	0·14	-0·33	0·49	-0·40	1·0	-0·29
Males in non-manual occupations	-0·61	0·16	0·58	0·53	-0·41	-0·43	0·30	-0·04	-0·14	-0·09	-0·56	-0·40	0·24	0·88	-0·75	-0·28	-0·29	1·0

———— highest coefficient in each column
‑ ‑ ‑ second highest coefficient in each column

at the time of the 1960 census. The most important educational grades are set out in Table I.

It is impossible to find quantifiable, ecological surrogates for Smith's systems of property and recreation. However, occupation may be used as an adequate proxy for his wider term 'economy'. The distinction between manual and non-manual occupations is known to be highly diagnostic of socio-economic variations in the Caribbean (Table I).[20] The Spearman rank correlation between this variable and the percentage of males who are in professional and managerial occupations is 0·92. This high correlation demonstrates the reliability of the non-manual variable as an indicator of high status areas. Elite districts are often difficult to determine by a general occupational variable in West Indian towns because of the many domestic servants.[21]

CORRELATION AND LINKAGE ANALYSIS

The eighteen variables listed in Table I have been used to construct a matrix of possible interrelationships (Table II). Many of the variables are either skewed or bi-modal, and a non-parametric technique of measuring association (Spearman rank correlation) has been used. All the variables were ranked from low to high. By inspecting the correlation matrix it is possible to examine the relationship between, for example, negroes and all the other variables, or to compare selected pairs of variables. But the object in the first instance is to establish broad patterns of interrelationship. This can be done by linkage analysis.[22] The highest and second highest coefficients in each column of the correlation matrix have been underlined, and a linkage diagram constructed to show the nature, strength and direction of these major statistical bonds (Fig. 1). The groups created by linking the highest coefficients are characterized by the fact that each variable in any group is more highly correlated with another variable in the same group than it is with any variable in any other group. In almost all cases the second highest correlation for any variable also falls within the same group; and in some instances members of the same group are highly inter-linked, with little or no significant correlation outside the group.

The linkage diagram clearly depicts two groups (Fig. 1). One focuses on the strong negative correlation between negroes and East Indians; the other is structured by the emphatic bond between secondary education and males in non-manual occupations, and by the strong negative relationship between these two variables and persons having less than standard six education. The former group reflects the most important pluralistic qualities of the urban community, the latter the principal features which pertain to stratification. Examination of the correlation matrix shows that the two groups are not completely un-correlated. Furthermore, the linkage diagram (Fig. 1) shows that the two groups are linked by various aspects of the family. Family structure reflects both pluralism and stratification, as the earlier descriptive material has already suggested. The common-law union is associated with low occupational status and poor education. Many lower-class Hindus and Moslems (as well as negroes) resort to consensual cohabitation, but only after their original marriage has foundered (Table II). Female headship is a negro phenomenon which is associated with visiting relationships rather than with marital or common-law unions.[23]

Between them the two statistical groups depicted in Figure 1 incorporate seventeen of the eighteen variables used in the analysis. Using the highest and second highest co-efficients for each variable, five nodes may be identified. In rank order of the number of

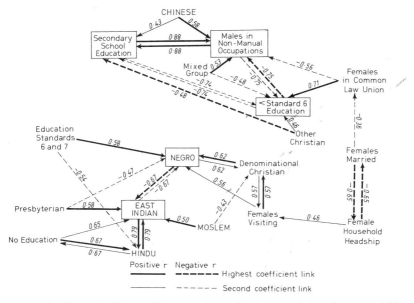

FIGURE I. San Fernando: linkage of highest and second highest correlations for each variable

correlation bonds, these nodes are East Indian and non-manual occupations; negro; less than standard six education; and secondary schooling. Examination of these nodes and their satellite variables provides a preliminary survey of the social structure of San Fernando.

Negroes are positively associated with the orthodox Christian churches (0·62), standard six and seven education (0·58) and females in visiting unions (0·56); they are negatively correlated with East Indians (−0·67) and Presbyterians (−0·47). As expected, East Indians form the hub of a series of strong positive bonds with Hindus (0·79), Presbyterians (0·58) and Moslems (0·50). The possession of no formal education is a peculiarly East Indian trait (0·65). Not only do negroes and East Indians load heavily and negatively on one another, but the links between their respective satellite variables are negative too. The variables linked to these two contraposed racial groups include aspects of religion and education, though family differences are of lesser importance. The plural hypothesis is further confirmed by inspecting the two top rows of the correlation matrix (Table II). Thirteen of the sixteen cases where the negroes and East Indians are correlated with other variables involve a change of sign as one moves from the one group to the other. Moreover, the matrix shows that the two groups are significantly different in family structure, especially where visiting and marriage are concerned.

Males in non-manual occupations are positively correlated with secondary education (0·88) and with the Chinese (0·58) and mixed groups (0·53). They are negatively associated with less than standard six schooling (−0·75) and females in common-law unions (−0·56). Secondary schooling is positively related to non-manual occupations (0·88) and to the Chinese (0·43), and negatively correlated with less than standard six education (−0·74) and other Christians (−0·48). Finally, less than standard six education is positively related to females in common-law unions (0·71) and other Christians (0·46), but negatively correlated with males in non-manual occupations (−0·75), secondary schooling (−0·74) and the mixed group (−0·48). This set of linkages indicates the low status of persons belonging to the Christian cults and sects, and those involved in common-law unions. The mixed population is confirmed as a relatively high status group; so, too, are the Chinese, the majority of whom are retailers.

SOCIAL AND SPATIAL PATTERNS

Although the linkage analysis is extremely helpful in clarifying the overall pattern of correlation it does not, of course, explore all the most important interrelationships. Some of these are capable of further investigation through the correlation matrix.

The mixed population has already emerged as a relatively high status group within the creole segment. Negroes record a negative correlation with non-manual occupations (−0·61) and comprise the base of the creole stratification. Comparison of the correlations for the mixed and negro populations supports the plural hypothesis (Table II); eight of the sixteen cases where the mixed and negro populations are correlated with other variables involve a change of sign as one moves from one group to another. East Indians achieve a small positive correlation with non-manual occupations (0·16), and appear at all levels of the employment scale. Presbyterians (0·30) form a slightly higher status group, and Hindus (−0·04) and Moslems (−0·14) rank beneath them. As the census provides no cross-tabulations between occupation and race and between occupation and religion for San Fernando, this is useful evidence. It confirms earlier work on San Fernando which demonstrates the approximately parallel ranking of creoles and East Indians using indices of dissimilarity.[24]

The spatial aspects of some of these ecological correlations may be explored by mapping the distribution of the three most important nodes in the linkage analysis—East Indians (Fig. 2), males in non-manual occupations (Fig. 3) and negroes (Fig. 4). Negroes and East Indians are highly polarized but not spatially segregated: they record an index of dissimilarity of only 27.2.[25] Hindus, Moslems and Presbyterians are as segregated from one another as this;[26] the correlation coefficients between them are positive but low (Table II). The distribution of males in non-manual occupations shows the spatial distribution of social statuses. Comparison of Figures 2, 3 and 4 confirms the location of East Indians at all levels of the occupational hierarchy, and depicts two high-status areas which are spatially divorced from those neighbourhoods which are predominantly negro. At this stage in the study it is possible to reintroduce the white population (Fig. 5). They are the most highly segregated of all the racial and religious groups in San Fernando[27] and form the occupational and social élite (Fig. 3). These data confirm that the creole segment comprises whites, coloureds and negroes, who rank in decreasing order of socio-economic status and increasing order of numerical size. In most cases the racial and religious groups that are adjacent to one another in the socio-economic scale are also close to each other spatially. Similar socio-economic positions imply similar jobs and equal opportunities to obtain housing. It must be emphasized, however, that while the Presbyterians represent the most highly acculturated element in the East Indian population, the differences between them and the Hindus and Moslems are more a question of education and occupation (and religion) than of family structure (Table II).

QUESTIONNAIRE DATA

Many anthropologists will remain unconvinced by the foregoing analysis. Behaviour

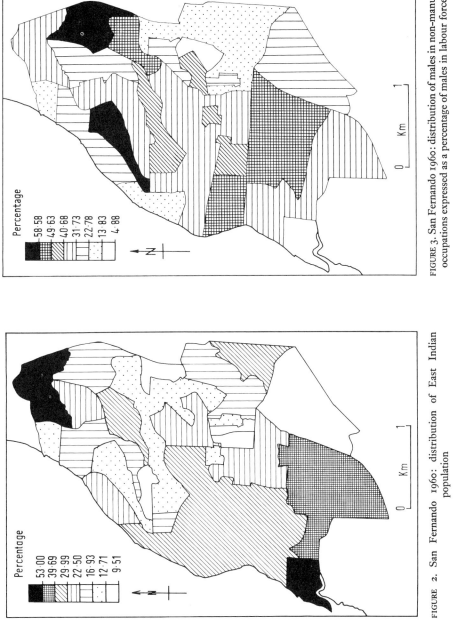

FIGURE 3. San Fernando 1960: distribution of males in non-manual occupations expressed as a percentage of males in labour force

FIGURE 2. San Fernando 1960: distribution of East Indian population

FIGURE 5. San Fernando 1960: distribution of white population

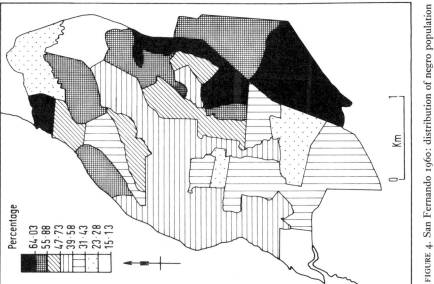

FIGURE 4. San Fernando 1960: distribution of negro population

TABLE III

Occupation among the sample populations

Group	Professional		Manager or administrator		Other non-manual		Skilled worker		Semi-skilled worker		Unskilled and personal service		Farmer		Agricultural labourer		Total	
	No.	%	No.	%	No.	%	No.	%	No.	%	No.	%	No.	%	No.	%	No.	%
Creole	4	1·9	22	10·4	58	27·5	68	32·2	27	12·8	31	14·7	1	0·5	0	0·0	211	100·0
Total East Indian	16	3·0	85	16·0	155	29·3	99	18·7	76	14·4	99	18·7	1	0·2	1	0·2	530	100·0
Hindu	5	3·4	29	19·5	13	8·7	21	14·1	25	16·8	56	37·6	0	0·0	0	0·0	149	100·0
Moslem	2	1·6	20	15·9	35	27·8	33	26·2	19	15·9	16	12·7	0	0·0	1	0·8	126	100·0
Christian East Indian	9	3·5	36	14·1	107	41·9	45	17·6	32	12·5	26	10·2	0	0·0	0	0·0	255	100·0

Creole —East Indian $X^2 = 18.9$; d.f. = 7; $p. < 0.01$

Creole —Hindu $X^2 = 53.6$; d.f. = 6; $p. < 0.001$

Creole —Moslem $X^2 = 5.7$; d.f. = 7; $p. > 0.50$

Creole —Christian East Indian $X^2 = 22.4$; d.f. = 6; $p. < 0.01$

Hindu —Moslem $X^2 = 38.0$; d.f. = 6; $p. < 0.001$

Hindu —Christian East Indian $X^2 = 73.3$; d.f. = 5; $p. < 0.001$

Moslem—Christian East Indian $X^2 = 11.7$; d.f. = 6; $p. > 0.05$

TABLE IV

Education among the sample populations

Group	University No.	%	Secondary with School Certificate No.	%	Secondary without School Certificate No.	%	Standard 6 or 7 No.	%	Standard 4 or 5 No.	%	Standard 3 or less No.	%	Not given No.	%	None No.	%	Total No.	%
Creole	2	0·9	28	13·3	37	17·5	110	52·1	24	11·4	8	3·8	1	0·5	1	0·5	211	100·0
Total East Indian	10	1·9	69	13·0	89	16·8	195	36·8	71	13·4	56	10·6	4	0·8	37	7·0	530	100·0
Hindu	2	1·3	13	8·7	17	11·4	33	22·1	27	18·1	29	19·5	3	2·0	25	16·8	149	100·0
Moslem	2	1·6	13	10·3	23	18·3	49	38·9	21	16·7	12	9·5	0	0·0	6	4·8	126	100·0
Christian East Indian	6	2·4	43	16·9	49	19·2	113	44·3	23	9·0	15	5·9	0	0·0	6	2·4	255	100·0

Creole —East Indian $X^2 = 30·7$; d.f. = 7; p.< 0·001

Creole —Hindu $X^2 = 81·3$; d.f. = 7; p.< 0·001

Creole —Moslem $X^2 = 17·4$; d.f. = 7; p.< 0·02

Creole —Christian East Indian $X^2 = 9·5$; d.f. = 7; p.> 0·20

Hindu —Moslem $X^2 = 24·7$; d.f. = 7; p.< 0·001

Hindu —Christian East Indian $X^2 = 74·1$; d.f. = 7; p.< 0·001

Moslem—Christian East Indian $X^2 = 10·7$; d.f. = 6; p.> 0·05

TABLE V
Educational aspirations for sons

Group	University No.	%	Secondary No.	%	Technical No.	%	Don't know No.	%	Total No.	%
Creole	189	89·6	18	8·5	2	0·9	2	0·9	211	100·0
Total East Indian	483	91·3	34	6·4	2	0·4	11	2·1	530	100·0
Hindu	129	86·6	18	12·8	0	0·0	2	1·3	149	100·0
Moslem	117	92·9	4	3·2	1	0·8	4	3·2	126	100·0
Christian East Indian	237	92·9	12	4·7	1	0·4	5	2·0	255	100·0

Creole —East Indian	$X^2 = 3·0$; d.f. = 3; p. > 0·30
Creole —Hindu	$X^2 = 2·7$; d.f. = 3; p. > 0·30
Creole —Moslem	$X^2 = 5·8$; d.f. = 3; p. > 0·10
Creole —Christian East Indian	$X^2 = 4·1$; d.f. = 3; p. > 0·20
Hindu —Moslem	$X^2 = 9·3$; d.f. = 3; p. < 0·05
Hindu —Christian East Indian	$X^2 = 1·3$; d.f. = 3; p. > 0·70
Moslem—Christian East Indian	$X^2 = 1·3$; d.f. = 3; p. > 0·70

has been measured in aggregate form. But what of the individual and his values? It is possible to meet these objections by using questionnaire material collected during field-work in San Fernando in 1964. A list of adults of both sexes was obtained from the electoral roll for San Fernando. East Indians were distinguished from creoles on the basis of their names, and a sample of individuals was selected at random from each group. The East Indian sample was divided into three components—Hindu, Moslem and Christian—and these can be treated as independent samples. The data for these respondents have been analysed to check some of the ecological evidence and to probe the value systems of the major racial and cultural groups.

Comparison of the sample populations shows that the creoles and East Indians achieve rather different occupations (Table III).[28] Considerable differences, too, are recorded between Hindus and Moslems, and Hindus and Christians. But Moslems are similar to Christian East Indians and to the creoles. Christian East Indians have strong 'white collar' associations; Hindus are more highly polarized occupationally than the Moslems. Educational patterns repeat the distinctions in employment. Creoles and East Indians are significantly different from each other (Table IV). Variations between the East Indian religious groups are almost as great, though the Christians emerge as similar both to the Moslems and to the creoles. Christians are the best-educated among the East Indians, while Hindus are outstanding for their poor schooling (Fig. 1). Nevertheless, both Tables confirm the appearance of some creoles and East Indians at every level of the social hierarchy.

Virtually all the distinctions between groups are eradicated when the respondents' aspirations for their sons are examined. The groups are extremely ambitious (Table V); almost everyone wants their son to go to university, though Hindus have set their sights slightly lower than the others in this respect. There is no significant difference between most of the groups when occupational aspirations for sons are considered (Table VI), but over two-thirds of all the samples want them to enter professional employment. No one gives a favourable mention to manual tasks. Parents are just as ambitious for their daughters. Aspirations among all groups soar well above the levels of likely attainment.[29]

Research in San Fernando has shown that creoles and East Indians are highly endo-

TABLE VI
Occupational aspirations for sons

Group	Profess-ional		Mechanical and techanical		Civil Service		Teaching		Office Job		Police		Don't know and other		Total	
	No.	%	No.	%	No.	%	No.	%	No.	%	No.	%	No.	%	No.	%
Creole	146	69·2	4	1·9	5	2·4	10	4·7	5	2·4	2	0·9	39	18·5	211	100·0
Total East Indian	395	74·7	10	1·9	13	2·6	30	5·7	21	4·0	0	0·0	61	11·5	530	100·0
Hindu	133	75·8	6	4·0	4	2·7	8	5·4	5	3·4	0	0·0	13	8·7	149	100·0
Moslem	96	76·2	2	1·6	2	1·6	7	5·6	6	4·8	0	0·0	13	10·3	126	100·0
Christian East Indian	186	72·9	2	0·8	7	2·7	15	5·9	10	3·9	0	0·0	35	13·7	255	100·0

Creole —East Indian $X^2 = 12.4$; d.f. $= 6$; $p. > 0.05$
Creole —Hindu $X^2 = 9.5$; d.f. $= 6$; $p. > 0.10$
Creole —Moslem $X^2 = 6.9$; d.f. $= 6$; $p. > 0.30$
Creole —Christian East Indian $X^2 = 6.6$; d.f. $= 6$; $p. > 0.30$
Hindu —Moslem $X^2 = 2.3$; d.f. $= 5$; $p. > 0.80$
Hindu —Christian East Indian $X^2 = 7.2$; d.f. $= 5$; $p. > 0.20$
Moslem—Christian East Indian $X^2 = 2.1$; d.f. $= 5$; $p. > 0.80$

TABLE VII

Why are there proportionately fewer East Indians than Negroes in the civil service?

Group	Racial pressure No.	%	Fail entrance No.	%	Don't want this job No.	%	No inequality No.	%	Don't know and no reply No.	%	Total No.	%
Creole	8	3·8	24	11·4	45	21·3	69	32·7	65	30·8	211	100·0
Total East Indian	334	63·1	71	13·4	42	7·9	31	5·9	51	9·6	530	100·0
Hindu	94	63·1	15	10·1	11	7·4	6	4·0	22	14·8	149	100·0
Moslem	75	59·6	25	19·9	9	7·1	7	5·6	10	7·9	126	100·0
Christian East Indian	165	64·7	31	12·2	22	8·6	18	7·0	19	7·4	255	100·0

Creole —East Indian	$X^2 = 261·9$; d.f. $= 4$; p.$< 0·001$
Creole —Hindu	$X^2 = 163·4$; d.f. $= 4$; p.$< 0·001$
Creole —Moslem	$X^2 = 157·6$; d.f. $= 4$; p.$< 0·001$
Creole —Christian East Indian	$X^2 = 204·0$; d.f. $= 4$; p.$< 0·001$
Hindu —Moslem	$X^2 = 7·7$; d.f. $= 4$; p.$> 0·10$
Hindu —Christian East Indian	$X^2 = 7·0$; d.f. $= 4$; p.$> 0·10$
Moslem—Christian East Indian	$X^2 = 11·1$; d.f. $= 4$; p.$< 0·05$

TABLE VIII

Percentage in each sample who would oppose intermarriage with specified race or religion

Group	Negro %	±2 S.E.%	East Indian %	±2 S.E.%	Presbyterian %	±2 S.E.%	Hindu %	±2 S.E.%	Moslem %	±2 S.E.%	N
Creole	3·3	2·4	8·5	3·8	10·4	4·2	20·9	5·6	21·3	5·6	211
Total East Indian	60·1	4·2	—		—		—		—		530
Hindu	85·2	5·8	—		36·2	7·8	—		28·9	7·4	149
Moslem	77·8	7·4	—		28·6	8·0	28·6	8·0	—		126
Christian East Indian	36·5	6·0	—		4·3	2·6	19·6	5·0	20·8	5·6	255

gamous and politically opposed.[30] One of the major political issues is the composition of the civil service, which has been traditionally a creole preserve. The reasons given for the alleged dearth of East Indians in the bureaucracy are highly and significantly polarized between creoles and East Indians (Table VII). Most East Indians, irrespective of religion, attribute their under-representation to racial pressure; the majority of creoles either find no inequality or refuse to reply.

Racial and religious antipathies are expressed obliquely in attitudes to intermarriage (Table VIII). Creoles are favourably disposed to unions with East Indians, but appear far more content about links with Presbyterians than with Hindus and Moslems. More than three-quarters of the Hindus and Moslems oppose intermarriage with negroes, but the majority of Christian East Indians do not. A continuum of cultural attributes and attitudes emerges among the sample populations. The Christian East Indians stand between the creoles and the oriental religions. However, their place in that continuum shifts with the situation.

CONCLUSION

This study generally supports Smith's hypothesis about cultural pluralism. It shows that both the creole and East Indian elements are divided into several cultural segments. The creole segments are ranked, but among the East Indians hierarchical and parallel positions are recorded. Both the major elements in the population are stratified, and the Christian East Indians achieve an occupational status comparable with that of the creole mixed group. In some cases the minor cultural segments are distinguished by two or three institutions alone; in others the entire range of institutional differences is involved, and the institutional practices themselves are quite distinct if not mutually incompatible. Each segment is highly endogamous and tends towards closure.

The plural model provides a valuable frame of reference. Nevertheless, it is the racial and cultural confrontation between creoles and East Indians that is so important. Although the Christian East Indians are partially acculturated to creole standards, they continue to ally themselves with the Hindus and Moslems on crucial issues. These issues are racially and culturally defined. Christians may express liberal attitudes towards intermarriage, but in practice they are almost as endogamous as the Eastern religious groups.[31] There is little difference between creoles and East Indians in their material aspirations. Their goals are identical, but the means of securing them bring the two major segments into competition. Consequently, when political factors are involved or when scarce resources, such as jobs, are in dispute, the Christians form part of the East Indian alignment.

Exactly the same closing of the ranks has taken place between the mulattoes and negroes within the creole segment, and many whites, too, have come to terms with this coalition. The smaller cultural elements have sunk their differences in the greater creole-East Indian struggle for political power and personal advancement. Cultures have not clashed in San Fernando; but the individuals, who form the segments, have had competitive interests which have brought the two major groups into conflict. These interest groups have become deeply entrenched. In recent years certain black power organizations have sought to fragment the creole population by isolating the middle and upper strata, and have attempted to forge links between the negroes and the East Indian population. Both schemes have so far proved abortive. The forces of law and order have maintained the *status quo*; negroes of low status have continued to support the creole-dominated government; and East Indians have remained suspicious of black power.[32]

The ecological correlations and the questionnaire material are, for the most part, mutually supporting: individuals conform to group norms. However, the map evidence shows that creoles and East Indians are not highly segregated. Although the social structure is reflected in the urban mosaic, social boundaries are more clearly expressed in individual behaviour than in residential patterns. Creoles and East Indians may live in close proximity and share similar aspirations; yet their behaviour and attitudes are often poles apart.

ACKNOWLEDGEMENT
The author acknowledges a grant from the Research Institute for the Study of Man, New York, to cover the cost of field-work in Trinidad and a grant from the Department of Geography, University of Liverpool, towards the cost of illustrations.

NOTES
1. Both L. BRAITHWAITE, 'Social stratification in Trinidad', *Soc. econ. Stud.* (1953), 5–175, and F. HENRIQUES, *Family and colour in Jamaica* (1953), couch their analysis in terms of colour-class.
2. J. LOBB, 'Caste and class in Haiti', *Am. J. Sociol.* 46 (1940), 23–34
3. M. G. SMITH, *The plural society in the British West Indies* (1965)
4. J. S. FURNIVALL, *Colonial policy and practice* (1948)
5. Ibid., 304, 308

6. M. G. SMITH, op. cit. (1965) 87–8

7. Ibid., 82

8. Ibid., 53

9. Ibid., 84

10. Ibid., 86

11. V. RUBIN, 'Social and cultural pluralism in the Caribbean', *Ann. N. Y. Acad. Sci.* 83 (1960), 783, discusses the point during the symposium which forms the basis of this volume.

12. C. WAGLEY expresses this opinion in a discussion reported in V. RUBIN, op. cit., 778.

13 R. T. SMITH, review of V. RUBIN, op. cit., in *Am. Anthrop.* 63 (1961), 155

14. L. A. DESPRES, *Cultural pluralism and nationalist politics in British Guiana* (1967)

15. M. G. SMITH, op. cit.; idem. *Stratification in Grenada* (1965)

16. M. G. SMITH, 'A structural approach to comparative politics' in *Varieties of political theory* (ed. D. EASTON) 1966, 113–28; M. G. SMITH, 'Institutional and political conditions of pluralism' and 'Some developments in the analytical framework of pluralism', chapters in *Pluralism in Africa* (ed. L. KUPER and M. G. SMITH) 1969, 27–65 and 415–58

17. C. G. CLARKE, 'Residential segregation and intermarriage in San Fernando, Trinidad', *Geogrl Rev.* 61 (1971), Table I, 200

18 For an excellent comparative study see M. G. SMITH, *West Indian family structure* (1962). A geographical enquiry into family composition is incorporated in C. G. CLARKE, 'Aspects of the urban geography of Kingston, Jamaica', unpubl. D.Phil. thesis, Univ. of Oxford (1967), 34?–7

19. M. G. SMITH, op. cit. (1962), 170

20. C. G. CLARKE, op. cit. (1967)

21. Ibid.

22. For a discussion of the use of linkage analysis see L. L. McQUITTY, 'Elementary linkage analysis for isolating orthogonal and oblique types and typal relevancies', *Educ. psychol. Measur.* 17 (1957), 207 and S. GREGORY, 'Rainfall over Sierra Leone', Dept. of Geography, Univ. of Liverpool, Research Paper No. 2, 1965.

23. C. G. CLARKE, op. cit. (1967)

24. C. G. CLARKE, op. cit. (1971)

25. Ibid., Table II, 207

26. Ibid.

27. Ibid.

28. Tables III–VII contain data for independent samples. Chi-square has been used to test the significance of the difference between selected pairs of samples. In each case the null hypothesis states that there is no significant difference between the values recorded in the two populations. When necessary, adjacent columns have been amalgamated to secure the minimum number of observed or expected frequencies demanded by the test.

29. This is a common phenomenon in the Caribbean. A pioneer study of the problem appears in M. G. SMITH, 'Education and occupational choice in rural Jamaica', *Soc. econ. Stud.* 9 (1960), 332–54. For a detailed account of youth aspirations in Trinidad see V. RUBIN and M. ZAVALLONI, *We wish to be looked upon* (1969).

30. C. G. CLARKE, op. cit. (1971), 213–5; 'The political ecology of a town in Trinidad' in *International Geography 1972* (ed. W. P. ADAMS and F. M. HELLEINER), papers submitted to the 22nd International Geographical Congress, Montreal, 798–801

31. C. G. CLARKE, op. cit. (1971), 213–4

32. D. NICHOLLS, 'East Indians and Black Power in Trinidad', *Race* 12 (1971), 443–59

RÉSUMÉ. *Le pluralisme et la stratification à San Fernando, Trinidad.* Cette étude emploie l'idée générale du pluralisme pour examiner les relations sociales à San Fernando, une communauté urbaine et complexe de Trinidad. On converge sur les groupes racials et religieux de la ville et considère leurs institutions plus importantes. Les techniques de corrélation et de l'analyse à lien sont employés pour faire la comparaison entre les données du rencensement pour la race, la religion, l'occupation, la famille, et l'éducation. Plusieurs modèles s'élèvent; les uns ont rapport à la «stratification», d'autres au «pluralisme». Ensuite on introduit l'information d'une questionnaire pour corrober la preuve cartographique, et pour examiner certaines valeurs et opinions tenues des éléments les plus importantes de la population. On discute les résultats en référant à l'hypothese plurale; et la conduite individuèle est comparée avec des modèles spatiaux dans la ville

FIG. 1. San Fernando: les liens entre les plus hautes corrélations et les plus hautes corrélations sauf une pour chaque variable

FIG. 2. San Fernando 1960: la répartition de la population indienne

FIG. 3. San Fernando 1960: la répartition des hommes dans les travaux non-manuels exprimés comme pourcentage des hommes qui travaillent

FIG. 4. San Fernando 1960: la répartition de la population nègre

FIG. 5. San Fernando 1960: la répartition de la population blanche

---

ZUSAMMENFASSUNG. *Der Pluralismus und die Gesellschaftsschichtung in San Fernando, Trinidad.* Diese Arbeit benützt den Begriff von Pluralismus, um das Sozialvorbild in San Fernando, eine komplizierte Stadtgemeinschaft in Trinidad zu untersuchen. Man untersucht die rassichen und religiösen Gruppen der Stadt und von ihren wichtigen Institutions. Man benützt die Methoden der Wechselbeziehung und Bindegliedanalyse, um Rasse, Religion, Beruf, Familie und Erziehung zu vergleichen. Einige soziale und kulturelle Vorbilde kommen heraus; einige sind mit der ‚Gesellschafts-schichtung‘, andere mit dem ‚Pluralismus‘ verwandt. Ein Fragebogen fördert das Bewcismaterial von dem Karten, und untersucht bestimmte Werte und Haltungen von dem wichtigsten Elementen der Gemeinschaft. Man beschreibt die Ergebnisse mit Bezug auf die Hypothese der Pluralismus; und man vergleicht individuelles Betragen mit räum-lichen Vorbildern in der Stadt.

ABB. 1. San Fernando: das Bindeglied von der höchsten und nächsten Wechselbeziehung für jede Variable
ABB. 2. San Fernando 1960: die Verteilung von Indern
ABB. 3. San Fernando 1960: die Verteilung von Kopfarbeitern als Prozente von dem Männern die angestellt sind
ABB. 4. San Fernando 1960: die Verteilung von Negern
ABB. 5. San Fernando 1960: die Verteilung von Weissen

The urban dimensions of Leicester, England

W. K. D. DAVIES

Associate Professor of Geography, University of Calgary

AND G. J. LEWIS

Lecturer in Geography, University of Leicester

Revised MS received 2 August 1972

ABSTRACT. Oblique and higher-order factor analysis is used to isolate the basic dimensions of a data set consisting of fifty-six variables and 143 areas in Leicester, England. The paper emphasizes the problems of isolating the eight basic dimensions which explain 70 per cent of the variance of the original data set. These eight dimensions include the standard factors of socio-economic status, life cycle and ethnic origins as well as others measuring sub-standard characteristics, economic participation, mobility of young adults, mobility and urban fringe characteristics. The study confirms that the standard North American pattern of urban social structure is applicable to British cities but demonstrates that the descriptive utility of the socio-economic, life cycle and ethnic dimensions primarily depends on the scale of generalization.

DESPITE the flexibility of the family of related technical procedures known as factor analysis, most factor ecologists have adopted a rather rigid frame of reference in their case studies which has limited the comparison of individual studies of urban social structure. Although many of the problems confronting the factor analyst have been isolated, as C. A. Jansen, L. Rummel and F. L. Sweetser[1] have shown, standard solutions to these issues are still some distance away. Out of all these problems two seem to be particularly important in factor ecology. The first is that of the widespread adoption of the Principal Component or Component-Varimax rotation solution. By imposing orthogonality upon the abstracted factor dimensions, a relatively rigid descriptive structure is used, whereas on *a priori* grounds we might expect the individual factors themselves to be correlated and subject to higher-order generalizations. The second problem relates to the restricted set of data used by most analysts; and the restrictions apply to the balance between the variables as well as to their overall scope. As the factor dimensions produced by any study only refer to the initial set of data, any inadequacies in this direction could miss important features of the internal structure of the city being investigated and may hinder the comparison of results between studies. This paper explores some of the issues associated with these two problems by means of a case study of the urban dimensions of Leicester, a major regional centre in England with a population of 283 260 in 1966.

THE DATA

Table I describes the fifty-six variables used in the case study of Leicester. All the variables were derived from the unpublished Enumeration District data of the 1966 10 per cent sample census of the United Kingdom. The variables were grouped into six broad categories:

TABLE I
Variables used in the analysis

Variable number	Short title	Loadings over 0·3	Detailed description of the variables	Communality
	Demographic			
1	Young adults	2	Percentage of the total population between 15 and 24 years of age	0·65
2	Mature adults	2	Percentage of the total population between 25 and 44 years	0·73
3	Middle aged	1	Percentage of the total population 45 years to 59 years	0·69
4	Old age	2	Percentage of the total population over 60 years	0·87
5	Females	1	Percentage of females in the total population	0·45
6	Fertile: female ratio	1	Percentage of females in the total population between 15 and 44 years	0·44
7	Single ratio	1	Percentage of total single persons in the adult population	0·84
8	Married females	2	Percentage of married females in the adult female population	0·54
9	Children	1	Percentage of persons 0–14 years in the total population	0·87
	Migration			
10	Born overseas	1	Percentage of persons born outside Britain excluding N. Ireland and Eire	0·89
11	Irish	2	Percentage of persons born in Eire or Northern Ireland	0·54
12	Commonwealth-colonial	1	Percentage of persons born in the British commonwealth or colonies—excluding the former White Dominions (Australia, Canada, New Zealand)	0·74
13	Foreign	1	Percentage of persons born in foreign countries	0·50
14	Recent movers	2	Percentage of persons moving residence within the last year	0·68
15	Five-year movers	1	Percentage of persons moving residence within the past 5 years	0·86
16	Local movers	2	Percentage of persons moving residence *within* their local authority area during the past 5 years	0·78
17	New residents	3	Percentage of persons moving their residence *into* a new local authority area during the past 5 years	0·86
18	Female movers	1	Percentage of movers within the past 5 years that are female	0·87
19	Single person movers	1	Percentage of movers within the past 5 years that are not married	0·81
	Economic			
20	Economically active	1	Percentage of economically active male and females within the adult population	0·64
21	Employed persons	1	Percentage of the adult population gainfully employed on census day	0·83
22	Unemployed ratio	0	Percentage of the total economically active persons who are unemployed	0·30
23	Employed females	2	Percentage of the adult females who are employed	0·70
24	Agricultural workers	1	Percentage of the employed population engaged in agricultural occupations	0·57

TABLE I (*cont.*)

25	Industrial workers	3	Percentage of the employed population who are engaged in manufacturing, construction and utilities	0·77
26	Transport workers	2	Percentage of the employed population engaged in the transport industry	0·38
27	Distribution & service	I	Percentage of the employed population engaged in the distribution and service industries	0·71
28	Government workers	2	Percentage of the employed population engaged in national or local government service	0·47

Social-occupational

29	High social class	I	Percentage of heads of families in Social Classes I and 2	0·94
30	Medium social class	2	Percentage of heads of families in Social Class 3	0·84
31	Low social class	I	Percentage of heads of families in Social Classes 4 and 5	0·77
32	Households with pensioners	2	Percentage of households with persons of pensionable age	0·80
33	Professional workers	I	Percentage of economically active males in Economic Groups 3 and 4	0·79
34	Employers and managers	I	Percentage of economically active males in Economic Groups 1, 2, and 13	0·86
35	Foremen & skilled workers	2	Percentage of economically active males in Economic Groups 8, 9, 12, and 14	0·87
36	Non-manual workers (intermediate)	I	Percentage of economically active males in Economic Groups 5 and 6	0·63
37	Personal service, agricultural workers	I	Percentage of economically active males in Economic Groups 7, 10, and 15	0·68
38	Unskilled manual workers	I	Percentage of economically active males in Economic Group 11	0·71

Commuting, cars

39	Crossing-commuters	I	Percentage of employed persons working outside the local authorities in which they live	0·81
40	Car-commuters	2	Percentage of employed persons travelling to work by their own personal transport (cars and motorcycles)	0·87
41	Works transport commuters	I	Percentage of employed persons travelling to work by private bus or van provided by their employers	0·17
42	Car ratio (area)	I	Number of cars in the enumeration district divided by the total population of the district	0·68
43	Households without cars	2	Percentage of households without cars	0·88
44	Two-car households	I	Percentage of households with two or more cars	0·73
45	Pedestrian commuters	3	Percentage of employed persons walking to work	0·72
46	Non-residents	I	Number of people enumerated on census day who are not usually resident in the enumeration district	0·68

Household

| 47 | Owner-occupiers | 4 | Percentage of households (tenure known) owning and occupying their own residence | 0·82 |

TABLE I (*cont.*)
Variables used in the analysis

Variable number	Short title	Loadings over 0·3	Detailed description of the variables	Communality
48	Council tenants	2	Percentage of households renting property from their local authority (council)	0·87
49	Tenants of un-furnished property	3	Percentage of households renting unfurnished property	0·69
50	One-person households	2	Percentage of households containing only one person	0·80
51	Large households	2	Percentage of households containing six or more persons	0·80
52	Sharing dwellings	3	Percentage of households sharing dwellings	0·69
53	Sub-standard houses	1	Percentage of households without exclusive use of hot water, W.C. or fixed bath	0·86
54	Rooms per person (area)	2	Number of rooms in the enumeration district expressed as a percentage of the total population of the area	0·63
55	Dense occupancy households	1	Percentage of households in which the average occupancy rate is	
			(a) over 1·5 persons per room	0·90
56	Sparse occupancy households	2	(b) under 0·5 persons per room	0·93

1. Demographic   4. Social and occupational
2. Migration   5. Commuting, cars
3. Employment   6. Households, dwellings

With the exception of the work of B. T. Robson, C. F. Schmid and K. Tagashira,[2] few factor ecologists have explicitly grouped the initial data into a broad range of categories that contain approximately equal numbers of variables. Without such a procedure it is sometimes difficult to appreciate the extent to which one type of variable dominates the rest, with the inevitable restriction of the factor dimensions to this dominant category. Examples are not hard to find: for instance, in the U.S.A., twenty out of the fifty-seven variables used by P. H. Rees[3] were ethnic and religious, so it is not surprising to find that five of the ten factors were concerned with race, national origin or religion; in Sweden, Jansen[4] identified no less than three separate 'familial' dimensions in his study of Swedish cities, but again, as nineteen out of the forty-four variables were concerned with demographic or family status, this emphasis might have been expected; in England, the list of variables recommended by the Centre for Urban Studies (London)[5] in 1961 includes no less than seven ethnic variables out of a total of twenty-six.

Most factor ecologies of British cities have only dealt with the administrative city and the results have been distorted by the extent to which the predominantly middle-class fringe areas have been excluded from consideration. In this article, the built-up areas immediately adjacent to the county borough of Leicester were added to the list of 136 city enumeration districts. Altogether 143 areas were analysed, in which the sample population mean was 267. Since this figure was derived from the 1966 10 per cent sample census, all enumeration districts with a sample population of under 100 were combined with adjacent units.

The 143 × 56 data set was transformed into standard scores and Pearson's Product Moment Correlation coefficients were calculated between each pair of variables to provide an *R* mode 56 × 56 similiarity matrix. R. J. Johnston[6] has recently pointed out that factor ecologists should transform the original variables into normal or linear distributions, but as yet few ecologists apart from R. A. Murdie[7] have attempted anything more sophisticated than a blanket logarithmic transformation. In this study, the data were used in their raw percentage forms. Although this meant that the study followed the majority opinion, it must be emphasized that the decision not to transform the variables was taken on other grounds. Thus the study was only one of a series of comparable case studies of large British provincial cities and it seemed possible that transformations suitable for the distribution within one centre may be different from those required by another city. In addition it might be suggested that statistically accurate transformations may tend to complicate the interpretation of the variables.[8] Given these problems, it was decided to use the raw percentage data and accept the lower correlations that are produced as a consequence of using untransformed variables. These will represent an under-estimate of the true degree of association between any set of variables; it was therefore hypothesized that any factors that the analysis produced would represent the minimum dimensions of the urban social structure.

THE INITIAL SOLUTION

An *R* mode Principal Components Analysis with unities in the diagonal of the similarity matrix produced nine components explaining 72·2 per cent of the original variance (Table II). Rigid comparison of the level of explanation of this example with the results of other studies is difficult because of the differences in the number and composition of the input variables. The effect of incorporating such a wide variety of variables is seen in levels of explanation that compare most closely with American studies that used similar numbers of variables, rather than with previous British studies.[9] This is particularly marked in relation to the cumulative variance shown by the first three components and emphasizes that any increase in the number and scope of variables in a set of data is likely to decrease the size of the largest eigenvalues.

As almost three-quarters of the variance can be explained by the nine component space compared with the fifty-six variable space, it is not surprising to find that the communalities are uniformly high (Table I). No less than thirty-four variables have communalities of over 0·7 and only three variables lie below 0·4. The three variables that demonstrate their independence of the nine dimensions are: the percentage unemployed (22), the percentage employed in the transport industry (26) and the percentage of workers who commute in transport provided by their employers (41).

ROTATION PROCEDURES

Mathematically, the initial component solution abstracts the vector producing the highest amount of variance and then produces successively lower amounts of variance. Factor ecologists are usually, though not always, interested in the series of separate dimensions rather than one overall general factor.[10] Hence analytical rotation techniques have been increasingly used in the search for a simpler structure that isolates the separate dimensions of the city. Unfortunately, few of the problems associated with the various rotation procedures have been discussed in the geographical literature, primarily because most geo-

TABLE II

Problem of factor isolation and naming

| | | Eight-factor solutions | | | | Nine-factor solutions | | | | Direct Oblimin | |
| | | Biquartimin 2 | | Varimax 2 | | Biquartimin 2 | | Varimax 9 | | 2 | 6 |
Factor:	Variable name	Residential mobility (1)	Ethnic-migrant 6 (2)	Residential mobility (3)	Ethnic-migrant 6 (4)	Migrant (5)	Ethnic 6 (6)	Sub-stan-dardness 9 (7)	Mobile young adult 5 (3)	Migrant (9)	Ethnic (10)
10	Born Overseas		0·69	0·70	0·39		-0·82	0·85		0·80	
12	Commonwealth born		0·52	0·53	-0·48		-0·79	0·77		0·76	
17	New residents	0·38	0·74	0·72		-0·48	-0·45	0·56	0·44	0·51	0·42
13	Foreign born		0·54	0·55			-0·44	0·49		0·43	
47	Owner occupiers						-0·39			0·33	
49	Tenants unfurnished property	0·32	0·35	0·37	-0·34		-0·36	0·49		0·42	
11	Irish		0·53	0·52			-0·34	0·45		0·37	
52	Households sharing dwellings		0·66	0·67	0·37	-0·40	-0·33	0·50	0·40	0·38	0·36
48	Council tenants	-0·35	-0·39	-0·43	0·60	-0·72	+0·53	-0·55	0·40	-0·54	0·72
16	Local movers	-0·83	0·31	0·28		-0·72	+0·62	-0·33	0·67	-0·50	0·72
15	Movers within 5 years		0·87	0·84		-0·91		0·29	0·83		0·85
18	Female movers		0·85	0·81		-0·94			0·86		0·89
19	Single movers		0·82	0·81		-0·83			0·78		0·79
14	Movers within last year		0·77	0·76		-0·61		0·42	0·57		0·56
2	Mature adults		0·43	0·40		-0·37			0·30		0·33
50	One person households		0·31						0·32		
45	Pedestrian commuters				0·40			0·39		0·32	
30	Medium social class	-0·35			-0·36			-0·31			
38	Unskilled manual				0·38			0·30			
4	Old age				0·33						
5	Females										
24	Agricultural workers	0·37									
26	Transport workers	-0·35									
39	Crossing commuters	0·50									
Correlation between factors Angles		+0·17 81°12'		Orthogonal		+0·27 75°20'		Orthogonal		+0·27 75°20'	
Name of factors		Residential mobility v. Ethnic-migrant				Migrant v. Ethnic				Migrant v. Ethnic	

Principal components	1	2	3	4	5	6	7	8	9	total 9 factor
% variance	21·83	16·06	9·05	6·44	5·34	4·15	3·61	3·13	2·61	72·24

graphers have employed the varimax solution. However, before the initial solution can be rotated and interpreted, a decision has to be made over two cut-off points, namely, the minimum size of factor loading that is worth interpreting and the number of factors to rotate. Ideally, one might consider that some of the statistical tests proposed by C. L. Burt[11] in respect to factor loadings, or by M. S. Bartlett[12] with respect to the number of factors may be used. Experience with these tests[13] led to the conclusion that their utility has yet to be finally established and they may be most appropriate in conditions where other procedures break down. Interpretation was, therefore, based upon a series of 'rule of thumb' procedures leading to a series of iterations designed to search for the simplest and most stable structure.

Most geographers have only interpreted those factors with eigenvalues over 1·0. This approach was rejected since it would provide a cut-off point of 1 per cent in a 100-variable analysis and 5 per cent in a twenty-variable analysis.[14] More appropriate procedures would seem to be R. Cattell's[15] scree test in which breaks in the patterns of eigenvalues are used to justify the cut-off point, or Burt's[16] suggestion that only components having more than one in twenty important loadings should be interpreted. As the distribution of first-order eigenvalues in the Leicester study (Table II) did not show any obvious breaks, several parallel procedures were adopted:

(a) First, attention was focused on an arbitrary range of eigenvalues isolating between 5 and 2 per cent of the total variance; the pattern of first-ranking loadings on these components was then isolated.

(b) Successive rotations of six, seven, eight and nine components revealed that the eight- and nine-component solutions were marginal in the sense that less than three (1 in 20) variables had their highest loadings on these factors.

(c) An eight-component solution was initially chosen but further analysis revealed that the rotation of nine components separated the ethnic-migrant dimension of the eight-factor solution[17] into distinct ethnic and migrant dimensions (Table II). This strengthened the rather indistinct 'residential mobility' dimension produced by the eight-factor solution (Column 1, Table II) by converting it into a distinct migrant dimension (Column 5, Table III). In addition, it removed the influence of variables twenty-four and thirty-nine (Column 1) from factor II and concentrated them upon factor VIII, the 'urban fringe' factor.

Table III shows the distribution of the variance associated with each of the nine factors as well as the pattern of correlation between the oblique factors. In this particular study the varimax solution produced quite good interpretations of the basic dimensions, but at this stage in the analysis the assumption of orthogonality could not be justified, so attention was focused upon oblique solutions that allowed the possibility of higher-order solutions being obtained. Two different types of oblique rotation, the oblimin solution of the reference structure matrix, and the direct oblimin solutions of the primary pattern matrix were used in the analysis.[18] As both solutions have a variable parameter that has to be specified, it proved possible to manipulate the data in different ways in order to test the stability of the oblique solution.

The results of the rotation iterations demonstrated that a fairly stable pattern of factor dimensions was present. This is particularly marked in relation to the direct oblimin solutions. Comparatively minor changes occur in the distribution of variances for, as the value of the direct oblimin δ increases, the amount of overall explanation decreases.

TABLE III
Differences between the oblique solutions

(a) *Distribution of direct variance for the first-order solutions*

	I	2	3	4	5	6	7	8	9	Total 9
Orthogonal										
Principal Components	21·83	16·06	9·05	6·44	5·34	4·15	3·61	3·13	2·61	72·24
Varimax	18·20	7·78	9·73	8·78	6·07	6·98	6·38	4·86	3·07	71·85
Oblique (a) Reference										
Structure Biquartimin (0·5)	17·63	8·21	9·89	8·06	5·98	6·42	6·09	4·68	3·13	70·08
(b) Primary Pattern										
Direct Oblimin (0·0)	14·73	6·25	9·44	8·31	5·71	7·30	6·52	4·89	3·06	66·21
Direct Oblimin (− 1·0)	11·03	6·75	9·39	8·53	5·91	7·23	7·18	5·74	3·16	64·92

(b) *Distribution of correlations between the factors in the oblique solutions*

	0 to 0·09	0·10 to 0·19	0·20 to 0·29	over 0·30	Total for half a 9 × 9 matrix
Biquartimin	15	14	5	2	36
Direct Oblimin (0·0)	22	10	4		36
Direct Oblimin (− 1·0)	21	11	4		36

This is because Table III only accounts for the direct variance and does not show the indirect variance associated with the correlations between the factors. Only one example of the reference structure type of solution, the biquartimin solution, is shown in Table III, because previous workers[19] have observed that the covarimin and quartimin procedures tend to produce dimensions that are consistently too orthogonal or too oblique respectively. Although the biquartimin solution produced two highly correlated sets of axes (factors 2 and 6 as well as factors 5 and 6), this was not held to be a point in favour of abandoning the solution since the comparison of the eight- against a nine-factor solution had already revealed a close association between the factors (Table II). In addition, the reference structure solution produced higher levels of overall explanation than the primary pattern solutions. Therefore we preferred the biquartimin solution to the direct oblimin techniques although in practice the two sets of factor loadings, or saturations, revealed little of substantive difference. In short, we examined some alternative factor solutions and rotational techniques, and concluded that a nine-factor principal components analysis subjected to oblique rotation using the biquartimin method represented best the structure of associations between the characteristics of enumeration districts in Leicester in 1966. The substantive nature of these nine factors, called urban dimensions, is next examined.

THE URBAN DIMENSIONS

Recent years have seen an increasingly uniform interpretation of the factor loading matrix with most factor ecologists adopting approximately 0·3 or 0·4 as the cut-off points for distinguishing significant from non-significant loadings. In this study, 0·3 was chosen as the absolute cut-off point, but three sets of positive and three sets of negative loadings were identified by grouping all the significant loadings into three categories: high (1·00 to 0·70), medium (0·69 to 0·50) and low (0·49 to 0·3). This procedure made it easier to focus attention upon the high as opposed to the low loadings and eased the problems of interpreting and naming the factors. This lessened the impact of an arbitrary choice of factor loading cut-off point and produced a simple structure in statistical terms. Thus in the biquartimin solution, fifty of the fifty-six variables had loadings of over 0·3 only on one or two factors. Moreover, only one variable, the percentage of owner occupiers (47), was spread over four factors while the only variable failing to achieve a loading over 0·3 was the percentage of unemployed (22).

Table IV shows the distribution of the loadings over the nine factors, together with a short descriptive title of the dimension. The amount of explanation associated with each factor depends partially on the rotation procedure but the primary influence comes from the initial input of variables. Hence, there seemed little point in making a rigid comparison between these eigenvalues and those reported by other factor ecologists, since different sets and combinations of variables have been used. In Leicester, the two largest eigenvalues, accounting for 17·6 and 9·9 per cent of the variance respectively, represent dimensions that can be described as socio-economic status (factor I) and life-cycle status (factor III). Both dimensions provide a typical factor scale with values ranging from high positive to high negative. In the case of the socio-economic status factor, this means that positive values indicate areas with high percentages of two-car households (44), social classes 1 and 2 (29), and professional and managerial groups (34, 33), as opposed to high negative values that are associated with high percentages of social classes 4 and 5 (31), personal service and agricultural workers (37), and unskilled workers (38). The life-cycle dimension, on the other hand, provides high percentages of middle- and old-age people (3, 4) on the positive side of the scale, with high percentages of children (9), large households (51) and a high single-person ratio (7) representing the negative end of the scale. It is worth noting that the large council (public) housing sector typical of the British city is accommodated on this dimension since these low-income housing areas usually have households that are larger than average.

It could be argued that many of the variables on these two scales complement one another and may be considered redundant. At this stage in our understanding of factor ecology this seems to be a worthwhile risk to take. Indeed, in defence of the set of variables, one could suggest that it not only provides an objective demonstration of our previous work but it avoids the problem of failing to isolate vital dimensions if the initial set of data is not sufficiently comprehensive. Probably this latter point is primarily responsible for the failure of previous British workers[20] to recognize clear-cut socio-economic and life-cycle dimensions in their studies.

The third major dimension that has usually been found in studies of North American cities[21] is an ethnic one and this factor is also found in Leicester. Comparatively small (6·4 per cent) because of the limited number of ethnic variables and the amount of ethnic mixing in British cities, it does represent the impact of large-scale Commonwealth immigration into the United Kingdom[22] in the last 15 years. In this sense the result has been to move the social structure of British cities closer to the North American pattern. Unlike factors I and III, the ethnicity factor (VI) does not provide as clear cut and complete a factor scale since only two associated variables, the percentage of Commonwealth migrants (10) and percentage born overseas (12) load highly on the dimension.

TABLE IV
First-order dimensions of Leicester

Factor I: Socio-economic status (19)
Positive   High: 44. Two car households; 29. High social class; 34. Employers/managers; 42. High car ratio;
               33. Professional workers
               Medium: 36. Intermediate non-manual workers; 27. Distribution and service workers; 40. Car com-
               muters; 47. Owner occupiers
               Low: 28. Government workers
Negative   Low: 11. Irish
               Medium: 45. Pedestrian commuters; 35. Foremen-skilled workers; 49. Tenants of unfurnished property;
               43. Non-car households; 25. Industrial workers; 38. Unskilled-manual workers
               High: 31. Low social class; 37. Personal service and agricultural workers

Factor II: Mobility (99)
Positive   High: None
               Medium: None
               Low: None
Negative   Low: 50. One-person households; 2. Mature adults; 17. New residents; 52. Households sharing
               dwellings
               Medium: 14. Recent movers
               High: 16. Local movers; 19. Single person movers; 15. Movers within 5 years; 18. Female movers

Factor II: Stage in life cycle (13)
Positive   High: 3. Middle aged; 4. Old age
               Medium: 54. Rooms per person (area)
               Low: 32. Households with pensioners; 49. Tenants of unfurnished property; 47. Owner occupiers;
               45. Pedestrian commuters; 56. Sparse occupancy households
Negative   Low: None
               Medium: 2. Mature adults; 48. Council tenants
               High: Children; 7. Single ratio; 51. Large households

Factor IV: Substandardness (9)
Positive   High: 55. Dense occupancy households; 53. Sub-standard houses; 56. Sparse occupancy households
               Medium: 50. One person households; 32. Households with pensioners; 43. Non-car households
               Low: 45. Pedestrian commuters; 51. Large households
Negative   Low: 54. Rooms per person (area)
               Medium: None
               High: None

Factor V: Mobile young adult (11)
Positive   High: None
               Medium: None
               Low: 8. Married adult females; 41. Commuters by works transport 47. Owner occupiers; 25. Industrial
               workers; 26. Transport workers; 30. Medium social class
Negative   Low: 52. Households sharing dwellings; 23. Employed females; 14. Recent movers
               Medium: None
               High: 46. Non-residents; 1. Young adults

Factor VI: Ethnicity (10)
Positive   High: None
               Medium: 16. Local movers; 48. Council tenants
               Low: None
Negative   Low: 52. Households sharing dwellings; 11. Irish; 49. Tenants of unfurnished property; 47. Owner
               occupiers; 13. Foreign-born; 17. New residents
               Medium: None
               High: 10. Born overseas; 12 Commonwealth-colonial born

Factor VII: Economic participation (9)
Positive   High: 21. Employed; 23. Employed females

TABLE IV (*cont.*)

Medium: 20. Economically active
Low: 30. Medium social class; 35. Foremen-skilled workers; 1. Young adults; 26. Transport workers
Negative Low: 4. Old age; 28. Government workers
Medium: None
High: None

Factor VIII: Urban fringe (5)
Positive High: 39. Crossing-commuters 24. Agricultural workers
Medium: None
Low: 25. Industrial workers; 40. Car commuters; 17. New residents
Negative Low: None
Medium: None
High: None

Factors IX: Females (3)
Positive High: None
Medium: 6. Fertile female ratio; 5. Females
Low: None
Negative Low: 8. Married females
Medium: None
High: None

Both are negative loadings, the former with a value of -0.75, the latter with -0.77. A set of low negative loadings confirms these immigrant characteristics and their association with poor housing conditions. Inversely related to these indicators, although only with medium loadings of $+0.65$ and $+0.52$ respectively, are the percentages of local movers (16) and council tenants (48). Although it is tempting to regard this component as a 'public housing' dimension, the higher values and greater spread of the negative loadings make it more appropriate to label it as an 'ethnicity' dimension. This is particularly apt since the operation of public housing policy[23] among the lower income groups makes it very difficult for coloured migrants to qualify for housing assistance. The result is an ethnic differentiation, with native-born white Britons in council house estates being picked out by the positive side of the axis, while areas occupied by recent immigrants are identified by the negative values.

The mixture of variables used in this analysis ensures that factors II and IV, called the mobility and sub-standard dimensions respectively, are of greater overall importance than the ethnic factor. In both cases the variables only load highly on one side of the factor, thereby measuring a specific association of variables rather than providing an overall factor scale. To identify the mobility dimension is simple because it is related to all the variables measuring some type of recent change of address. It is not surprising to find this particular dimension ignored by most other factor ecologists, since few workers other than Rees[24] have incorporated any comparable data in their study. Given the importance of the developing literature in intra-urban mobility[25] it is to be hoped that the discovery of this dimension will lead to closer links between factor ecological and migration studies.

The sub-standard dimension is more familiar since it is represented by variables measuring some aspect of obsolescent property, whether by reference to the lack of modern facilities (53), to some index of over-crowding (55), or to above-average levels of household under-occupancy once the family has grown up and left (56). Since this factor is also related to the percentage of person households (50), and households with pensioners (senior citizens) (32) and without cars (43), it becomes additionally a statement of the completed family group, the association with sub-standard property being similar to Jansen's 'aged-family equipment' factor.[26] Hence, factor IV provides an index of those household groups who are least able to cope with the pressures of modern urban living.

The presence of a set of economic variables in the original data provides another means of picking out areas with an above-average level of employed people (21, 23, 20). Although described as an economic participation factor (VII), it may be also considered to represent one aspect of the family life cycle, the stage in which middle-income households in the middle stage of life have working children or working mothers.

Factor V is a 'mobile young adult' dimension that emphasizes the fact that Leicester is a large commercial city with a university and other higher educational facilities. The influx of students as well as young office and sales staff provides the explanation for the high association with non-residents (46) and young adults between the ages of 15 and 24 years (1). The other loadings are comparatively low, being positively linked with the percentage of households sharing dwellings (52), recent movers (14) and employed females (23), but inversely linked with a series of variables relating to stable, middle-income households (41, 47, 25, 26, 30). In some ways this factor represents the transitional stage in life prior to family formation. Although the basis for this factor is different and the individuals are more integrated within the particular urban society, they may be considered as being somewhat similar to the transient zone of immigrants, characteristic of cities in the U.S.A.[27] It might be suggested, therefore, that the affluence and specialization of existing Western society increasingly provides an opportunity for the presence of this 'youth' factor.

The decision to incorporate the peripheral built-up areas of the city in the analysis provides the basis for factor VIII, the urban fringe factor. The high correlations associated with agricultural workers (24) and commuters crossing administrative boundaries (39) are particularly important in demonstrating the extent to which the factor provides an identifiable rural-urban dimension delimiting the city.

It has already been noted that nine, rather than eight, factors were rotated in order to clarify the description of the ethnic and migrant dimensions. It is also usual to make sure that one more factor is rotated than is interpreted so that it can act as a 'catch-all' for the random loadings that cannot be accommodated on the primary set of axes. Factor IX which acted in this capacity was remarkably clear, being associated with three female variables (6, 5, 8). The low level of variance associated with the factor, its association with such a limited set of variables, and the fact that it was only abstracted as a 'catch-all' factor, lead to the conclusion that the general relevance of the dimension is in doubt. Also it provided additional confirmation that a simple factor structure was isolated from the initial component solution.

HIGHER-ORDER SOLUTIONS

A major advantage of using oblique rotation is that the relationships between the first-order factors may be used to search for higher-order descriptive generalizations. The matrix of correlations between the eight oblique factors of Leicester was factorially analysed according to the Principal Components model. Exploration of a series of rotation solutions revealed that the three-factor biquartimin procedure of the reference structure matrix produced the clearest pattern of association and accounted for 55·2 per cent of the variance

TABLE V
Association between the dimensions of Leicester

Successive levels of generalization

Second-order title	Loadings	First-order title (Communality)	First-order variance	Examples of important variables
2. Social status	−0·61 / +0·76 / +0·69	4. Sub-standardness (0·51)	8·1%	+ Overcrowding; sub-standard housing − Rooms per person (L)
		8. Urban fringe (0·61)	4·7%	+ Cross commuters; agricultural workers − None
	+0·54	1. Socio-economic status (0·72)	17·6%	+ Two-car households; employers & managers − Low social class; personal service workers
3. Family status	+0·74 / −0·64	3. Life cycle (0·56)	9·9%	+ Middle age; old age − Children; large households
		7. Economic participation (0·49)	6·1%	+ Employed persons − Old age (L)
	+0·50	5. Mobile young adults (0·34)	5·9%	+ Owner occupiers (L) − Non-residents: young adults
1. Ethnicity-migrants	+0·87 / +0·66	6. Ethnic origins (0·74)	6·4%	+ Local movers; council tenants (M) − Born overseas
		2. Mobility (0·45)	8·2%	+ None − Migrants

◄─────── First-ranking correlation

◄ ─ ─ ─ ─ Second-ranking correlation

Loadings are greater than 0·7 unless shown by: (M) 0·5 to 0·69
(L) 0·3 to 0·49

(0·51) The communalities of the first-order dimensions in the second-order analysis

(b) Higher-order Principal Components solution

Components	1	2	3	4	5
% variance	21·86	15·93	13·03	10·95	9·74
Cumulative variance	21·86	37·82	50·84	61·79	71·53

Second-order correlations matrix: biquartimin solution

	1	2	3
1. Ethnic migrant	1·00		
2. Social status	0·10	1·00	
3. Family status	−0·15	−0·07	1·00

of the oblique factor correlation matrix. In this case, 'clearest' means that as many of the first-order factors as possible were exclusively allocated to one of the higher-order dimensions.

Table V shows all the reference structure loadings over 0·3 for the biquartimin solution, together with the first-order dimensions and examples of the most important variables associated with them. The most distinct second-order dimension is one on which three of the first-order dimensions have their highest loadings. The first-order socio-economic status and urban fringe factors load positively on the higher-order axis, whereas the sub-standard characteristic loads negatively. Although labelling may be rather premature, given the fact that few high-order solutions have been reported in the literature, it would seem that this dimension could be conveniently described as social or socio-urban status.

The most complex second-order factor is called family status since the life-cycle dimension loads most highly upon it, with economic participation in negative association. Socio-economic status is also linked with the factor but only with a second-ranking connection. Overall, these attributes seem to confirm the association of this cluster with the first-order dimensions that measure aspects of the family life cycle.

A third factor, the ethnic-migrant factor, is positively associated with the highest loadings of the ethnic and the two mobility dimensions. This factor brings together the association that was separated by the choice of the nine- rather than the eight-factor solution, so it can be seen that the effect of this analysis has not been artificially to separate the characteristics of a particular set of variables within the city. Instead, it has simplified the description of these related features by presenting an explanation that applies to two scales, one represented by the first-order analysis and the other by the second-order study.

The second-order correlation matrix also shows that the three second-order dimensions are only slightly related to one another. However, it is dangerous to infer from this that the results confirm the existence of a simple orthogonal and hierarchical relationship in which each variable is uniquely absorbed by one first-order factor, and each first-order factor is uniquely linked with a second-order dimension. The results come very close to this, but the persisting variation of family size with economic status in western society produces the ambivalent relationship shown of the socio-economic status dimension of Leicester, a feature which is likely to be characteristic of other cities.

CONCLUSION

The emphasis of this study of Leicester has been deliberately related to some of the problems of deriving comparable oblique factor solutions since comparatively few of these major issues have been explored by factor ecologists. Despite this orientation towards the technical problems of the analysis, however, it has proved possible to demonstrate that the basic urban dimensions of Leicester conform much more closely to the standard North American patterns than has hitherto been suggested.

In addition, a parallel study[28] dealing with the distribution of factor scores shows that the typical concentric, sectoral and clustered patterns are typical of the life-cycle, socio-economic and ethnic dimensions respectively. Probably, most of the difficulty of relating British studies with those of other western societies stems from the initial choice of variables which restricted the number and type of dimensions that can conceivably be identified. Although the problem of redundancy does crop up, it is further suggested that the advantages of using such a wide variety of variables makes it possible to distinguish factor scales for the major dimensions. These may prove to be especially useful in indicating the continuity of the dimensions throughout the city, as well as providing a more logical basis for the choice of indicator variables in any analysis of a reduced data set.

In addition to the three standard factors for Western cities, six other dimensions, measuring the extent of sub-standard characteristics, the urban fringe, economic participation, household mobility and mobile young adults, were identified. The stability of the factor solution in the case study of Leicester suggests that they represent important clusters of associations but comparable studies of other cities are needed before they can be recognized as general factors. The incorporation of these six dimensions into the three standard general factors in the higher-order analysis means that they are more properly regarded as sub-sets of the social status/family/migrant-ethnic dimensions and their isolation as separate entities is primarily a function of the scale of generalization. However, there is a danger that descriptions that only deal with these three high-level generalizations may miss some of the developing aspects of Western urban society such as the presence of an inner city pre-family dimension, or the increasing mobility of certain groups, while the relevance of identifying sub-standard characteristics in relation to projects for urban renewal needs no emphasis. At present, identification of these features is still either at the subjective level or is controlled by the study of one or two relevant variables. It should be the objective of factor ecologists to make their analysis flexible enough to incorporate these features, thereby providing an objective basis for inter-city and cross-cultural comparisons.

ACKNOWLEDGEMENTS

The authors record their appreciation to the Leicester City Planning Office and the Leicestershire County Planning Office for kindly allowing them access to the relevant data.

NOTES

1. C. A. JANSEN, 'Some problems of ecological factor analysis structure' in M. DOGAN and S. ROKKAN, *Quantitative ecological analysis in the social sciences* (Cambridge, Mass., 1969); L. RUMMEL, *Applied factor analysis* (Evanston, 1970); F. L. SWEETSER, 'Factor structure as ecological structure', *Acta Sociol.* 8 (1965), 202–25

2. B. T. ROBSON, *Urban analysis: a study of city structure* (Cambridge, 1969); C. F. SCHMID and K. TAGASHIRA, 'Ecological and demographic indices: a methodological analysis', *Demography* 1 (1964), 194–211

3. P. H. REES, 'The factorial ecology of metropolitan Chicago, 1960' in B. J. L. BERRY and F. W. HORTON, *Geographic perspectives on urban systems* (1970)

4. C. A. JANSEN, 'A preliminary report on Swedish urban spatial structure', *Econ. Geogr.* 47, 2 (Supplement, June 1971), 249–57

5. Centre for Urban Studies (University College London). 'A note on the Principal Component analysis of 1961 Enumeration District data for London Administrative County'. Unpublished. No date. See also B. T. ROBSON, op. cit.

6. R. J. JOHNSON, 'Some limitations of factorial ecologies and social area analysis', *Econ. Geogr.* 47, 2 (Supplement, June 1971), 314–23

7. R. A. MURDIE, 'The factor ecology of Metropolitan Toronto, 1951–1961', Dept. of Geography, Univ. of Chicago Res. Pap. 116 (1969)

8. P. J. TAYLOR, 'Distance transformations and distance-decay functions', *Geogrl Anal.* 3, 3 (July, 1971), 221–38

9. D. T. HERBERT, 'Principal Components analysis and British studies of urban social structure', *Prof. Geogr.* 20 (1968), 280–3

10. W. K. D. DAVIES, 'Varimax and the destruction of generality', *Area* 3, 2 (1971), 112–8. See also *Area* 3, 4 (1971) for a discussion of these problems between P. Mather and W. K. D. Davies. In this paper, 'factor' is used in the popular and widest sense to include component analysis and factor analysis *sensu strictu*. Factor analysis proper is designated as 'common factor analysis'.

11. C. L. BURT, 'Tests of significance in factor analysis', *Br. J. Psychol. statist. Sect.* 5 (1952), 109–33

12. M. S. BARTLETT, 'Tests of significance in factor analysis', *Br. J. Psychol. statist. Sect.* 3, II (June, 1950), 77–85. See also the discussion in the same journal, 4 (1951), 1–2

13. W. K. D. DAVIES, 'Conurbation and city region in an administrative borderland', *Reg. Stud.* (1972, forthcoming)

14. W. K. D. DAVIES, 'Urbanization and interaction', *Proc. I.B.G. Urban Study Grp* (Keele, September, 1969)

15. R. CATTELL, 'The scree test for the number of factors', *Multivariate Behavioural Res.* 1, 245–76

16. C. BURT, op. cit.

17. W. K. D. DAVIES, 'The factor ecology of British cities: a preliminary report', *International Geography 1972* (ed. W. P. ADAMS and F. M. HELLEINER, Montreal 1972), 805–8

18. The reference structure matrix and the primary pattern matrix both provide measures of the co-ordinates or saturations of the variable and the factor despite the differences in the orientation of the axes used in the procedure. By contrast, the reference pattern and primary structure provide examples of the correlations between variable and factor, and include direct and joint variance.

19. H. H. HARMAN, *Modern factor analysis* (Chicago, 1968)

20. E. GITTUS, 'The structure of urban areas', *Tn Plann. Rev.* 35 (1964), 5–20; D. T. HERBERT, 'Principal Component analysis and urban social structure' in H. CARTER and W. K. D. DAVIES (eds.) *Urban essays: studies in the geography of Wales* (1970), 79–100; B. T. ROBSON, op. cit.

21. R. A. MURDIE, op. cit.; P. D. SALINS, 'Household location patterns in American metropolitan areas', *Econ. Geogr.* 47, 2 (Supplement, June 1971), 234–48

22. B. E. COATES, 'The distribution of the overseas born of the British Isles', *Trans. Inst. Br. Geogr.* 43 (1968). 37–43

23. J. CULLINGWORTH, *Housing needs and planning policy* (1961)

24. P. H. REES, op. cit., footnote 6

25. J. W. SIMMONS, 'Changing residence in the city: a review of intra-urban mobility', *Geogrl Rev.* 58 (1968), 622–51

26. C. A. JANSEN, op. cit. (1971)

27. R. E. PARK, E. BURGESS and R. D. MCKENZIE, *The city* (Chicago, 1925)

28. G. J. LEWIS, 'Leicester—urban structure and regional relationships' in N. PYE (ed.) *Leicester and its region* (Leicester, 1972)

RÉSUMÉ. *Les dimensions urbaines de Leicester, Angleterre.* Des procédés d'analyse factorielle obliques et d'ordre supérieur sont employés afin d'isoler les dimensions fondamentales d'un ensemble de données recueillies sur 143 secteurs et en fonction de cinquante-six variables à Leicester, Angleterre. Sont mises en valeur les difficultés rencontrées en isolant les huit dimensions fondamentales qui expliquent 70 pour cent de la variance dans l'ensemble de données. Ces huit dimensions se composent des facteurs normaux de situation socio-économique, groupe d'âge et groupe ethnique ainsi que de ceux qui mesurent les conditions d'habitation, la participation économique, les jeunes adultes mobiles, la mobilité de la population, et les particularités de la banlieue urbaine. Cette étude corrobore l'applicabilité aux grandes villes britanniques du modèle type nord-américain de la structure sociale urbaine mais démontre que l'utilité descriptive des dimensions socio-économiques, d'âge et ethniques est fonction du degré de généralisation de l'enquête.

ZUSAMMENFASSUNG. *Die städtischen Dimensionen Leicesters, England.* Analyse-Verfahren mittelbarer und hochgradiger Faktoren werden angewandt, um die fundamentalen Dimensionen eines 56 Variabel × 143 Flächen-Daten-Satzes in Leicester, England, zu isolieren. Besonderer Nachdruck wird auf die Probleme der isolierung der acht basischen Dimensionen, die 70 prozent der Abweichung der originell gegebenen Daten erklären, gelegt. Diese acht Dimensionen schliessen die Faktoren der durchschnittlichen-soziologisch-wirtschaftlichen Stände des Lebenszyklus und der Rassen ein, und messen ausserdem auch die Merkmale von ärmlichen Wohnverhältnissen, wirtschaftlicher Anteilnahme, der Mobilität der Jung-Erwachsenen, der Mobilität der Bevölkerung und der städtischen Peripherie. Diese Untersuchung bestätigt die Anwendbarkeit des typisch nord-amerikanischen Musters städtisch-sozialer Struktur für englische Städte, beweist aber auch, dass die beschreibende Nutzbarkeit der sozial-wirtschaftlichen, lebenszyklischen und ethnischen Dimensionen im wesentlichen eine Funktion des Ausmasses der Verallgemeinerung der Untersuchung ist.

A comparative study of urban social structures in South Wales

D. J. EVANS

Research Student in Geography, University College of Swansea

Revised MS received 23 May 1972

ABSTRACT. The paper analyses the factorial ecology of the three major cities in South Wales by applying factor techniques to forty variables drawn from the 1966 census data. A social status component, a tenure and stage in family-life cycle component and a residential quality component are differentiated in each of the three cities. The results are then compared with those of other recent British studies. It is suggested that it is now possible to predict the major dimensions of urban social structure from factorial analysis of British census data for any major city. The need now is for new directions in research which may lead to an explanation of why and how these dimensions are arranged.

ONE of the basic problems of the existing literature in factorial ecology is the lack of comparability between individual case studies. One may cite numerous examples to support such a claim ranging from the factorial analysis by E. Gittus of twenty-seven indices from the 1951 census sub-divisions of Merseyside and South-East Lancashire,[1] to the forthcoming report from the Centre for Urban and Regional Studies of such an analysis of the 1966 census data for Birmingham and the West Midlands.[2] In each case a unique set of indices is used making the precise comparison of results difficult. Some attempts have been made to produce a set of universally applicable indices, notably by the Centre for Urban Studies, whose list of indices originally used in an analysis of Greater London[3] was also employed by D. T. Herbert in South Wales.[4] In an analysis of the 1961 census data for Cardiff and Swansea, Herbert showed the fallibilities of using the same set of indices in two different contexts; for example, one problem was that the multitude of ethnic groups, so important in London, proved to be relatively unimportant in South Wales. However, if meaningful generalizations are to be made about urban social structure from factorial ecologies, further attempts at comparability must be made in Britain. This paper endeavours to relieve the position by applying factor analysis to a similar range of variables selected from the 1966 census for the three largest cities in South Wales: Swansea (167 000), Cardiff (253 000) and Newport (111 230).[5] By comparing the components which emerge from such an analysis, it is hoped that valid generalizations can be made about the urban social structure of cities in South Wales. These results can then be compared with the results of other recent British studies, and similarities and divergencies in the emerging factors noted. It will be shown that the major differentiating factors of British urban social structure in general can be evaluated and that this in turn will help to establish a model of British urban social structure.

PREPARATION OF THE DATA

From the multiplicity of possible variables which can be selected from a variety of sources, each differentiating the urban social system in a particular way, one is led inevitably to

TABLE I
Variables used in the analysis of Cardiff, Swansea and Newport

1. Population total
2. Overall sex ratio
3. Percentage of economically active females
4. Percentage of economically active males employed in government
5. Percentage of economically active males in social classes I and II
6. Percentage of economically active males in social classes IV and V
7. Percentage of cars garaged in the curtilage
8. Percentage of persons living at a density of more than $1\frac{1}{2}$ per room
9. Percentage of households lacking a fixed bath
10. Percentage of households who share a dwelling
11. Percentage of dwellings which are multi-dwellings purpose-built
12. Percentage of dwellings which are multi-dwellings converted
13. Percentage of total population who are foreign born
14. Percentage of total population who are single
15. Fertility ratio of children aged 0–4 years to women aged 15–44 years
16. Percentage of population aged 0–4 years
17. Percentage of population aged 15–24 years
18. Percentage of population aged 65 and over
19. Percentage of persons moving within the local authority during the last 5 years
20. Percentage of persons moving into the local authority during the last 5 years
21. Percentage of economically active males
22. Percentage of economically active males in construction etc.
23. Percentage of economically active males in services
24. Percentage of economically active males in socio-economic groups 1, 2, 3, 4 and 13
25. Percentage of economically active males in socio-economic groups 7, 10, 11 and 15
26. Percentage of households with no car
27. Percentage of households with two or more cars
28. Percentage of persons travelling to work by public bus
29. Percentage of persons travelling to work by car
30. Percentage of persons travelling to work on foot
31. Percentage of dwellings which are owner-occupied
32. Percentage of dwellings which are rented from the council
33. Percentage of dwellings which are privately rented
34. Percentage of households with no family
35. Percentage of households with six or more persons
36. Ratio of persons per room
37. Percentage of persons living at a density of less than $\frac{1}{2}$ per room
38. Percentage of households with 1–3 rooms
39. Percentage of households with 7 or more rooms
40. Percentage of households with exclusive use of all amenities

rely on census data. Much has been written about the faults of census data, especially of the 1966 10 per cent sample census, notably by B. T. Robson[6] and D. W. G. Timms,[7] emphasizing especially the probable lack of homogeneity of the enumeration districts, owing to the arbitrary nature of their limits. In this study precautions were taken so that districts were only included in the analysis if their total size was greater than 750 persons and if their institutional population was less than 25 per cent. In spite of the criticisms put forward, the census is still a unique source of information, covering a wide range of topics, demographic, socio-economic and household and, as such, merits being used to differentiate urban social structure on a sub-area framework.

As a preliminary step, fifty-two variables, theoretically thought to be important and covering a wide cross-section, were selected from the 1966 Census for Swansea and an unrotated component analysis was carried out. As a result of the inspection of the correlation matrix, the number of variables was reduced from fifty-two to forty, on the grounds that some of the variables duplicated the other variables and were thus redundant to the analysis. It has been stressed repeatedly by nearly every worker undertaking a factorial ecology from Gittus[8] onwards, that the original selection of variables preconditions the eventual results, so that a careful selection of variables will considerably improve the chances of useful results being obtained. Here every variable admitted to the final analysis was included for a specific technical reason, namely, that it contributed to the original correlation matrix. The variables used were in the form of percentages or ratios and were standardized to a comparable range (Table I).

In addition to care being taken in the selection of variables, caution must also be exercised in the selection of the urban area included in each analysis. It is a well-known fact, emphasized by the recent re-organization of local government boundaries, that such boundaries do not always include what is generally recognized as the complete built-up area of a city; suburbs usually sprawl over the fringes. In this study an attempt was made to include these outer suburbs since they form an integral part of each of the urban systems and their exclusion would have considerably biased the results. F. L. Sweetser[9], analysing the factors found in differently defined areas of Boston and Helsinki, concludes that great caution should be paid to delimiting the outer boundaries of metropolitan communities if they are to be used for comparative ecological studies. In this analysis the author consulted the respective planning authorities and examined journey-to-work data before deciding on the final areas of study. Caution was thus exercised in delimiting the respective study areas, so that they represented as nearly as possible a complete urban system.

CHOICE OF TECHNIQUE

In analysing the internal structure of such a system, an appropriate technique has to be chosen and justified. Authors of factorial ecologies rarely justify their choice of technique, but factor analysis is only one of several possible techniques of urban analysis.

The Shevky-Bell typology is perhaps *the* traditional method of sub-area analysis,[10] and as such has suffered much criticism on both theoretical and empirical grounds. Looking only at the empirical applications in this country one can see why factor analysis is to be preferred. Herbert's original work in Newcastle-under-Lyme shows the difficulty of applying the technique to British census data and even then, when an improvised technique is used, the outcome is far from that predicted by Shevky and Bell.[11] This technique has in fact been applied to one of the cities included in this study (Cardiff) by R. Inder, who concludes by saying, 'In this way, the additional results for Cardiff have served to add weight to the argument that there is an individualistic British context for Social Area Analysis, which stands apart from other countries'.[12] It seems that the Shevky-Bell typology is tied to a particular society, namely North America, and cannot easily be translated into a different society, such as that of Britain, where different forces are at work, notably the building of houses by local authorities. This is confirmed by the author's experience in Wolverhampton C.B., where an attempt was made to apply the Shevky-Bell technique to the 1966 census data.[13] It was found that a multivariate technique not only accounted for more variation but produced more precise results than the Shevky-Bell analysis. The particular form of multivariate technique used in that case was elementary linkage analysis but, whatever the particular type of multivariate technique used, it is reasonable to expect such a technique to be more appropriate in view of the complex nature of urban areas.

Factor analysis is one of the more sophisticated forms of multivariate analysis about which much has already been written.[14] One need only give details of the particular technique used in this instance, where an indirect approach was adopted since no *a priori* hypotheses were made about the possible outcome. The particular type of program used was a principal components analysis with varimax rotation.[15] An important point to note is that components are mathematical constructs and often have no intuitive meaning. As an aid to the interpretation of the components produced in this study, they were orthogonally rotated according to the varimax criterion to give what L. L. Thurstone has termed a 'simple structure',[16] of a few high loadings and some near-zero loadings. Recently there has been much debate on the relative merits of orthogonal and oblique rotations, as in the discussion between W. K. D. Davies and P. M. Mather extending over several issues of *Area*.[17] This is not the place to be drawn into such a discussion but simply to say that varimax rotation has been the most widely used form of rotation in factorial ecologies and was used as such here, though experimentation with other rotations may affect future approaches. The loadings given to each component by varimax rotation show how each variable contributes to each of the components in turn and thus meaning can be assigned to each of the components in terms of their highest loading variables. The component scores, on the other hand, show how the components are distributed with respect to the enumeration districts and thus their spatial variation can be examined. However, it is the former task, an analysis of the structure of urban social space, which is the priority here and a detailed examination of the spatial patterns of component scores merits a separate exercise.

COMPONENT STRUCTURES

Five components were extracted from the data matrix and subsequently rotated, each of these contributing more than 5 per cent to the total variance. The five components accounted for the amounts of variance shown in Table II.

The amount of variance accounted for by the first five components compares reasonably with those reported in previous studies though precise comparisons are difficult because the number of variables is not constant. However, the amounts of variance accounted for by the first five factors extracted by Gittus in Merseyside[18] and Robson in Sunderland[19] were respectively 69 and 77 per cent. More relevant to the present study areas, the amounts accounted for here by the first five components are very similar to the amounts extracted by Herbert for Cardiff and Swansea, using 1961 data, when the amounts were 73·0 and 63·2 per cent respectively.[20] So, at a general level, the results seem comparable with other recent British studies. It remains to be seen if a more detailed examination of component structures will also produce similarities.

In looking at the important loadings on each component, several alternatives are available which could significantly affect the interpretation of results. It must be noted with K. Hope[21] that every loading is of some importance but in order to select the most diagnostic variables some choice must be made. Significance tests[22] are available in setting limits on the loadings chosen but these have rarely been used by geographers. Here a limit of $+0.4$ was taken to indicate an important loading. By setting such a limit one has at least a standard base for comparison of the component loadings. The nature of each com-

TABLE II

Percentage variance accounted for by components 1 to 5

Component:	1	2	3	4	5	1–5
Swansea	25·6	14·9	12·7	7·4	6·5	67·1
Cardiff	28·7	17·3	10·6	7·7	6·2	70·6
Newport	21·5	19·6	10·4	8·9	8·4	68·8

TABLE III

Component loadings on the social status dimension

Variable loading	*Title*

Swansea: Component I = 25·6 per cent of the total variance

5 = +0·92	economically active males in social class I and II
29 = +0·91	travelling to work by car
26 = −0·91	households with no car
24 = +0·89	economically active males in socio-economic groups 1,2,3,4,13
6 = −0·85	economically active males in social classes IV and V
25 = −0·83	economically active males in social classes, 7,10,11,15
27 = +0·79	households with 2 or more cars
20 = +0·77	persons moving into L.A. during last 5 years
7 = +0·76	cars garaged in the curtilage
28 = −0·69	travelling to work by public bus
23 = +0·67	economically active males in services
31 = +0·64	dwellings which are owner-occupied

Cardiff: Component I = 28·7 per cent of the total variance

5 = +0·92	economically active males in social classes I and II
24 = +0·92	economically active males in socio-economic groups 1,2,3,4,13
29 = +0·91	persons who travel to work by car
26 = −0·90	households with no car
27 = +0·85	households with 2 or more cars
6 = −0·82	economically active males in social classes IV and V
7 = +0·82	cars garaged in the curtilage
25 = −0·81	economically active males in socio-economic groups 7,10,11,15
20 = +0·76	persons moving into L.A. during last 5 years
22 = −0·74	economically active males in construction, etc.
40 = +0·73	households with exclusive use of all amenities
23 = +0·71	economically active males in services

Newport: Component I = 21·5 per cent of total variance

26 = −0·89	households with no car
29 = +0·88	travelling to work by car
6 = −0·86	economically active males in social classes IV and V
25 = −0·86	economically active males in socio-economic groups 7,10,11,15
27 = −0·78	households with 2 or more cars
7 = +0·77	cars garaged in the curtilage
24 = +0·73	economically active males in socio-economic groups 1,2,3,4,13
5 = +0·72	economically active males in social class I and II
9 = −0·71	households lacking a fixed bath
40 = +0·67	households with exclusive use of all amenities
21 = +0·55	economically active males
33 = −0·54	dwellings which are private rented

All variables are expressed as percentages unless otherwise stated.

TABLE IV

Component loadings on the tenure and stage in the family life-cycle dimension

Variable loading	Title
Swansea: Component II = 14·9 per cent of the total variance	
18 = −0·80	population aged 65+ years
36 = +0·78	* ratio of persons per room
16 = +0·78	population aged 0–4 years
37 = −0·75	* persons living at a density of less than ½ per room
35 = +0·71	households with 6 or more persons
1 = +0·65	population total
32 = +0·58	dwellings which are council rented
8 = +0·52	* persons living at more than 1½ per room
31 = −0·48	dwellings which are owner-occupied
40 = +0·47	households with exclusive use of all amenities
33 = −0·46	dwellings which are private rented
9 = −0·46	households lacking a fixed bath
Cardiff: Component II = 17·3 per cent of the total variance	
37 = −0·85	persons living at a density of less than ½ per room
36 = +0·85	ratio of persons per room
18 = −0·83	population aged 65+
35 = +0·77	households with 6 or more persons
16 = +0·76	population aged 0–4 years
31 = −0·69	dwellings which are owner-occupied
32 = +0·68	dwellings which are council rented
1 = +0·57	population total
34 = −0·51	households with no family
8 = +0·49	persons living at more than 1½ per room
10 = −0·44	households who share a dwelling
39 = −0·43	households with 7 or more rooms
Newport: Component II = 19·6 per cent of the total variance	
32 = +0·89	dwellings which are council rented
31 = −0·78	dwellings which are owner-occupied
11 = +0·76	dwellings which are multi-dwellings purpose-built
33 = −0·70	dwellings which are private rented
16 = +0·68	population aged 0–4 years
19 = +0·68	persons moving within L.A. during the last 5 years
37 = −0·67	persons living at less than ½ person per room
30 = −0·66	persons who travel to work on foot
28 = +0·65	persons who travel to work by bus
40 = +0·64	households with exclusive use of all amenities
9 = −0·58	households lacking a fixed bath
39 = −0·56	households with 7 or more rooms

All variables are expressed as percentages unless otherwise stated.

ponent was thus interpreted on the basis of values above ±0·4 though no more than twelve variables are shown in the respective Tables for space reasons.

Component I

The first component accounted for 25·6, 28·7 and 21·5 per cent of the variation in the data matrices for Swansea, Cardiff and Newport respectively. It was interpreted as a 'social status' component in each case since the variables loading highest positive on the first component are the percentage of economically active males in social classes I and II

(V.5) and the percentage of economically active males in the professional, managerial and service socio-economic groups (V.24) (Table III); conversely, the variables loading negatively indicate the percentage of economically active males in the lower socio-economic groups (V.25). Car ownership supports this contention since variables 27 and 29 (households with two or more cars and the percentage who travel to work by car) both have high positive loadings above +0·4 while the percentage of households with no car (V.26) and the percentage who travel to work by bus (V.28) both have high negative loadings less than −0·4. Thus variables with high positive scores on this component show a high rate of ownership of cars which, more often than not, are garaged within the curtilage (V.7), giving an indication of the morphology of the houses. One of the few population measures included by this component is that of recent movement into the local authority area (V.20), revealing something of the mobility of this population group. Household amenities are usually good and the houses owner-occupied, as shown by the positive loadings on variables 40 and 31 and the negative loadings on variables 9, 32 and 33. In general, then, each of the first components for each of the three towns may be interpreted as a 'social status' dimension.

Component II

Component II, which accounts for 14·9, 17·3 and 19·6 per cent of the variance in Swansea, Cardiff and Newport respectively, can be interpreted as a 'Tenure and stage in family life cycle component' in each case. Thus, tenure variables play a large part in this component with a high percentage of the dwellings being rented from the council (as shown by the positive loading on variable 32 and the negative loadings on variables 31 and 33: Table IV). In addition, one finds a high positive loading on a high density of occupation (variables 36 and 8) and a high negative loading on a low density of occupation (variable 37). This is perhaps a reflection of the family life-cycle element since variables with positive scores reflect a tendency for large families, with the age structure weighted towards children and adolescents rather than old people. Such families probably live in large households. This can be inferred from the positive loadings on variables 35, 16, 15 and 17 and the negative loadings on variables 34, 18 and 39. The amenities of the households are, however, generally good and the households may be purpose-built, as signified by the positive loadings on variables 40 and 11 and the negative loading on variable 9. Socio-economic status is relatively low, as can be inferred from the positive loadings on variables 22 and 28 and the negative loadings on variables 23 and 29. Of the population measures included in the Swansea component, one can see a positive loading on recent movement within the local authority area (V.19), probably because of the movement involved in redevelopment, and negative loadings on the percentages of single persons (V.14) and foreign born (V.13), both of which one would not expect to reside in council-rented houses. Thus, in general, variables with positive scores on this component show council-rented accommodation and an early stage in the family life cycle as characteristics, and variables with negative scores show the opposite characteristics.

Component III

The third major dimension differentiated in this study was one of 'residential quality'. It must be stressed at the outset that none of the variables relating to household amenities is involved but this does not invalidate the interpretation since the variables loading above

TABLE V

Component loadings on the residential quality dimension

Variable loading	Title
Swansea: Component II = 12·7 per cent of the total variance	
10 = +0·84	households who share a dwelling
12 = +0·77	dwellings which are multi-dwellings converted
38 = +0·77 ←households with 1–3 rooms	
13 = +0·67	total population who are foreign born
34 = +0·67	households with no family
39 = +0·56 ←households with 7 or more rooms	
33 = +0·54	dwellings which are private rented
23 = +0·43	economically active males in services
30 = +0·43	persons who travel to work on foot
Cardiff: Component III = 10·6 per cent of the total variance	
38 = +0·76	households with 1–3 rooms
13 = +0·72	total population who are foreign born
34 = +0·71	households with no family
12 = +0·63	dwellings which are multi-dwellings converted
10 = +0·57	households who share a dwelling
33 = +0·51	dwellings which are private rented
14 = +0·48	total population who are single
39 = +0·43	households with 7 or more rooms
Newport: Component IV = 8·9 per cent of the total variance	
10 = +0·75	households who share a dwelling
12 = +0·73	dwellings which are multi-dwellings converted
38 = +0·72	households with 1–3 rooms
14 = +0·60	total population who are single
17 = +0·44	total population aged 15–24 years
3 = +0·43	economically active females
39 = +0·40	households with 7 or more rooms
16 = −0·40	population aged 0–4 years

All variables are expressed as percentages unless otherwise stated.

±0·40 *indirectly* signify poor residential quality. This component which accounted for 12·7, 10·6 and 8·9 per cent of the total variation in Swansea, Cardiff and Newport respectively, was the third most important component in the case of the former two towns but the fourth most important in the latter case, reasons for which will be advanced later. As may be expected from the descriptive label given to this dimension, housing variables figure prominently in each of the component structures (Table V). Thus, variables with positive scores show a high percentage of households who share a dwelling, of multi-dwellings which are converted, and of both small flat-type households with one to three rooms and large households with more than seven rooms, as is shown by the positive loadings on variables 10, 12, 38 and 39. The dwellings are more likely to be privately rented as indicated by the positive loading on variable 33. With regard to the demographic structure, variables with positive scores reveal a family structure weighted towards households with no family and an age-structure weighted towards adolescents, as is shown by the positive loadings on variables 34 and 17. Also, the variable representing foreign-born people has a high positive loading (V.13) in both the Swansea and Cardiff component structures. Some indication is given of the economic activity by the high positive loading

TABLE VI
Loadings on the fourth set of components interpreted

Variable loading	Title
Swansea: Component IV = 7·4 per cent of the total variance	
19 = −0·69	persons moving within the L.A. during the last 5 years
11 = −0·59	dwellings which are multi-dwellings purpose-built
4 = −0·55	economically active males employed in government
30 = +0·45	persons travelling to work on foot
9 = +0·44	households lacking a fixed bath
40 = −0·42	households with exclusive use of all amenities
2 = −0·41	overall sex ratio
Cardiff: Component IV = 7·7 per cent of the total variance	
19 = −0·58	persons moving within the L.A. during the last 5 years
28 = −0·56	persons travelling to work by public bus
33 = +0·55	dwellings which are private rented
32 = −0·53	dwellings which are council rented
9 = +0·52	households lacking a fixed bath
40 = −0·50	households with exclusive use of all amenities
11 = −0·44	dwellings which are multi-dwellings purpose built
39 = +0·44	households with 7 or more rooms
Newport: Component III = 10·4 per cent of the total variance	
36 = −0·73	ratio persons per room
34 = +0·68	households with no family
2 = +0·65	overall sex ratio
37 = +0·62	persons living at a density of less than $\frac{1}{2}$ per room
35 = −0·61	households with six or more persons
22 = −0·59	economically active males in construction, etc.
23 = +0·51	economically active males in services
1 = −0·44	population total

All variables are expressed as percentages unless otherwise stated.

on the proportion of economically active males who work in services in the Swansea component structure. In that structure too an indication is given that a high proportion of people travel to work on foot (V.30). Generally one builds up a picture of this component as a continuum of residential quality with poor quality 'bed-sitter land' at the positive end and better residential areas at the negative end of the spectrum.

The variables loading positively on Newport Component III, which accounts for 10·4 per cent of the variance, are those which one would expect to find at the negative end of the 'tenure' and 'stage in family life cycle' component. The variables indicate a later stage in the family life cycle, higher socio-economic status and a lower density of occupation not in council-rented dwellings but in owner-occupation (Table VI). Thus, this component may be considered a sub-set of Newport's Component II which has already been described; therefore the structure of this component does not warrant separate consideration.

Similarly, the variables which load highly on the Swansea and Cardiff Component IV structures, which account for 7·4 and 7·7 per cent of the variance respectively, are the ones which are expected at the negative end of the 'tenure' and 'stage in family life cycle' component (Table VI). Poor household amenities, larger households and a lack of purpose-built multi-dwellings, a lack of movement within the local authority, travel to work by

TABLE VII
Loadings on the fifth set of components interpreted

Variable loading	Title
Swansea: Component V = 6·5 per cent of the total variance	
15 = +0·75	fertility ratio
17 = −0·57	population aged 15–24 years
14 = −0·48	total population who are single
3 = −0·47	economically active females
16 = +0·44	population aged 0–4 years
Cardiff: Component V = 6·2 per cent of the total variance	
14 = +0·72	total population who are single
3 = +0·65	economically active females
17 = +0·63	population aged 15–24 years
15 = −0·58	fertility ratio
Newport: Component V = 8·4 per cent of the total variance	
20 = +0·79	persons moving into L.A. during the last 5 years
15 = +0·70	fertility ratio
23 = +0·54	economically active males in services
1 = −0·53	population total
5 = +0·51	economically active males in social classes I and II
22 = −0·49	economically active males in construction, etc.
18 = +0·48	population aged 65+

All variables are expressed as percentages unless otherwise stated.

foot rather than by bus and a prevalence of other types of tenure, such as privately rented rather than council tenure, are characteristic. Such component structures do not represent new major dimensions of the urban social structure of the cities under consideration and therefore more detailed explanation is omitted at this stage.

When the fifth set of components is reached the amount of variance they account for is very small. Thus the fifth component for Swansea, Cardiff and Newport accounts for 6·5, 6·2 and 8·4 per cent of the total variation respectively. In addition, the number of variables loading above ±0·40 is also becoming very small. In the case of Swansea and Cardiff only five variables load above this figure, making the interpretation of the components rather hazardous. However, for the sake of completeness some consideration will be given to the structures of the fifth set of components.

In the fifth component structures for Swansea and Cardiff the variables associated with Shevky and Bell's[23] urbanization or family life index are to be found, though the emphasis in the two cities is different (Table VII). Thus, in the case of Swansea one finds the variables 3 (women in the labour force), 14 (single persons) and 17 (young persons 15–24) together with 15 (fertility rates) and 16 (young children), but here the positive emphasis is on the children while in Cardiff the reverse obtains. This can perhaps be explained by the relative sizes of Swansea and Cardiff, 167 000 and 253 000 in 1966 respectively. Although the presence of these variables associated with the urbanization index of Shevky Bell may give some comfort to proponents of that method it must be noted that such variables are not as important in Britain as in North America and certainly do not merit consideration as one of the three major differentiating axes of urban social structure.

The fifth component for Newport may be considered as a sub-set of the social status component which has already been described. Here the variables load positively on the higher social classes and socio-economic groups (Table VII) together with the associated characteristics of recent movement in the local authority, retired persons over 65 years, and a greater proportion of women than men, and therefore the fifth component does not merit separate detailed consideration.

It can be said, therefore, from an examination of the five principal component structures for each of the three cities that there are three major dimensions which present themselves from each city. These are a 'social status' dimension, a 'tenure' and 'stage in family life cycle' dimension and a dimension of 'residential quality'. The other components which have been interpreted are either sub-sets of these three major dimensions or components which account for a small proportion of the total variation and do not appear in all three cases. The five sets of components are represented in diagrammatic form in Table VIII.

TABLE VIII
A diagrammatic representation of the components interpreted

	Swansea	Cardiff	Newport
Component 1	Social status	Social status	Social status
Component 2	Tenure—Stage in family life cycle	Tenure—Stage in family life cycle	Tenure—Stage in family life cycle
Component 3	Residential quality	Residential quality	Tenure—Stage in family life cycle
Component 4	Tenure—Stage in family life cycle	Tenure—Stage in family life cycle	Residential quality
Component 5	Urbanization	Urbanization	Social status

Although similar meaning can be given to the three major dimensions in each case, the dimensions are not necessarily of the same order of importance. Thus, the residential quality component of Newport is the fourth rather than the third most important component as in the other two cases. One explanation which could be put forward to account for this is that Newport is much smaller than the other two cities and may be considered to rank lower in the urban hierarchy. Therefore one would not expect to find such well developed areas of residential decline in Newport as in Swansea and Cardiff, so that this component explains less of the total variation in Newport than in the other two cities.

Even so, there is a remarkable similarity in the major dimensions differentiating urban social structure which have emerged from each of the three cities. This is the more remarkable when one remembers that there is no mathematical reason why the same dimensions should emerge, as each factorial analysis is a unique solution of the variation between the individual variables over the respective areas. So within the limitations of the data used, the common dimensions which emerge are the measures by which the urban social structure of the cities of South Wales may be gauged. Whether they are the same measures that have been produced by other British studies remains to be seen in a comparison with the results of those studies.

COMPARISONS

In making the comparison only the results of recent *British* factorial ecologies will be considered since, although the range could well be extended to North America, it was felt safer to remain on common cultural ground within the British Isles and to thus restrict the comparison. Similarly, only the results pertaining to the factorial ecology of cities as opposed to regions will be reviewed as it is the major dimensions of *urban* social structure which are being investigated. The results of this analysis are not really comparable with those of Gittus, who analysed thirty-one variables drawn from the 1961 census for sub-divisions of Merscyside,[25] since most of the variables included were housing variables with a lack of socio-economic indices. More comparable are the results of P. Norman's component analysis of thirty-eight variables from the 1961 census for enumeration districts in London,[26] where two major components were interpreted. The first of these was a socio-economic dimension, with the positive emphasis on low status, and the second a rooming-house component, both of which have equivalents in the present analysis, with the social status dimension and the dimension of residential quality. Similarly parallels can be seen with the components which emerged from Robson's analysis of thirty variables drawn from the 1961 census for Sunderland.[27] Here the two principal components, which accounted for nearly two-thirds of the total variation, were a social class component, isolating high-class areas, and a component of housing conditions, highlighting poor housing conditions. Thus the two major dimensions found in London and replicated in Sunderland have parallels in the results of this study, though not necessarily in the same order of importance.

One omission from these studies, however, is an axis representing council renting. Such a component is not, however, lacking from Herbert's analysis of twenty-six variables extracted from the 1961 census for Swansea and Cardiff,[28] since that is the most important component which emerges in both cases. The council renting component, embodied in the 'tenure' and 'stage in family life cycle' dimension, is not such a dominating influence in the present analysis, but even so the other components discerned in the analysis of 1961 data, namely a component representing poor housing conditions, a component representing social status, and a component associated with family status, do find their parallels in the present study. Similarities can also be seen in the results of J. A. Giggs's analysis of another town in South Wales, Barry.[29] If one looks just at the socio-economic and household components, the first to emerge is one of social status, the second is one of municipal rented housing and associated characteristics, and the third is one of 'low family cohesion', which includes many of the variables included in the present study's residential quality component. Thus, just from the results of the factorial analysis of census data for the towns of South Wales, using only the 1961 census data, similar dimensions can be seen to be emerging.

Extending the range of comparison to other British cities and the later 1966 sample census data, further similarities can be seen. When C. J. Thomas analysed twenty-four variables for the Greater Nottingham area using 1966 data,[30] the three major components which emerged were ones representing social class, family life cycle and tenure, and decline in residential status, which are very similar to the main dimensions of this study, even though a different set of variables was analysed for Nottingham. A recent factorial analysis of the 1966 census data for Hull by H. R. Wilkinson, R. N. Davidson and M. K. Francis[31] produced three principal components similar in structure to the three main dimensions distinguished in this study. The first was interpreted as an index of social class and overcrowding, the second of housing tenure and amenities and the third of 'rooming-house' or 'zone in transition' characteristics. These components have close parallels in the principal components already described. A forthcoming factorial ecology is a report of the analysis of the 1966 census data for the city of Birmingham carried out by the Centre for Urban and Regional Studies.[32] Here the first factor was one representing socio-economic status, the second was a dimension representing stages in the family life cycle, the third factor identified rooming-house or transience areas, and the fourth type of domain was that representing council ownership, all of which find their equivalents in the present study.

In all these studies, even though the respective factors may vary in importance and slightly different emphases of interpretation may be put on the factors owing to the theoretical predilections of individual workers, similar major dimensions of urban social structure can be seen to be emerging repeatedly from recent British factorial ecologies.

CONCLUSIONS

These dimensions representing socio-economic status, tenure and stage in the family life cycle and residential quality need perhaps to be confirmed by further comparative studies using 1971 census data. The stage has almost been reached, however, at which the major dimensions which will emerge from a factorial ecology of British census material can be predicted with some degree of confidence. Although the results from the analysis of the cities in this study have a narrow base in both time and area when compared with the results of recent British studies, similar dimensions are shown to be emerging recurrently. Given that these analyses have taken us as far as they can, what new directions are opened for research towards a set of generalizations attempting to explain British urban social structure?

One direction has been mentioned by Timms, namely, a decision-making approach to the study of the residential selection process.[33] This would help to explain the influences affecting people's choice of which particular area of the city to inhabit, and would provide some depth of evidence for the importance of the different dimensions of urban social structure already established by factorial ecologies. A second direction would be to undertake factorial ecologies at different periods of time in order to evaluate changes in urban social structure and its main dimensions. Such studies in Britain have so far been few, possibly because of the changing area base of British censuses but, with the introduction of grid-square information in 1971, more comparable time-span analyses should be possible. A third direction would be to use the social area framework established by factorial ecology as a sampling frame for the study of other aspects of urban behaviour. Such new directions of research, as they are consolidated, will lead towards a greater understanding of British urban social structure.

ACKNOWLEDGEMENTS

The author thanks Dr D. T. Herbert and Dr C. J. Thomas of the Department of Geography, University College of Swansea, and Mr J. R. Edwards of the Centre for Urban and Regional Studies, University of Birmingham, for making constructive criticisms at various stages in the preparation of this paper. Thanks are also due to the referees whose comments did much to improve the final draft of the paper and to Miss Jennifer Davies of the Department of Geography, University of Swansea, for typing the completed paper.

NOTES

1. E. GITTUS, 'The structure of urban areas—a new approach', *Tn Plann. Rev.* 35 (1964), 5–20
2. J. R. EDWARDS *et al.*, 'Social area analysis', forthcoming report of the Centre for Urban and Regional Studies

3. *Centre for Urban Studies, London*, 'A note on the principal component analysis of 1961 e.d. data for London administrative county', unpublished report, no date

4. D. T. HERBERT, 'Principal components analysis and urban social structure, a study of Cardiff and Swansea' in *Urban essays: studies in the geography of Wales* (ed. H. CARTER and W. K. D. DAVIES, 1970), 79–100

5. *General Register Office, Sample Census 1966 England and Wales, County Report Glamorgan* (1967)

6. B. T. ROBSON, *Urban analysis: a study of city structure* (1969), 39–45

7. D. W. G. TIMMS, *The urban mosaic—towards a theory of residential differentiation* (1971), 39–44

8. E. GITTUS, 'An experiment in the identification of urban sub-areas', *Trans. Bartlett Soc.* 2 (1963–64), 109–35

9. F. L. SWEETSER, 'Ecological factors in metropolitan zones and sectors' in *Quantitative ecological analysis in the social sciences* (ed. M. DOGAN and S. ROKKAN, 1969), 413–56

10. E. SHEVKY and W. BELL, *Social area analysis* (1955)

11. D. T. HERBERT, 'Social area analysis: a British study', *Urban Stud.* 4 (1967), 41–60

12. R. INDER, 'Social area analysis', *Swansea Geogr.* 9 (1971), 73–82

13. D. J. EVANS, 'Social area analysis: a case study', unpublished dissertation submitted to the Centre for Urban and Regional Studies, University of Birmingham, October 1970, for a Diploma in Urban and Regional Studies

14. B. J. RUMMEL, 'Understanding factor analysis', *J. Conflict Resolution* (1967), 444–97

15. All the component analyses were carried out on the University College of Swansea ICL 1905 Computer between January and July 1970 using a principal component analysis and varimax rotation programme, by Klovan (Calgary) out of Hill (Aberdeen) revised for Clark and Davies (Swansea) by Viner *et al.*

16. L. L. THURSTONE, *Multiple factor analysis* (1947), 35

17. W. K. D. DAVIES, 'Varimax and the destruction of generality: a methodological note', *Area* 3 (1971), 112–18; P. M. MATHER, W. K. D. DAVIES, 'Comment on "Varimax and Generality"', *Area* 3 (1971), 252–9; *Area* 4 (1972), 27–30

18. E. GITTUS, op. cit. (1963–64)

19. B. T. ROBSON, op. cit. (1969)

20. D. T. HERBERT, op. cit. (1970)

21. K. HOPE, *Methods of multivariate analysis* (1968)

22. W. K. D. DAVIES, 'Urbanisation and interaction; problems in the study of the Greater Swansea Area', unpublished paper presented at the IBG urban study group meeting at the University of Keele (1964)

23. E. SHEVKY and W. BELL, op. cit. (1955)

24. *General Register Office*, op. cit. (1967)

25. E. GITTUS, op. cit. (1963–64)

26. P. C. NORMAN, 'Third survey of London life and labour: a new typology of London districts' in *Quantitative ecological analysis in the social sciences* (ed. M. DOGAN and S. ROKKAN, 1966), 371–96

27. B. T. ROBSON, op. cit. (1969)

28. D. T. HERBERT, op. cit. (1970)

29. J. A. GIGGS, 'Socially disorganised areas in Barry: a multivariate analysis' in *Urban essays: studies in the geography of Wales* (ed. H. CARTER and W. K. D. DAVIES, 1970), 101–43

30. C. J. THOMAS, 'Geographical aspects of the growth of the residential area of Greater Nottingham in the twentieth century', unpubl. Ph.D. thesis, Univ. of Nottingham (1968)

31. H. R. WILKINSON, R. N. DAVIDSON and M. K. FRANCIS 'Kingston upon Hull and Haltemprice—social area analysis 1966: Part I—Atlas', Univ. of Hull, Department of Geography, Misc. Ser. No. 10

32. J. R. EDWARDS *et al.*, op. cit. (1971)

33. D. W. G. TIMMS, op. cit. (1971), Chapter 3

RÉSUMÉ. *Une étude comparative des structures sociaux urbaines.* Cet article donne une analyse de l'écologie factorielle de trois villes majeures au Pays de Galles du Sud, en appliquant les techniques de l'analyse factorielle à la même liste quarante grandeurs variables qui se trouvent parmi les données du recensement de 1966. Les composantes du rang social, de la tenure et de la phase du cycle de la vie domestique, et aussi de la qualité résidentielle sont différenciées pour chacune des trois villes. On compare ensuite ces résultats avec ceux des nouvelles études Britanniques. Par conséquent, il est maintenant possible de prédire les dimensions principaux qui sortiront d'une analyse factorielle des données du recensement Britannique pour des villes majeures: il faut déveloper une modèle théorique qui explique pourquoi et de quelle manière en espace ces dimensions sont distribuées.

ZUSAMMENFASSUNG. *Eine Vergleichungsuntersuchung der städtischen Sozialstrukturen in Südwales.* Man analysiert die faktorielle Ökologie der drei grösseren Städte in Südwales durch die Anwendung von Faktoranalyse auf dieselbe Liste von vierzig veränderlichen Grössen aus den 1966 Volkszählungangaben. Eine Sozialzustandskomponente, eine Dauer und Etappe Familienkreislaufkomponente und eine Wohnungsgutekomponente wurden in jeder Stadt differenzierten. Man vergleicht diese Ergebnisse mit den in neuen britischen Versuche erlangten Schlussfolgerungen. Nun hat man das Vermögen zu vorhersagen die grössere Faktoren der städtischen Sozialstruktur, die aus irgendeinen, faktoriellen Analyse der britischen Volkszählungangaben fur eine grössere Stadt emporkommen, und man brauchte nun neue Versuchslinien die zur Formulierung eines theoretischen Modell die erklärt warum, und zeigt im Raum wie, diese Grössen anordnet werden.

Residential mobility and preference: a study of Swansea

D. T. HERBERT

Lecturer in Geography, University College of Swansea

Revised MS received 11 May 1972

ABSTRACT. Mobility at the intra-urban level is essentially the process of residential selection in which decisions are made and ordered social geographical patterns emerge. Although studies using aggregate data have a continuing importance, recent research has emphasized the importance of analysis at the individual scale and the possibilities of adapting behavioural concepts. These micro-scale studies have successfully produced several conceptual frameworks but have not so far tested them in a convincing way. The objectives of the Swansea studies were essentially preliminary in nature and empirical rather than theoretical. Using Census data, it is demonstrated that some useful aggregate analyses can be made. Household survey data from several parts of the city are used to examine the nature of residential mobility in a British context, with particular emphasis on levels of mobility, motivations for moves and the basic spatial patterns which emerge. Information on residential preferences from the same surveys enables the spatial evaluations of both general residential districts and local authority estates within the city to be analysed.

RESIDENTIAL mobility has always been an integral part of urban-social geography but it is only in recent years that it has received a significant amount of attention at the intra-urban scale. At this scale, residential mobility is now recognized as a potentially crucial process in the formation of residential patterns and in understanding the overall socio-spatial structure of cities. The development of new analytical approaches has involved the use of data at several scales of investigation and has stimulated methodologies derived from the behavioural sciences. More traditional studies have operated at what might be termed the aggregate scale and have often been concerned with the gradual shift of residential areas over time.[1] Cumulatively, this type of residential shift can display distinctive spatial patterns which are explicable in terms of the general characteristics of urban growth. In some contrast to this type of study, recent emphasis has been placed upon the individual household as a decision-making unit and upon the necessity for analysis at this micro-scale.[2] The methodologies and concepts involved at this individual level and the associated behavioural approaches have drawn geographers into contact with literature, such as that of social psychology, with which they have had little previous acquaintance. The full effects of this have yet to be seen, but it is already clear that not the least of the problems facing social geographers is that of integrating their findings at the micro-scale with those at the more traditional or aggregate scale. Residential mobility has become a rapidly expanding and clearly open-ended field of study, but it is probably fair to say that, to date, behaviouralist approaches have been much more successful in forming conceptual frameworks and hypotheses than they have been in putting them into operation or testing them. Research objectives, which are now being stated in the context of devised conceptual frameworks, will doubtless provide substantial new insights when they are fulfilled, but at the present time real knowledge of mobility within the city is derived from relatively few empirical studies.

The objectives of this particular study are in a sense preliminary and empirical rather than theoretical: within each sub-section, opportunities for further research suggest themselves. One objective is to offer a British case-study in a field in which most published results refer to North American examples; another is to explore the qualities of analysis at both aggregate and individual scales. At the aggregate scale, Census data are used to measure the patterns of statistical association between measures of mobility and selected variables; in the main part of the paper, based upon a survey of individual households, the basic nature of mobility and patterns of residential preference are investigated. The city of Swansea (population 172 566 in 1971) and its adjacent districts have inspired some substantive social studies which provide a sound contextual framework for the present analysis.[3]

ECOLOGICAL PATTERNS: THE AGGREGATE SCALE

Despite the recent proliferation of behavioural approaches, macro-scale analyses still have a valid contribution to make in the study of intra-urban mobility. E. G. Moore, who has provided some of the clearest statements on this contribution, described the possible roles of aggregate data in terms of short-term predictions and in identifying indicators which might be investigated by more intensive study.[4] An analysis of Brisbane, using H. M. Blalock's causal model, identified a basic measure of turnover, defined as 'percentage of population leaving specific dwellings within a given area in a single year who are replaced by other migrants', and examined its statistical relationships with a set of variables which comprised age-differential, single females, private house index, owner-occupied dwellings, Australian-born, and accessibility. Although Moore recognized several deficiencies in his model, he did suggest that it offered a plausible statement regarding existing ecological relationships in South Brisbane.

The 1966 Sample Census for England and Wales contained information at the level of the enumeration district on the turnover of population for the preceding 5-year period. A mover was defined as an individual 'whose usual address at census was different from that on 24 April 1961'.[5] Movers were also classified according to whether their change of residence occurred within the same local authority area or was from another area. It was thus possible to distinguish between intra- and inter-urban movers, though the latter may include changes of residence between contiguous municipalities which are effectively part of the same city. As the Census also recorded many socio-economic, housing and demographic variables for each enumeration district, it is possible to test for the statistical correlates of the two types of mobility. A full analysis of these data is beyond the scope of the present paper, but some results are described which demonstrate the apparent patterns and which provide an ecological setting to the analysis based upon individual households.

A definition of Swansea was taken which could be described as the formal city, comprising the county borough and its effective suburban extensions in Gower R.D. and Llwchwr U.D. Eighty-six enumeration districts made up the study area and, for each of these, nineteen variables were calculated. Results available from general factorial studies in South Wales—which had included the two measures of turnover in inputs of over forty variables—enabled variables which identified the likely correlates to be chosen.[6] Choice of variables was also influenced by previous literature, particularly the work of P. H. Rossi[7] and Moore,[8] and Table I shows the full list arranged in the two sub-sets within which associations were hypothesized.

TABLE I
Variables

1 *Inter-urban movers 1961–66*	11 *Intra-urban movers 1961–66*
2 Owner occupiers	12 Local Authority tenants
3 Social classes I and II	13 Social classes IV and V
4 Socio-economic groups 5 and 6	14 Sex ratio
5 Women at work	15 Fertility ratio
6 Single-person households	16 Persons per room
7 Single adults	17 Households with six or more persons
8 Working outside Local Authority of residence	18 Privately rented unfurnished tenancies
9 Use of all amenities	19 Without cars
10 Aged over 65 years	20. F. Born. Pevians

All variables are expressed as percentages except 14, 15 and 16: all variables were tested for normality and transformations were employed where appropriate.

TABLE II
Patterns of significant ecological correlation

(*a*) *Variables correlated with inter-urban mobility :*
  significant at the 0·1 per cent level

Social classes I and II	+0·62
Owner occupiers	+0·60
Socio-economic groups 5 and 6	+0·41
Without cars	−0·63
Social classes IV and V	−0·57
Local authority tenants	−0·47
Six-person households	−0·39

(*b*) *Variables correlated with intra-urban mobility :*
  significant at the 5·0 per cent level

Without cars	+0·23
Fertility ratio	+0·22
Sex ratio	+0·22
Local authority tenants	+0·21
Owner-occupiers	−0·25
Social classes I and II	−0·25

The correlation matrix on the transformed variables provided the first evidence of ecological associations among the pairs of input variables.

As Table II shows, whereas inter-urban mobility was strongly associated with a distinctive set of variables, the correlation of variables with intra-urban mobility was only marginally significant at the 5 per cent level. Inter-urban mobility is effectively a measure of migration—fundamentally different in character from the process of residential selection within a city—but some of its connotations are relevant to residential change in Swansea and its main characteristics can be briefly noted. The strong positive associations with measures of high social class and owner-occupance in large part reflect the career mobility of professional and business groups, while negative correlations with local authority tenancy demonstrate both the constraints upon migration which such tenancy imposes—because of its relative non-transferability—and also the comparative stability of lower-income groups given adequate opportunities for employment in the locality. These findings accord with the considerable literature on inter-regional migration.[9]

TABLE III
Loadings on Principal Component I (30·4%)

Owner-occupiers	+0·83
Social classes I and II	+0·80
Inter-urban mobility	+0·74
Socio-economic groups 5 and 6	+0·67
Social Classes IV and V	−0·81
Local Authority tenants	−0·80
Persons per room	−0·68
Without cars	−0·68

   Although the correlates of intra-urban mobility shown in Table II are statistically weak, they do show a measure of association with low social class, with fertility, and with local authority housing tenure. A possible explanation of this pattern is that the two main ingredients of local mobility are stage in life cycle—for which fertility is a key indicator—and local authority housing tenure which, by its terms of reference, involves movement within a city as long as vacancies occur. Low social class is not necessarily a key variable in itself but is most likely to be an associated characteristic of local authority tenancy.

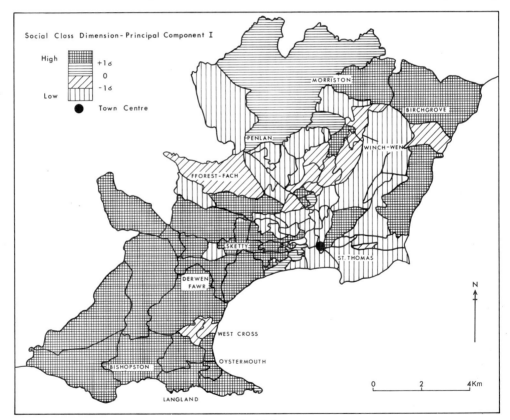

FIGURE 1. Social class areas

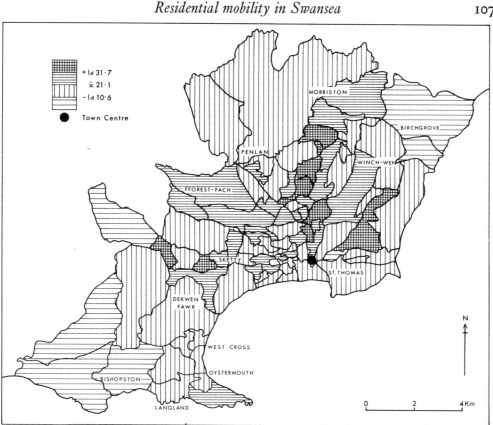

FIGURE 2. Rates of intra-urban mobility, 1961–66

These statistical correlates of intra-urban mobility were confirmed by the general factorial studies of Cardiff and Newport in which the variables were included[10] and a further tentative conclusion was that an immobile section of the population associated with old age, single-person households and lack of car ownership, could be recognized. These results from the correlation matrix helped to justify the initial choice of variables in that the main positive correlations in each case were with key variables in the respective sub-sets.

The Swansea variables were analysed by Principal Components Analysis and Varimax Rotation and although the results are not discussed here—they add little to the patterns identified in the correlation matrix—Principal Component One (Table III) provided a clear social class dimension and scores were mapped to provide a basic ecological framework.

Figure 1 shows the basic contrast within Swansea between the high-status west and the lower-status centre and east of the city. Low-status enclaves in the west correspond with local authority estates and with old village nuclei such as Oystermouth, while higher-status districts in the north-east reflect more recent suburban growth. While rates of inter-urban movement showed a close correspondence with these social class differences, rates of intra-urban movement (Fig. 2) were less easily comprehended.

Areas of contemporary housing construction showed high rates of intra-urban mobility and offered one obvious explanation but otherwise the pattern was variable. Rates of intra-urban mobility were high in districts which contained many local authority houses, such as Sketty Park, Blaenymaes and a part of Penlan, but were also high in some high-status areas, such as Derwen Fawr, part of the Uplands and Mumbles. Low rates occurred throughout most of the older terraced housing areas in districts such as St Thomas and in the north-east where older industrial villages incorporated in the modern borough attracted few local movers. Although rates of mobility were low in the western high-status areas, such as Bishopston, these districts are outside the city boundary and their recorded high levels of inter-urban movement undoubtedly reflect a significant inflow from the city of Swansea.

Evidence from Census data revealed rates of turnover which were appreciably lower than those recorded for North American cities. Large parts of Swansea showed a comparative stability which probably reflects both the limited range of vacancies in some sectors of the housing market and an inclination to adapt existing homes rather than change residence at various stages of the life cycle. Nevertheless, reference to individual variables showed that about 80 per cent of the enumeration districts with high rates of intra-urban movement had above-average fertility ratios, suggesting a link with increasing family-size and stage in life cycle. Other characteristics of those districts with high rates of movement indicated two main types, local authority estates on the one hand and higher-status districts of owner-occupance on the other. The nature of movement in these type-areas and the contrasts between them were among the topics investigated by direct survey methods.

The patterns of intra-urban movement in Swansea were partly explicable in terms of local knowledge and by reference to the basic ecological structure but an explanation based solely on aggregate data was insufficient, and some spatial patterns did not accord with the statistical associations. Spatially, for example, high rates occur in some high-status areas, though the statistical correlation with high social class was negative. This type of discrepancy and the comparatively weak statistical correlations suggested that further analysis at the aggregate scale was not justified. Despite the deficiencies of the data, analysis at the aggregate scale could usefully be taken further with a comparative set of cities or with a city larger than Swansea but for present purposes it has been sufficient to review movement and the ecological background against which analysis at the individual scale can be discussed.

HOUSEHOLD SURVEY DATA

Residential mobility

Most recent research on residential mobility has been primarily concerned with specifying behavioural concepts and there have been comparatively few empirical studies published. Much of the American literature, for example, refers to the seminal work by Rossi[11] and recognition of the importance of stages in the life cycle as reasons for moves is related to his work. G. Sabagh and others have defined the several life-cycle stages and have suggested that mobility is particularly high, for example, in child-bearing and child-launching stages, but is low during the child-rearing stage.[12] Life-cycle stages are not, of course, the only reasons for change of residence and Rossi provided an overall measure with his 'mobility potential' and 'combined complaints' indices.[13] The former was based on three variables—age, household size and renters' preference for renting or owning—while the latter contained six variables—dwelling unit space, dwelling facilities, accessibility,

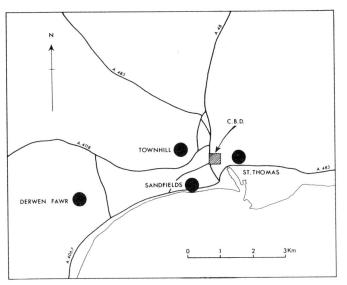

FIGURE 3. Location of survey areas

physical environment, social environment and costs. Rossi showed that almost half the voluntary movers in his sample survey had moved because of complaints relating to dwelling-unit space (thus confirming life-cycle stage as a factor) while a further 25 per cent had some complaint relating to cost or neighbourhood.

Recent geographical studies in this field have been less concerned with disputing the basic facts identified by Rossi than with emphasizing the importance of the behavioural context and the individual scale. J. Wolpert provided an initial stimulus with his critique of macro-models and his exposition of basic behavioural concepts such as place utility and the mover-stayer dichotomy.[14] Others have elaborated these concepts; L. A. Brown and Moore have suggested the need for more data and emphasized the decision-making characteristics of the individual household.[15] Furthermore, it should be possible to compare the characteristics of movers and non-movers rather than concentrate upon mobility alone. While these were not explicit objectives in Swansea, the survey was conceived on similar lines.

Figure 1 and other available maps of the urban structure of Swansea provided a sampling framework and five contrasted sub-areas were chosen for social survey investigation. Within each of the sub-areas, a sampling technique based upon random numbers was used.[16] The sample populations were chosen without previous knowledge of movers and non-movers and one objective was to study the levels of residential mobility in the different sub-areas. The five sub-areas selected were all established parts of the urban structure— the most recent was the part of Derwen Fawr which was completed in the early 1950s— and included two local authority estates (Townhill and St Thomas), two terraced housing districts (Sandfields and St Thomas) and the high-status private area of Derwen Fawr in west Swansea. Figure 3 shows the locations of the survey areas and Table III allows the compositions of the sample populations to be compared.

The figures in Table IV indicate the basic contrast between Derwen Fawr and the other areas, notably in terms of social class. Derwen Fawr also contained higher proportions

D.T.HERBERT

TABLE IV
*Sample populations**

Age groups	Derwen Fawr	Sandfields	St Thomas	Townhill	St Thomas L.A.
15–24	0	0	3	7	3
25–34	23	14	19	8	7
35–44	31	17	20	22	10
45–54	24	16	17	18	29
55–64	11	24	16	17	10
65 and over	11	29	25	28	41

Household size:					
1 person	3	8	14	8	15
2 persons	24	37	28	34	31
3–4 ,,	48	36	38	34	31
5–6 ,,	25	17	17	18	21
>7 ,,	0	2	3	6	2

Social class:					
I	33	0	0	0	0
II	35	3	0	3	0
III	32	55	64	61	48
IV	0	20	21	21	27
V	0	22	15	15	25

* All figures are percentages

in the younger age groups and had fewer small households than the other districts. These features were probably related to the higher levels of turnover in Derwen Fawr which are discussed below. Younger families continue to move into Derwen Fawr—giving representatives at several life-cycle stages—while the other areas with low inward mobility tend to be dominated by households in later stages of the life cycle. Some of the contrasts among the sample populations could be confirmed by reference to data for the enumeration districts in which they were located.

Residential mobility among the sample populations was first investigated by questions related to length of residence, to previous addresses, and to reasons for moving. The four lower-status areas showed several common features in terms of residential mobility, which all reflected the stability and local origins of their population. A preponderance of older people in both local authority housing areas indicated that a more recent estate might have been usefully included in the survey, but it is suggested that whereas this would have revealed differences in length of residence, degree of local origins would not have been different. Between 45 and 62 per cent of the sample populations in the four lower-status areas had lived at their present addresses for over 20 years; only 13 to 26 per cent had moved within the past 5 years. Very high proportions had lived in Swansea for over 20 years and the data on previous addresses showed a predominance of short-distance moves. For the three areas which included older housing, over 60 per cent of the sample populations had previous addresses in the same district; over 80 per cent in all four areas had previous addresses in Swansea. Derwen Fawr showed marked contrasts with the other four areas in each of these aspects of mobility. Over 60 per cent had moved within the past 5 years, only one-third had lived in Swansea for more than 20 years and a similar number had previous addresses in the city. There were clear indications of two elements within the Derwen Fawr sample population which could be termed local and non-local.[17] One element was composed of people who were born in Swansea, or at least in South Wales,

TABLE V

Enumeration District data

	Social Classes I & II	IV & V	Percent over 65	1 or 2 person households
261015 (Derwen Fawr)	50	5	7	5·6
261009 (Townhill)	6	45	10	5·0
260805 (Sandfields)	4	41	16	23·5
260920 (St Thomas)	7	43	8	14·9

TABLE VI

Mobility characteristics

Length of residence at present address	Derwen Fawr	Sandfields	St Thomas	Townhill	St Thomas L.A.
12 months	10	4	6	2	4
1–3 years	37	9	8	7	7
4–5 years	14	5	12	4	7
6–10 years	30	8	15	15	11
11–20 years	6	19	14	22	9
Over 20 years	3	55	45	50	62
Length of residence in Swansea					
12 months	6	0	1	0	0
1–3 years	16	1	0	0	0
4–5 years	14	1	2	2	0
6–10 years	17	4	0	4	0
11–20 years	11	7	2	7	0
Over 20 years	36	86	95	87	100
Previous address					
Same district	5	64	60	15	62
Other in Swansea	30	20	31	75	22
Other in S. Wales	26	10	6	7	9
S.E. England	17	2	2	0	0
Other in England	15	2	0	0	4
Elsewhere	7	2	1	3	3
Reasons for moving					
Marriage	7	33	26	N/A	14
To own a house	1	30	24		14
House-size	22	5	20		28
Neighbourhood	10	5	3		7
Employment	50	10	9		19
Family	2	10	5		1
Health/retirement	8	2	4		1
Environment	0	5	9		16

and had local previous addresses; the other comprised a professional/businessmen group, with no local connections, who were mobile at an inter-city scale and were probably short-term residents in Swansea. Movements of the latter occur between neighbourhoods of similar or improving status in different cities in accordance with the requirements of their career. This was confirmed by information on reasons for moving; half of the Derwen Fawr respondents quoted employment as the reason for their most recent change of residence.

In a closer analysis of reasons for moving, however, that section of the Derwen Fawr population with previous addresses in Swansea was studied separately and employment as a motivation ceased to be relevant. Over half the reasons quoted among local movers in Derwen Fawr were related to stage in life cycle—with 40 per cent specifically stating dwelling-size—while about one-third quoted reasons related to the desire for better neighbourhood and environment. For the other survey areas, local movers were not analysed separately as in-migration from other parts of the country was insignificant. In each of these areas, life-cycle reasons accounted for about two-thirds of all movers; employment as a reason did occur—particularly in St Thomas L.A.—and was a stated reason for local moves as well as a reflection of the small amount of in-migration from outside Swansea. Reasons for moving were not recorded for the main local authority estate in the sample at Townhill, but here the normal set of reasons is not directly applicable. Individuals may seek local authority accommodation for reasons in part related to life-cycle stages—this is confirmed in information from St Thomas L.A.—but an actual move is determined by the availability of a vacant tenancy. A feature of the sample population in the St Thomas terraced housing district was that the present residence was the first home for at least half of all respondents, many of whom had long tenure. Constraints upon movement are clearly many for lower-income groups, imposed both by finance and by the limited availability of suitable housing alternatives.

Two contrasted sub-areas, Derwen Fawr and St Thomas, were selected for closer comparisons in terms of the spatial directions of local moves and levels of satisfaction with the neighbourhood. Figure 4 shows the origins and destinations of those respondents in Derwen Fawr and St Thomas who had previous addresses within the city. The St Thomas population was characterized by short-distance moves—including many within the district itself—and the great majority of moves from outside St Thomas originated in similar low-income areas near the city centre. For Derwen Fawr, distances involved in intra-city moves were appreciably greater and most moves showed a south-westerly shift towards the higher-status parts of Swansea. Levels of satisfaction with present residence were relatively high in both Derwen Fawr and St Thomas; just under half of the population in the former and one-third in the latter area could identify no particular disadvantage of neighbourhood. The main disadvantages quoted in Derwen Fawr were lack of shopping facilities and of bus services and the high costs; in St Thomas, qualities of the environment such as poor housing, noise, lack of cleanliness and modernity were frequently quoted. Advantages stated for Derwen Fawr were its neighbourhood and environmental qualities, such as quietness and proximity to beaches; while in St Thomas, nearness to the city centre and its facilities was the main advantage. A local issue in Derwen Fawr was residential qualification for the high-prestige neighbourhood schools.

That part of the survey concerned with reasons for residential mobility has thus produced several empirical findings which both illuminate the British case and provide some bases for comparison with North American literature. As the samples were selected

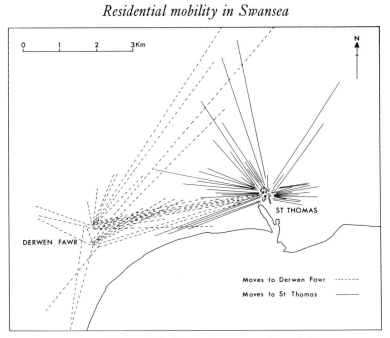

FIGURE 4. Moves within Swansea for two sample populations

from the total populations of each case-study area and were not confined to local movers, they contained a broad cross-section of individuals in what Wolpert has termed the mover-stayer dichotomy.[18] It became clear that in the low-income areas, including local authority housing estates, the relatively immobile section of the population was much larger than might be expected from North American experience. Although this survey did not examine in depth aspirations to moving, it is evident that people are much more 'stayers' than 'movers' and that large sections of British cities probably possess stable and essentially local populations. Even within Derwen Fawr where a sub-group of 'mobile professionals' existed, there was still a strong locally-based element with comparatively high stability. Questions on reasons for moving provided results which were wholly in accord with established generalizations. Most of Rossi's factors were valid though the importance he attached to renters' preference for owning was less obvious.[19] Local authority housing areas contained most of the renters and, for the lower-income groups, it appeared to be such tenancies which formed the desirable goal rather than owner-occuparship in the private sector. Specific factors which Rossi identified in his combined complaints index were again mostly confirmed. Dwelling-unit space, physical and social environments were all stated reasons for moving or for satisfaction with present residence. Accessibility was an advantage expressed in St Thomas and, to a lesser extent, a disadvantage of Derwen Fawr; dwelling-unit facilities and costs were not explicitly stated but appear to be an integral part of the process of residential selection. An interpretetion of this part of the survey data confirms the main factors suggested in previous literature, with the main divergences related to local authority tenure and the overall lower rates of mobility.

Residential preferences

The measurement of spatial preferences has proved one way in which geographers have been able to test and use concepts relating to perception and other behavioural approaches.[20] Preference on where to live is obviously relevant to an analysis of residential mobility and questions were included in the household surveys within Swansea. Most published studies of spatial preference have been conducted under laboratory conditions, often using student classes as respondents, and many more practical problems emerge with study in the field. The aim was to obtain a ranking of both general residential areas and of local authority estates within the city and it became clear that a fair amount of amalgamation was necessary in order to reduce the potentially large number of alternative areas to a reasonable number. A list of twelve general residential districts and of ten local authority estates was compiled and respondents were asked to rank the alternatives on each list according to residential preference. Each interviewer was provided with two highly simplified outline maps which showed the general location of the various areas and listed some of the main sub-districts of which they were composed. For each list of alternatives, respondents were requested to state reasons for their leading choices of area. A persistent problem in studies of spatial preference is the inability of many respondents to rank more than a few alternatives; this was of course the reason for amalgamating to a relatively few areas. Where this problem arose, interviewers were instructed to obtain positive leading choices and positive non-choices and to allocate any remaining unclassified areas to a mid-point in the rank. Spatial preference patterns within Swansea are not complex and basically reveal a west/east differential, together with some local affiliation dependent on the place of survey and a minority preference for a location in the town. Multivariate techniques of analysis were initially used on the preference data but more straightforward statistical analyses, which demonstrate the basic patterns equally well, are preferred in the present discussion.

Figure 5a was obtained by calculating the proportion of total respondents, over all the survey areas, which placed each district within the first three choices. The overall pattern presented by this map shows the strong advantage which is possessed by districts west of the city centre in terms of residential preference. Historically this pattern has developed from the growth of the city, particularly of course in the past two centuries.[21] Industrial development in Swansea, some of it dating from the early eighteenth century, has always been concentrated in the eastern part of the city and in the lower parts of the Swansea valley. The docks, located close to the city centre, have their main transport links with the industrial valleys of the South Wales coalfield to the north and east. Over a long period of time, a succession of industries, which includes non-ferrous metals, tin-plate and iron-working, has been associated with the eastern part of the city and has left its mark upon the cultural landscape. By contrast, the western parts of Swansea, several of which were not incorporated in the Borough until 1918, have been almost entirely free of industry and contain large expanses of beach and coastland which gradually merge into the rural landscapes of the Gower peninsula. Figure 5a, therefore, reflects the physical advantages of western districts through the expressed preferences of individuals. West Cross, Langland and Mumbles all possess high preference scores in contrast to the generally low scores of northern and eastern districts. A further characteristic shown in Figure 5a is the preference for town or central city areas over northern or eastern suburbs. Each of the preference surveys was influenced by the locality of interviewing, in that a fairly strong expression of allegiance to present residence was expressed. Figure 5b shows the preferences disaggregated to individual districts and, whereas the same general pattern is evident, the Townhill

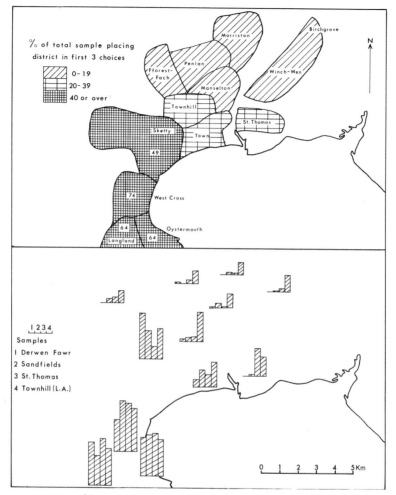

FIGURE 5 (a) *upper*, (b) *lower*. Residential district preferences in Swansea.

and St Thomas scores are noticeably higher for their respective sample populations. The response on preference for local authority housing estates is of particular interest in that it clearly mirrors the more general pattern. Figure 6a reveals a strong preference for the two estates in the western part of the city at Sketty Park and West Cross. The great bulk of local authority housing has taken place in the northern parts of the city, using large tracts of elevated land within the borough, but these western developments have been a deliberate attempt to provide low-price housing in formerly exclusive high-status areas.[22] There is a marked minority preference for local authority accommodation in central locations, much of which comprises multi-storey flats, and estates in eastern and northern locations are typified by low scores. The effects of survey localities are shown clearly in Figure 6b in which the high overall score for the Townhill estate is largely accounted for by the preferences of the sample population drawn from its own residents. To the extent that residential preferences indicate future residential mobility, there is a clear potential

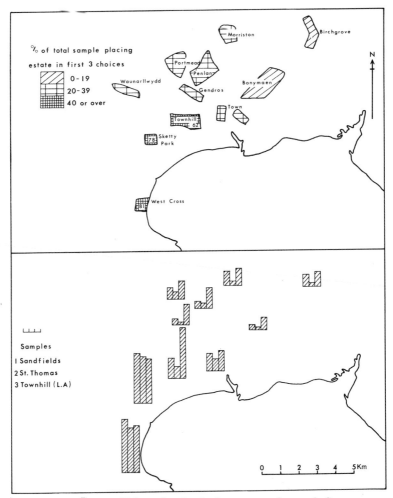

FIGURE 6 (a) *upper*, (b) *lower*. Local authority estates preferences in Swansea

for westerly drift with a minority preference for central locations in improved environments. That this pattern exists contemporarily is evidenced by recorded intra-city moves in the private sector and also by information which exists on applications for transfers in the public sector of housing.[23] Acting against this drift in both sectors are availability of land for new housing and increasing costs.

Measures of spatial preference based upon the ranking of residential districts form one of the most basic behavioural approaches,[24] but results in Swansea identified clear patterns which were in line with the findings of other local sources of information. The generalizations from this part of the analysis were that well-ordered patterns of residential preference did exist which in large part reflected objective variations in social status in the city. It was further evident that this ordered pattern extended to the local authority housing sector and although rents depended upon dwelling-size and modernity

TABLE VII

(a) Assessments of present residential area

	Derwen Fawr			St Thomas		
	1	2	3	1	2	3
Quietness	30	66	4	9	48	43
Space	56	41	3	22	38	40
Facilities	42	40	18	51	35	14
Expense	68	32	0	11	49	40
Status	45	55	0	2	74	24
Modernity	24	68	8	4	43	53
Localness	8	85	7	62	34	4
Friendliness	34	56	10	55	40	5
Accessibility	27	62	11	68	29	3
Cleanliness	47	48	5	10	54	36

(b) Assessment of Derwen Fawr by present 'local' residents

	1	2	3
Quietness	39	61	0
Space	61	36	3
Facilities	50	42	8
Expense	81	19	0
Status	47	53	0
Modernity	31	64	5
Localness	8	80	12
Friendliness	31	66	3
Accessibility	36	55	9
Cleanliness	50	47	3

Note: Each respondent was asked to rate his residential district on a three-point scale for several nominated qualities. On this scale, 1 was a positive rating (very quiet, plenty of space, a lot of facilities, very expensive, etc.) while 3 indicated an opposite rating and 2 an average position. Individual responses were aggregated and expressed as percentages on the three-point scale for each quality.

rather than upon location, estates tended to reflect the desirability rating of the general district in which they were located.

The most general reasons given for choice of general residential district were related to qualities of the environment, such as quietness and attractiveness, and to accessibility, particularly to city centre and to beaches. This overall pattern of reasons for choice varied little over the individual sample populations but the St Thomas and Sandfields populations quoted family and friendship ties in their home area as the reason for preferring their present district of residence. Reasons for local authority estate preferences were similarly weighted towards environmental qualities and access, with the additional element of better housing and other facilities. In order to examine the bases of residential choice in more detail, an attempt was made to record ways in which people perceived their present district.

Table VII (a) records the ways in which respondents in two of the survey areas perceived their district of present residence. Analysis was made in terms of the overall sample populations rather than in terms of individuals but an indication of significant patterns did emerge. Although it was evident that many individuals had adopted average positions, there was nevertheless a consistent neighbourhood consensus with reference to virtually all the qualities. Only in the case of responses on amount of space in St Thomas did a minority view of over 20 per cent appear (i.e. where scores of 1 are compared with 2 and 3 or of 3 with 1 and 2). This finding would seem to offer some support for the view that location is one of the factors which affects an individual's perception and that images are to a large extent shared by people in close geographical propinquity.[25]

Responses for the Derwen Fawr population showed that, although it was only in two cases—space and expense—that more than half placed the district in an above-average position, proportions rating it below average were consistently low with the exception of the availability of facilities. Table VII (b) records the responses for that part of the Derwen Fawr sample which had previous addresses in Swansea, i.e. the 'locals'. In all but two qualities—localness and friendliness—the local people rate Derwen Fawr higher than the non-locals. It can be hypothesized that, whereas the locals are judging by local standards and an awareness of comparisons within Swansea, the non-locals have a national frame of reference. Scores for the St Thomas population showed that over half the respondents rated the districts as above average on four of the nominated qualities. At first sight this was surprising as by an 'objective' judgement St Thomas is an unattractive and under-privileged district. It does, however, point to some of the difficulties of comparison—similar to that between locals and non-locals in Derwen Fawr—as contrasted sub-groups may well apply different criteria in rating the qualities of a residential district. Two of the qualities rated highly by the St Thomas population, facilities and accessibility, relate to the district's proximity to the city centre rather than to internal advantages; while friendliness and localness are qualities of working-class districts which are clearly recognized by the St Thomas population. Very few residents placed St Thomas above average in terms of quietness, cost, status, modernity and cleanliness.

From this analysis it is evident that Derwen Fawr, although a modern, well-provided and prestigious district by any objective measure is not rated particularly highly by its residents. Part of this may be explained by the fact that non-locals are judging qualities by national standards; part by local issues, such as the poor bus service and the proximity of a local authority refuse dump. The St Thomas population, with much more to com-plain about, recognize the deficiencies of their district, although in only one quality, modernity, was it assessed as below average by a majority of the sample.

Respondents in both Derwen Fawr and St Thomas were also asked to rate alternative residential districts of their first choice for the same qualities on a three-point scale. Detailed comparative analysis was difficult because the pairs of districts involved were not consistent but, in general, the Derwen Fawr respondents saw their alternative choices as more expensive and higher-status areas with more space and cleanliness; while St Thomas respondents saw their alternative choices as districts which possessed advantages of modernity, status and general environmental conditions but which involved some loss in terms of localness, friendliness and accessibility.

CONCLUSIONS

This study has explored several aspects of residential mobility in Swansea. Using aggregate data from the Census it has proved possible to identify statistical correlates of movement within the area though the patterns of association were not highly significant. Census definitions and territorial bases of the data are clearly far from ideal for the development of macro-scale models but the possibilities appear worthy of further investigation. Some of the statistical indicators in Swansea, such as the existence of a life-cycle factor and the association with local authority tenancy, could be confirmed by analysis of the household survey data. Further, the highly significant association of inter-urban movement with high social class was verified by the important non-local element in Derwen Fawr. As suggested earlier, aggregate scale analysis in Swansea was not sufficient in itself adequately to explain patterns of intra-urban mobility, but it provided useful indicators and an overall framework for study at the micro-scale.

Household survey data revealed that in broad terms the explanations for intra-urban movement advanced by previous literature are tenable. The contrast between the high-status district of Derwen Fawr and the other survey areas was great and, though basic factors of demographic structure and age of housing development could not be kept completely constant, differences in social class appear to be highly significant. High levels of stability and locality of origins which typified the four lower-status areas can be explained in such terms as the inadequacy of some sectors of the housing market and cost constraints, but would also suggest that the increasing mobility of urban populations reported in North American literature is not typical of sizeable sections of British society. As with so many other aspects of British urban structure, the impact of the public sector in housing is a major factor. Public sector housing activity accounts for the residential mobility of many low-income households, and for many others it offers the only real prospect of a change of residence. If life-cycle factors operate, it is over a protracted time scale, and the timing and direction of movement is strongly conditioned by the availability of local authority tenancy. Further, because of the possibility of choice and transferability within the public sector, a sub-market operates in which cost as a factor is minimized.[26] Even within the private sector, rates of intra-urban movement are comparatively low and relevant factors here include a preference for adapting dwellings, constraints of cost and available alternatives, and the contrasts between local and non-local elements in the population.[27]

Results from the studies of spatial preferences could be easily interpreted in Swansea in the context of many well-known features of the city's socio-spatial structure. The analytical techniques employed in this part of the survey were basic, and experimenting with more sophisticated methods, particularly in evaluating the qualities of districts, should prove rewarding.[28] As suggested at the beginning of this paper, several sections of this investigation contain possibilities for more detailed analyses; the present study offers an empirical basis from which they can proceed.

NOTES

1. H. HOYT, *The structure and growth of residential neighbourhoods in American cities* (1939); R. J. JOHNSTON 'The location of high-status residential areas', *Geogr. Annlr* B 48 (1969), 23–35

2. L. A. BROWN and E. G. MOORE, 'The intra-urban migration process: a perspective', *Geogr. Annlr* B 52 (1970); J. W. SIMMONS, 'Changing residence in the city: a review of intra-urban mobility', *Geogr. Rev.* 58 (1968), 622–51

3. T. BRENNAN, E. COONEY and H. POLLINS, *Social change in south-west Wales* (1954); C. ROSSER and C. C. HARRIS, *The family and social change* (1965); C. BELL, *Middle class families* (1968)

4. E. G. MOORE, 'The structure of intra-urban movement rates: an ecological model', *Urban Stud.* 6 (1969), 17–33

5. *1966 Sample Census for England and Wales* (1965), Migration Summary Tables

6. D. J. EVANS, Department of Geography, University College of Swansea, kindly provided this information.

I

7. P. H. ROSSI, *Why families move: a study in the social psychology of urban residential mobility* (1955)

8. E. G. MOORE, op. cit.

9. C. JANSEN, *Social aspects of internal migration* (1968); R. WELCH, *Migration research and migration in Britain: a selected bibliography* (1970)

10. Unpublished results from R. A. INDER and D. J. EVANS, Department of Geography, University College of Swansea

11. P. H. ROSSI, op. cit.

12. G. SABAGH, M. D. VAN ARSDOL and E. W. BUTLER, 'Some determinants of intrametropolitan residential mobility: conceptual considerations', *Social Forces* 48 (1969), 88–98

13. P. H. ROSSI, op. cit.

14. J. WOLPERT, 'Behavioural aspects of the decision to migrate', *Pap. Proc. reg. Sci. Ass.* 15 (1966), 159–69

15. L. A. BROWN and E. G. MOORE, op. cit.

16. The household surveys were carried out in four selected districts which were characterized by uniform internal morphology but provided some contrast in terms of types of residential area. Each district was selected with the E.D. framework in mind, though the St Thomas district contained both terraced rows and a local authority estate. Within each district, households were selected using a system based on random numbers and interviews were carried out by students, working in pairs, the great majority of whom had some previous survey experience. The refusal rates were highest in St Thomas (average 28%) and lowest (8%) in the Townhill local authority estate. Interviewers were given a period of one week to complete the survey and were instructed to call or recall at different times of the day. A large sample-size was chosen in order to reduce the possible bias of non-response and the final count showed that numerically-large samples had been obtained:

	Derwen Fawr	*Sandfields*	*Townhill*	*St Thomas*
Number of interviews obtained	88	83	180	109
Sample as percent of total households	31	28	34	24

17. C. BELL, op. cit., also made this distinction.

18. J. WOLPERT, op. cit.

19. P. H. ROSSI, op. cit.

20. P. R. GOULD and R. R. WHITE, 'The mental maps of British school-leavers', *Reg. Stud.* 2 (1968), 161–82; P. R. GOULD, 'The structure of space preferences in Tanzania', *Area* (1969), 29–35

21. W. G. V. BALCHIN (ed.), *Swansea and its region* (1971)

22. D. T. HERBERT, 'The twentieth century' in *Swansea and its region* (ed. W. G. V. BALCHIN) (1971)

23. From information held by the City of Swansea Housing Department

24. G. RUSHTON, 'Behavioural correlates of urban spatial structure', *Econ. Geogr.* 47 (1971), 49–58

25. F. E. HORTON and D. R. REYNOLDS, 'Effects of urban spatial structure on individual behaviour', *Econ. Geogr.* 47 (1971), 36–48

26. D. T. HERBERT, 'Public sector housing, residential mobility and preference', Unpublished discussion paper, Dept. of Geography, Swansea (1972)

27. C. BELL, op. cit.

28. R. M. DOWNS, 'Geographic space perception: past approaches and future prospect', *Progr. Geogr.* 2 (1970), 65–108

RÉSUMÉ. *La mobilité et la préférence résidentielles: une étude à Swansea.* La mobilité dans une zone urbaine peut être définie essentiellement comme le choix d'une résidence qui aboutit à la prise des décisions et l'émergence des dessins sociaux-géographiques réguliers. Bien que les études faisant usage des données collectives retiennent leur importance, la nouvelle recherche à souligne la valeur de l'analyse sur le plan de l'individu, et le possibilité d'adapter les concepts du behaviourisme. Ces études en miniature ont réussi à produire plusieurs cadres conceptuels, mais on ne les a pas mis à l'épreuve jusqu'ici. Le but des études à Swansea était d'une nature essentiellement préliminaire, et empirique plus que théorique. En faisant usage des données du recensement on montre qu'il se peut faire des analyses utiles. Les renseignements d'une recherche fondée sur les menages individuels de plusieurs quartiers de la ville ont été employées pour l'examen de la nature de la mobilité résidentielle dans les circonstances britanniques, tout en appuyant particulièrement sur les niveaux de la mobilité, les raisons des déplacements et les dessins spatiaux de base qu'on trouve. Les renseignements sur les préférences résidentielles de la même recherche permettent d'analyser les évaluations spatiaux des quartiers résidentiels généraux ainsi que les propriétés des autorités municipaux dans la ville.

FIG. 1. Les zones des catégories sociaux

FIG. 2. Les vitesses de la mobilité intraurbaine (1961–66)

ZUSAMMENFASSUNG. *Wohnungsbeweglichkeit und Vorliebe : ein Versuch in Swansea.* Die Beweglichkeit auf dem intra-städtischen Niveau ist im wesentlichen das Verfahren von Wohnungsauswahl wobei man zu bestimmten Entscheidungen kommt und ordentliche Modelle einer soziale-geographische Beschaffenheit entstehen. Es gibt keinen Zweifel dass die auf angehauften Angaben begründeten Studien behalten ihre Wichtigkeit, aber die neuen Untersuchungen haben den Einfluss einer individuum-orientierten Analyse und die Moglichkeiten der Betragensbegriffe im Zusammenhang hiermit nachdrücklich betont. Diese Forschungen in verkleinertem Massstab haben viele begriffliche Rahmen hergestellt, aber man hat diese nicht ganz entschieden geprüft. Die characteristische Beschaffenheit der Studien in Swansea war im wesentlichen einleitend, eher empirisch als theoretisch. Vermittels der Volkszählungsangaben zeigt man dass mehrere nützliche angehaufte Analysen möglich sind. Man kann die Angaben eines mehrere Stadtbezirke einschliessenden Haushaltungsfragebogen benutzen um die Beschaffenheit der Wohnungsauswahl zu untersuchen, mit dem Nachdruck auf dem Beweglichkeitsniveau, den Grunden zur Wohnortveränderung und den basischen räumlichen Modelle die emporkommen. Die Angaben über die Wohnortvorliebe von denselben Überblicke ermöglichen eine Analyse von den räumlichen Wertbestimmungen der allgemeinen Wohnbezirke und von den Gemeindeverwaltungsländereien in der Stadt.

Segregation in Kuwait

A. G. HILL

Lecturer in Geography, University of Aberdeen

Revised MS received 7 August 1972

ABSTRACT. In Kuwait marked residential segregation occurs between citizens and immigrants and is particularly pronounced in Kuwait City. Continual pressure on the excellent health, welfare and educational facilities has forced the government to give preference to citizens (Kuwaitis) as against non-Kuwaitis (immigrants). In addition, labour laws explicitly force employers to give preference to the native population for all grades of employment. Kuwaitis, although in a minority, remain the dominant force in the government and the administration. They command higher salaries and wages and have pre-empted certain quarters of the city as exclusive residential areas. Their patterns of movement and socio-demographic characteristics are distinctive and contrast sharply with those of the immigrant population. The non-Kuwaitis are not a homogeneous group but consist of various nationalities whose socio-economic and demographic attributes can be used to divide the group into sub-classes by means of factor analysis. Some results of an original survey of shopping patterns among the sub-groups show how these communities act as semi-independent cells within the overall urban structure. Parallels are drawn between residential and activity segregation in Kuwait, and in other areas where similar dichotomies have been observed. It is suggested that rapid growth of population may be an important factor in preventing one sub-group or community being absorbed by another.

As more detailed demographic statistics become available for enumeration districts or other small divisions of cities, it appears that segregation of communities within urban areas is an almost universal phenomenon. The basis for segregation varies widely and may include colour, class, or creed. In addition to segregation by place of residence, characteristic patterns of spatial behaviour by several sub-groups in the city may result in what has been recently called 'activity segregation'.[1] In both instances the effect of segregation is to break down the composite character of the city into a set of overlapping cells whose degree of independence may increase during times of inter-community rivalry and decrease during phases of harmony, possible in the face of a common enemy.

G. Sjoberg among others suggested that, in the pre-industrial city, social sub-division occurs along ethnic lines while ethnicity is in turn strongly associated with specific occupations.[2] Ethnicity is thus seen as the principal axis of differentiation of non-Western cities in marked contrast to most cities of Europe and the United Kingdom where, although race is important in certain specific instances, the major dimension of social differentiation and residential segregation is the socio-economic attributes of the inhabitants.[3]

The central problem in comparing segregation in non-Western and Western cities is thus how race replaces social class as a basis for differentiation. In Kuwait, most of the urban growth has been compressed into a period of less than 30 years so that there is a rare opportunity to study the evolutionary pattern of segregation in a non-Western city from both statistical documents and from reliable first-hand accounts.

PRE-INDUSTRIAL URBANISM

Urban areas in Arabia have in the past contained a surprisingly large proportion of the peninsula's total population and have exerted a powerful influence over the structure and organization of Arab society as a whole.[4] Most of the cities including Mecca and

123

Madina owe their origins to the early establishment of long-distance trading connections, which in the area of the Persian Gulf engendered the development of an urban-based community of seamen and merchants. The small coastal settlements—Basra, Bandar Abbas, Jask, Dubai and several others including Kuwait itself—thus became exotic, heterogeneous communities because of the immigration of tribes from the interior, together with peoples from the littoral areas of the Arabian Sea and the coast of East Africa.[5] Several Arab geographers refer to the mixed racial character of the ports of the Persian Gulf in the mediaeval period. Further evidence of the existence of these communities and their mercantile way of life in earlier periods is coming to light as a result of archaeological investigations in the Gulf area.[6]

The first detailed descriptions of the Gulf ports were made in the latter half of the nineteenth century as Great Britain began to sign a series of treaties and other engagements with the Gulf rulers. One official, J. G. Lorimer, was charged with the difficult task of taking stock of the area and people with whom Britain had become directly involved. Lorimer and his assistants produced a monumental survey—a *Gazateer of the Persian Gulf, Oman and Central Arabia*—which still provides useful and accurate information on some aspects of the contemporary Persian Gulf.[7] The *Gazateer* (sic) provides enough detail on Kuwait to indicate that in structure, morphology and function Kuwait City was very close to Sjoberg's archetypal non-Western city. Physically the city was compact, measuring about 3 km along the shore: 'The streets are irregular and winding, many of them blind alleys, and the town is not laid out on any general plan; the only street of apparent importance, besides the main bazaar which runs at right angles to the sea about the middle of the town, is one which leads from the Suq or market square, situated at the back of the town near the Murqab quarter, to the north-east end of the town, but it has no general name. Most of the houses have only a ground floor, but appear higher owing to a parapet-wall enclosing the roof; they are generally built surrounding a courtyard. The better sort are of stone plastered with *Juss* and have high arched gateways, sometimes with a wicket-door in the middle of the gate; a few arches appear also in upper storeys. The system of conservancy is rudimentary; the sewage is deposited in large, open public cesspools in the various quarters. There are between 20 and 30 mosques, of which 4 are Jami's or Friday congregational mosques; these are the chief mosque, which stands on the west side the main bazaar, the Shaikh's mosque on the sea's face near his residence, the mosque of Haddad, and the mosque of the Jana'at; none of these have any architectural pretensions'.[8]

Between the 1870s and the early 1900s Kuwait City doubled in size owing principally to immigrants from the interior so that it overspilled an older mud wall and spread out into the surrounding desert where the Shaikh was granting free plots of land. The lower and middle strata of society almost all lived by seafaring occupations, including pearl diving, fishing and the carrying trade. Long-distance maritime trading links were important in producing an ethnically mixed population in Kuwait consisting of loosely defined kinship groups owing allegiance directly to the Ruler. Some of these kinship groups were located in certain quarters within the city which Lorimer was able to identify: 'The population of Kuwait is now about 35 000, of whom the great majority are Arabs . . . The 'Utub are the tribe to which the Shaikhs of Kuwait belong, but they are reckoned to be only about 30 (another account says 250) families . . . More than 100 Arab households in the town are immigrants from Zilfi in Najd. The Persian community consists of about 1000 souls; its members do not inhabit a separate quarter but are scattered through the town; nearly all of them are permanently settled at Kuwait, nevertheless they go and come freely between Kuwait and the parts of Persia to which they originally belonged. Persian merchants are about a score; over 100 Persians are shopkeepers; 200 of the remainder are penniless labourers who live from hand to mouth. The Jews amount to between 100 and 200 souls; they have a synagogue of their own, called a Kanisah; at Kuwait they seem to be notorious chiefly for the distillation of spirituous liquors which some of the Muhammadan population consume secretly in dread of the Shaikh. Two of the Jews are well-to-do merchants; the rest are mostly cloth-sellers and goldsmiths. The Jana'at are a small colony of 150 souls; some are merchants, the others sailors and boatmen. The negroes are a very conspicuous element in the population; they number about 4000 altogether, and have social clubs of their own which are distinguished by peculiar sky-signs; about one-third are *Ma'tuq* or emancipated, while two-thirds are *Mamluk* or enslaved'.[9]

From this, it seems that both residential segregation and the tendency of some groups to specialize in certain trades were both established characteristics of pre-oil Kuwait. The puzzling dispersion of the Persians throughout the city may possibly be explained by their high mobility and by their employment as domestic servants living in their employers' houses. Lorimer's analysis is notable because of its stress on race and national origins as bases for differentiation among the urban population and for his lack of references to class divisions in Kuwait's pre-industrial society.

Throughout the first four decades of the twentieth century Kuwait's population grew steadily when trading links with the Arabian hinterland and Iraq were most secure and prolific. During wartime when blockades were imposed on Kuwait's trade because of the volume of smuggled arms and other supplies reaching Turkish Iraq, the whole community experienced periods of severe hardship and near starvation. With the beginning of oil exports, in 1946, however, Kuwait's fortunes began on a rapid upward spiral which produced radical changes in the structure of the city, the economy and society.

THE GROWTH OF POPULATION AND THE MODERN CITY

The modern state now consists of a settled area along the coast which in plan takes the form of an inverted L. Kuwait City, the capital, is by far the largest centre which held 58 per cent of the state's total population in 1970. Most of the recent increase of population has been accommodated on the outskirts of the Old City described by Lorimer, particularly in the south-eastern suburbs some of which are now 10 km from the centre of the Old City. Ahmadi, the town begun in 1950 by the Kuwait Oil Company, has grown very little in recent years, but Fahahil on the east coast has experienced a considerable expansion together with satellite centres nearby. The smaller villages of the east coast and Jahra west of the capital have altered little so that the dominance of Kuwait City remains unchallenged.

While Kuwait's population was never in the past homogeneous in composition, the growing oil industry stimulated the immigration of people from a wider variety of source areas than ever before. The small indigenous population grew by the return of expatriates from other countries and, as health facilities were improved in the late 1950s, by natural increase. Despite this expansion, the native population ('Kuwaitis') were soon outnumbered by the later arrivals ('non-Kuwaitis'). Strict nationality laws in force since 1948 carefully maintained the distinction between Kuwaitis and immigrants, a division which has proved of lasting significance. The government gives preference to the native population for

TABLE I

The population of Kuwait, 1904–70

Date	Males	Kuwaitis Females	Total	Males	Non-Kuwaitis Females	Total	Males	Total Females	Total
1904	—	—	—	—	—	—	—	—	35 000[1]
1944	—	—	—	—	—	—	—	—	70 000[2]
1952	—	—	—	—	—	—	—	—	160 000[3]
February 1957	59 154	54 468	113 622	72 904	19 947	92 851	132 058	74 415	206 473
May 1961	84 461	77 448	161 909	116 246	43 466	159 712	200 707	120 914	321 621
April 1965	112 569	107 490	220 059	173 743	73 537	247 280	286 312	181 027	467 339
April 1970	175 513	171 883	347 396	244 368	146 898	391 266	419 881	318 781	738 662

Notes: 1. J. G. Lorimer's estimate which excludes 13 000 Badu
2. Admiralty War Staff, *Handbook of Arabia* (1916), vol. 2, 400
3. H. R. P. DICKSON, *Kuwait and her neighbours* (1956), 40
All other figures taken from *Census of Population* (1957, 1961, 1965 and 1970), (Arabic)

employment and particularly in the civil service where certain higher grades are reserved for Kuwaitis only. Further discrimination gradually evolved in the educational, health, and welfare fields where serious pressures on the facilities by the growing population resulted in restrictions on their use by non-Kuwaitis.

The distinction between Kuwaitis and non-Kuwaitis has become the prime division within the population of Kuwait because of the preference system operated in favour of Kuwait citizens. For official purposes, citizens are distinguished from immigrants not on racial or religious grounds but only on the ability of the former to produce some proof, preferably written, of their habitual residence in the state of Kuwait. There are, however, strong racial contrasts between the citizens and the aliens and also within the alien population but these differences bore no relation to the evolution of the discriminatory system based on nationality. While nationality is a relatively recent concept in the Middle East, it is possible in most cases to distinguish the national origins of the immigrants in Kuwait on the basis of their physical characteristics and dress. The Iranians, for example, as a group are of relatively slight stature, rarely above 167 cm in height, with medium-brown skins and black or dark grey hair. They commonly wear a small felt skull cap and a loose-fitting gown hitched up to knee height. Thus the distinctions which are drawn on the basis of nationality between citizens and immigrants, and between the nationalities comprising the non-Kuwaiti population, are broadly coincident with racial and, to a lesser extent, religious differences within Kuwait's total population.

Detailed statistics on the characteristics and distribution of Kuwait's population in the period immediately after 1946 are sparse but the four censuses of population held in 1957, 1961, 1965, and 1970 provide a stronger factual base in the recent period. Two questions in the first census asking for nationality and period of residence in Kuwait make some retrospective population estimates possible. The results of the census reports and other population estimates are presented in Table I. They show a rapid increase in Kuwait's

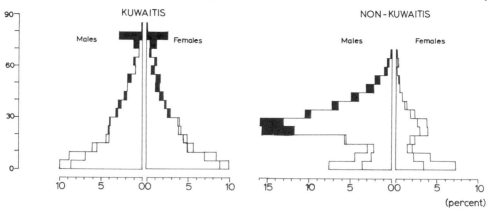

FIGURE I. Population pyramids for Kuwaitis and non-Kuwaitis in 1957 and 1965. The solid black portions indicate where the percentage figure for 1957 was greater than the figure for 1965. The Kuwaiti pyramid of 1957 provides clear evidence of erroneous age recording in the over-70 age group.

total population with the immigrant population gradually forming a higher proportion of the total. As naturalization of immigrants is almost impossible except for a maximum of fifty favoured individuals annually, there has clearly been some misrepresenting of nationality and under-recording in the earlier censuses.[10] These errors do not invalidate the general trends identified below although they do make detailed demographic projections difficult.

With heavy investment in health facilities, totalling K.D. 11·5 million[11] in 1965–66 and rising to K.D. 16·4 million in 1969–70, mortality rates (especially infant mortality rates) have been reduced to near European levels. Thus the Kuwaiti population in particular is one of the youngest in the world because of its rapid natural increase. The non-Kuwaiti population, while increasing at a faster rate principally by the influx of newcomers, is also growing rapidly by natural increase. There is some evidence to suggest that fertility is high among the immigrants because Kuwait's health facilities are cheap and of a high standard, thus forming an extra attraction for potential migrants in the reproductive age-groups.[12] The recent changes in the structure of the immigrant population include a trend towards more evenly balanced sex ratios and the addition of more dependants to the original population consisting mostly of young adult males. This trend suggests that the immigrants are becoming a more settled community although still distinguishable from the Kuwaitis by their age-sex characteristics (Fig. 1).

RESIDENTIAL SEGREGATION

Kuwaitis and non-Kuwaitis are strongly segregated in Kuwait City and in the outlying towns and villages. In 1970 for example, 38 per cent of the capital's population consisted of Kuwaitis but in eleven of the suburban blocks Kuwaitis comprised at least three-quarters of the total population. In Hawalli and the Old City, however, Kuwaitis were in a minority, comprising in the former area as little as 11 per cent of the 1970 population. There are several reasons for this pattern of marked segregation (Fig. 2).

Central to the issue of residential segregation is the government's programme of property acquisition established in 1952 as a means of expediting urban re-development in the Old City (Figs. 3 and 4). The government agreed to pay Kuwaiti owners of land or

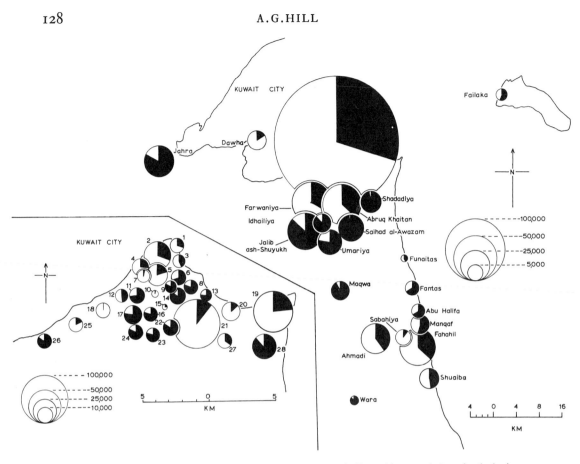

FIGURE 2. The distribution of Kuwait's population in 1970. Kuwait City, with a population of 456 562, is defined as the continuously built-up area enclosed within the fourth ring road. The capital governate administrative division is unsatisfactory for geographical purposes since it excludes, for example, the suburbs of Hawalli and Salimiya and includes outlying centres such as Jahra and Dawha. Areas in the inset: 1 Dasman, 2 Sharq, 3 Bnaid al-Qar, 4 Qibla, 5 Mirqab, 6 Dasma, 7 Salihiya, 8 Da'iya, 9 Mansuriya, 10 Abdulla Salim, 11 Shamiya, 12 Shuwaikh Suburb, 12 Sha'ab, 14 Qadisiya, 15 Nuzha, 16 Faiha, 17 Kaifan, 18 Shuwaikh industrial area, 19 Salimiya, 20 Maidan Hawalli, 21 Hawalli, 22 Sulaibikhat, 26 Sulaibikhat village, 27 Jabriya, 28 Rumaithiya. The black portions of the circles represent Kuwaitis.

property generous sums of money to sell up and move out of the Old City into the newer suburban neighbourhoods. Considerable amounts of money were disbursed, totalling K.D. 697·5 million for the period January 1952 to April 1971, which had the double effects of reducing the Old City's population and at the same time hastening the development of newer suburbs. Since Kuwaitis only were allowed to own property, they alone benefited from the liberal compensation paid and were thus in a strong financial position to build new villas beyond the old city wall. Government loans were available to assist those unable

FIGURE 3. This aerial view of the Old City in 1951 portrays the city much as Lorimer described it in the early 1900s. The Ruler's palace can be discerned on the waterfront overlooking the prominent jetties, and the covered lanes of the *Suq* can be traced inland from the palace to the smaller oval open space which is Safat square. Only the open spaces of the cemeteries break up the closely packed cellular structure of the city within the enclosing wall.

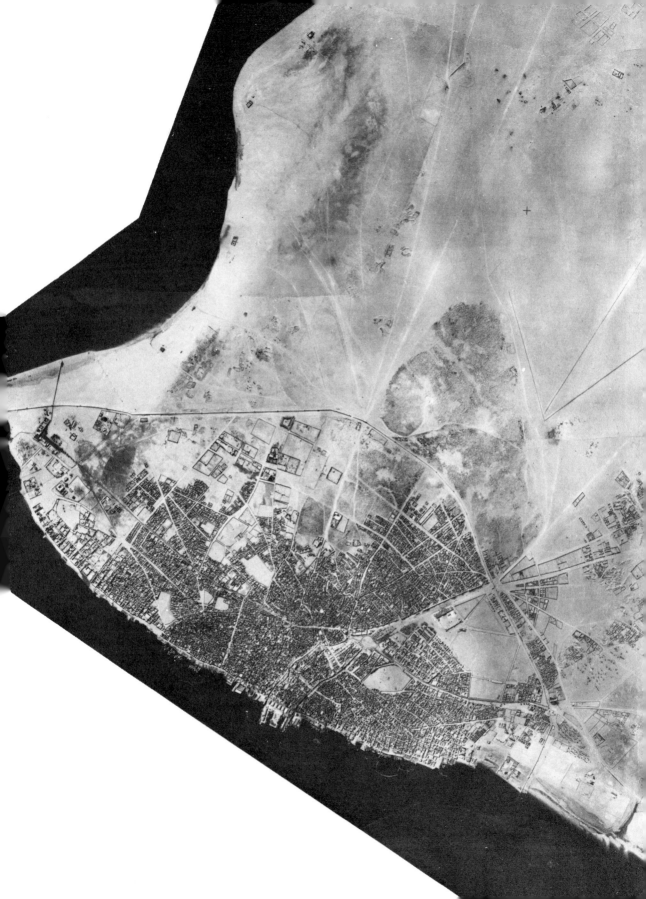

FIGURE 4. The Old City in 1967 has been transformed by the insertion of wide divided highways and the replacement of single storey houses by taller public buildings. New commercial centres have been inserted between the old *Suq* and the dhow harbour, while west of Safat Square the most prominent additions are the public park replacing an older cemetery and the canyon of tall apartment blocks and shops which is Fahad as-Salim street.

to afford the high cost of building their own houses. Plots of land were allocated to Kuwaitis by choice or by lottery in blocks of 750 or 1000 m² and sold at a nominal price.[13] In addition, almost 13 000 houses have been built by the government for low-income Kuwaitis who rent or buy the houses at subsidized rates.

Non-Kuwaitis, excluded from this development, filled the housing vacated by Kuwaitis in the Old City as well as moving into newer apartments built by Kuwaitis in the city centre and in the two suburbs of Hawalli and Salimiya which were not zoned for Kuwaitis. These factors largely account for the segregation pattern which has emerged today in Kuwait City.

Elsewhere in Kuwait, non-Kuwaitis and Kuwaitis also reside in different areas. The reasons for this segregation are different from those in Kuwait City. Instead, it is necessary to refer to the location of employment opportunities for Kuwaitis and non-Kuwaitis and to the various levels of skill required. Initially the immigrants were better educated and more skilled than the indigenous population so that employment in the oil industry and in the other technical fields was dominated by non-Kuwaitis. Remote rural areas of Kuwait

TABLE II
Male employment by profession, 1965 (percentages)

Profession	Kuwaitis	Non-Kuwaitis
1. Senior technical and scientific staff	2·5	6·1
2. Directors and senior administrative staff	3·4	1·7
3. Clerical staff	15·2	8·0
4. Workers in retail and wholesale sales	11·0	7·9
5. Farmers and fishermen	1·8	2·2
6. Quarrymen and workers in extractive industries	0·4	0·5
7. Transport workers	13·6	9·2
8. Artisans, production workers and porters	12·9	42·4
9. Workers in service trades, including policemen and guards	32·6	20·7
10. Not included above	6·6	1·2
Total =	100	100
Total employed =	41 933	133 617

Source: Census of Population (1965), Tables 6a and 6b (Arabic)

offer little attraction to the immigrants who mostly move either to the growing oil centres of Fahahil and Ahmadi or to Kuwait City. The situation has altered slightly since Kuwaitis are now aspiring to all levels of employment but the bulk of the village and small town population still consists of Kuwaitis. Thus the capital city and the industrial areas of Kuwait contain the majority of the immigrant population while Kuwaitis remain a more evenly distributed population, dominant in the villages and towns not directly associated with the oil industry and its ancillaries.

NATIONALITY AND EMPLOYMENT IN KUWAIT

With the government's close control over visas, work permits, and especially naturalization for the immigrant population, it was possible to carry through a policy of discrimination in employment by demanding that every employer should in the first instance offer a job vacancy to a Kuwaiti citizen. In addition, the oil companies were periodically asked to hasten the training and promotion of Kuwaitis to replace the expatriates employed at all levels. The civil service, Kuwait's principal source of employment, was also made to conform to the labour laws and in particular to reserve the senior administrative and executive positions for Kuwaitis. This policy has produced some anomalous situations, but there is evidence to support the earlier contention that there is a powerful link between the nationality group and their principal category of employment.

First, the distinction between Kuwaitis and non-Kuwaitis by employment status and branch of economic activity is clear-cut. From Table II, it is clear that Kuwaitis are dominant in the government and administration eschewing the manual and semi-skilled craftsmen grades of employment. These gaps in the employment spectrum are filled by non-Kuwaitis. (In the discussion of employment, only male workers are considered to

TABLE III

Non-Kuwaiti males by nationality and employment, 1965 (percentages)

Employment	Jordanians and Palestinians	Iranis	Omanis	Iraqis	Syrians	Lebanese	Indians	Pakistanis	Egyptians	Mahris
					Nationality					
1. Senior technical and scientific staff	10·6	0·2	0·4	2·2	5·0	7·9	7·3	1·8	41·9	0·1
2. Directors and senior administrative staff	1·7	0·4	0·1	0·9	2·4	6·7	2·3	0·6	6·7	0·0
3. Clerical staff	15·8	0·7	2·2	5·3	2·2	9·2	26·6	6·3	8·8	2·1
4. Workers in retail and wholesale sales	5·9	6·6	6·0	8·7	13·3	13·6	8·4	2·5	1·3	31·2
5. Farmers and fishermen	3·3	1·2	3·3	4·5	1·8	0·2	0·0	0·2	0·6	1·1
6. Quarrymen and workers in extractive industries	0·4	0·8	0·2	1·7	0·3	0·1	0·1	0·2	0·1	0·0
7. Transport workers	11·4	2·8	9·9	1·0	1·0	14·7	4·5	5·6	1·7	11·8
8. Artisans, production workers and porters	37·1	71·6	18·5	47·3	51·9	38·7	23·0	67·3	30·8	7·6
9. Workers in service trades, including policemen and guards	12·8	14·9	57·5	17·9	9·5	8·6	27·3	15·0	7·9	43·8
10. Not included above	1·0	0·8	1·7	1·1	2·4	0·2	0·4	0·5	0·1	2·2
Total =	100	100	100	100	100	100	100	100	100	100
Total male labour force	33 769	27 892	14 647	10 364	9715	8532	6175	5441	3913	3353

Source: Census of Population (1965), Table 30 (Arabic)

avoid the distorting effects of errors in the enumeration of females at work.) Few Kuwaitis work in agriculture or fishing or indeed in any of the primary sectors of the economy including the oil industry. It emerges that the immigrants not only fill the lowest employment grades but are also important at higher levels where persons with specialized technical and professional experience are required. At least two types of immigrant are thus required to meet these contrasting needs.

While educational status is generally closely associated with type of employment, Kuwaitis with only a moderate level of education have been able to pre-empt certain higher-status positions because of the declared policy of discrimination. For example, just over half of the Kuwaitis who were employed as professional persons, directors, and in senior positions in government departments had received only a basic primary level of education although more than four-fifths of the non-Kuwaitis similarly employed had been educated to a higher standard.[14]

Several notable cases of national specialization in one trade or industry are illustrated in Table III. At least four broad groupings of the foreign nationals in Kuwait can be identified. Iranis, Omanis and Mahris were employed as construction workers, labourers and craftsmen; Lebanese and Syrians, while still working as craftsmen in considerable numbers, also showed a preference for sales employment; other Arabs worked in services or in clerical positions; while British, Americans and Egyptians were employed in technical and professional tasks.

To determine the type of employment an individual migrant will take up on arrival in Kuwait is an impossible task but generalizations about groups from the same source area are valid because of their homogeneous socio-demographic attributes. Broadly it would seem that the migrants' level of education, type of employment at home, and their age-sex characteristics together determine the level of employment taken up in Kuwait. An important but intangible factor may be at work in bringing migrants from one source area together in the same employment in Kuwait, for information about new jobs and vacancies is relayed to potential migrants through workers returning from Kuwait on leave. In addition, there may be a slight preference shown by employers for workers from one area, since within Kuwait some foreign nationals may be less desirable as employees in senior positions than others.[15]

One notable repercussion of the discrimination in favour of Kuwaitis in employment is the discordance in income levels between citizens and aliens. In a family budget survey covering 1344 households in 1966, it was revealed that, while 7·8 per cent of Kuwaiti households had an income of over K.D. 6000 a year, the figure for non-Kuwaitis was 1·8 per cent.[16] At the lower income levels, non-Kuwaitis were more numerous than their Kuwaiti counterparts. Further, more Kuwaitis owned cars, refrigerators, washing machines and air-conditioning units than their non-Kuwaiti counterparts. One would expect there to be contrasts in income and variation in affluence as measured by possession of selected consumer durables between the individual national groups, but unfortunately detailed statistics are unavailable.

Summarizing, it can be seen how a traditional society, organized on the basis of kin groupings but without any pronounced ranking of its sub-groups, has been transformed into a highly structured community based on the dominant economic and political position occupied by the Kuwaitis. In several instances, this power has been used radically to alter the social geography of the city. Kuwaitis and non-Kuwaitis not only live apart but

TABLE IV

The composition of factors 1, 2 and 3

| Factor 1 | | Factor 2 | | Factor 3 | |
Variable	Loading	Variable	Loading	Variable	Loading
Kuwaitis	4·09	Density	5·60	Construction workers	2·82
Service employment	2·60	Males	1·07	Craftsmen	2·70
Muslims	2·17	Muslims	0·98	Illiterates	2·07
Illiterates	1·59	Age 15–39	0·93	Muslims	2·05
Age 0–14	1·45	Size of centre	0·86	Males	1·93
Married	1·12	Married	0·77	Age 15–39	1·60
Construction workers	−0·89	Craftsmen	0·72	Iranis	1·12
Craftsmen	−1·13	Kuwaitis	−0·48	Service employment	−1·14
				Density	−1·59

Notes: The factor scores are pseudo-standardized and can be used in a qualitative way only. A value of zero indicates that a factor contains roughly an average amount of that variable and a value of +1·0 means that the factor contains roughly one standard deviation above the average of that variable.

they also work at different levels in both the civil service and in the private sector. Just like Belfast, Kuwait's society is both ranked and polarized.[17] Further subdivisions are of importance particularly among the non-Kuwaiti population, posing the wider question as to whether or not some reasonably objective quantitative criterion can be conceived which adequately describes most of the characteristics of Kuwait's population and at the same time permits the distribution of these attributes to be interpreted. This problem of examining connected descriptive statistics and reducing the number of measures to a smaller derived set of indices is one commonly solved by factor analysis.

THE URBAN ECOLOGY OF KUWAIT

For detailed analysis, the state of Kuwait was divided into thirty-nine areas for which thirty-eight attributes, mostly drawn from the census of 1965, were available to describe the population characteristics of each area. Using Q mode factor analysis incorporating a varimax rotation to bring out the differences and similarities between the thirty-nine areas,[18] three factors were extracted which accounted for 92 per cent of the descriptive power of the original 39×38 matrix. The factor compositions are shown in Table IV. Figures 5, 6 and 7 illustrate the spatial significance of each of these major dimensions.

The analysis confirms several points established earlier in connection with the differentiation and spatial separation of sub-groups in Kuwait's population. Factor 1, summarizing many of the attributes of the Kuwaitis, effectively separates citizens from aliens. Non-Kuwaitis, the solution reveals, can be viewed as a group comprising two major sub-sets—the educated immigrants working in professional and technical occupations and, secondly, the largely illiterate arrivals who work in the construction industry and other fields where manual labour is in demand. Kuwait, it seems, is not so much a dualistic type of society but one with at least three major cleavages. Examination of Figures 5, 6 and 7 reveals that each of the three elements picked out by factor analysis has a distinctive pattern of distribution. For example, the Kuwaitis were concentrated in the new suburbs of the capital and in Idhailiya and Jalib ash-Shuyukh, while the higher-status immigrants predominated in the city centre. Low-status immigrants were clustered in areas where the construction

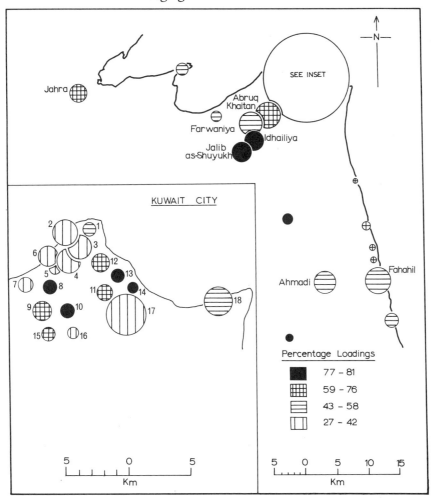

FIGURE 5. The distribution of Factor 1. The districts on the inset are as follows: 1 Dasman, 2 Sharq i, 3 Sharq ii, 4 Mirqab, 5 Salihiya, 6 Qibla, 7 Shuwaikh, 8 Shamiya, 9 Kaifan, 10 Faiha, 11 Qadisiya, 12 Dasma, 13 Da'iya, 14 Sha'ab, 15 Khaldiya, 16 'Idailiya, 17 Hawalli, 18 Salimiya

of new housing was in hand or else in the ports of Shuwaikh and the east coast where manual labour was similarly required.

The pattern of differentiation outlined by the factor analysis, while it was based largely on descriptive statistics concerning the demographic, occupational and economic status of the inhabitants, is an unfamiliar one to Western analysts. It shows how nationality becomes a summation of many other indices in the urban ecology of a Middle Eastern city. Although Kuwait is atypical because of the volume of foreign immigration, other Middle Eastern cities also display a cellular ecological structure that is broadly similar.[19]

SEGREGATION OF ACTIVITY IN KUWAIT

With a population consisting of separate units, each with a characteristic assemblage of demographic, economic and employment characteristics, independent and contrasting

K

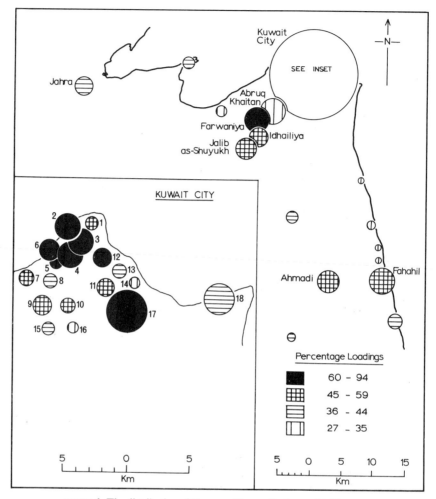

FIGURE 6. The distribution of Factor 2. Key to districts as for Figure 3

patterns of spatial behaviour in Kuwait are only to be expected. An examination of the
composition of the several shopping centres in the capital and in the smaller towns reveals
that several centres specialize in the supply of commodities to particular sections of the
population. One new street in Kuwait City, Fahad as-Salim street, consists of an assemblage of shops selling clothing and a wide variety of consumer goods largely derived from
the West or Japan. Since many of the shops themselves resemble in form their Western
counterparts (plate-glass fronts, elaborate window displays and air conditioning), this
area acts as a magnet for the educated élite, Kuwaitis and non-Kuwaitis, who are generally
Western-orientated in their attitudes and ambitions (Fig. 8).

   These retail specializations are complex to define and study in an objective manner
but one demonstration of the tendency of national groups to behave similarly when faced
with the problem of where to obtain a certain commodity can be demonstrated as a result
of a questionnaire survey of nearly 350 households. The study was carried out through

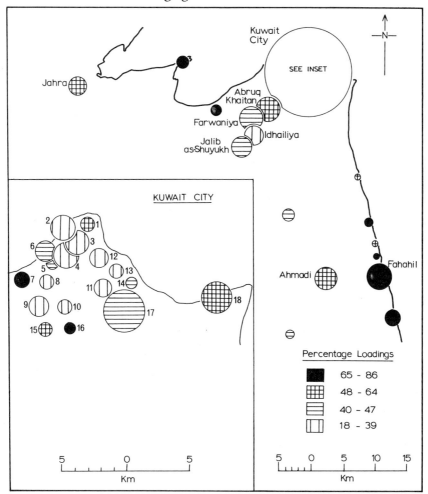

FIGURE 7. The distribution of Factor 3. Key to districts as for Figure 3

the ladies' clubs which acted as rallying points for the various resident foreign communities. The students at the University of Kuwait kindly arranged for a representative sample of Kuwaitis to answer the same questionnaire.

With low-order goods such as foodstuffs and other groceries, the purchases were generally made locally so that the journey to shop was closely related to the household's place of residence. One important difference between Kuwaitis and non-Kuwaitis was the way that the former patronized the suburban co-operatives where sizeable dividends were paid to members. Non-Kuwaitis were not eligible to join the co-operatives and therefore had less of an incentive to buy their groceries there. For example, among the respondents who bought most of their groceries at Kaifan co-operative, 79 per cent were Kuwaitis.[20]

For higher-order goods, and clothing and cloth in particular, the most popular shopping centres were Fahad as-Salim street and the Suq. Of the Suq users, just 53 per cent were Kuwaitis while in the more expensive area of Fahad as-Salim street the propor-

FIGURE 8. Fahad as- Salim street, here seen looking north-eastwards towards the Suq, was deliberately built to modernize the appearance of the Old City. Its shops, while not as costly to rent as some prized locations in the Suq, sell mostly luxury goods such as electrical goods, photographic equipment and expensive clothing.

tion of Kuwaiti users rose to 62 per cent. Few Britons or Americans made use of the Suq for purchases of cloth or clothing, compared with other Arab groups who made the majority of their purchases in this traditional retail nucleus of Kuwait (Fig. 9).

These conclusions have been confirmed by a firm of planning consultants who, in 1969, carried out their own independent survey of 1729 households. The survey highlighted some of the contrasts between the prosperity of the newer Kuwaiti neighbourhoods with household incomes as high as K.D. 388 per month and the older parts of the city where average monthly household incomes fell to K.D. 147. Despite the lack of a detailed cross-tabulation of the results of nationality, it is possible to identify a tendency of Kuwaitis from the new neighbourhoods to use both the Suq and Fahad as-Salim street for the bulk of their needs. In the Suq they constituted 29 per cent and in the latter area 22 per cent of all users. By comparison, the needs of the population of the strongly non-Kuwaiti areas of Hawalli and Salimiya were largely catered for within the two areas, for in the former case 68 per cent, and in the latter case 84 per cent, of all shopping trips both originated and terminated in the same area.

FIGURE 9. The Suq remains the retail focus of Kuwait. The products it sells and the form of the shops are attuned to a 'traditional' market. Of the female shoppers using the Suq, the majority wear the veil.

CONCLUSION

In many European or North American cities, geographical research has indicated that the urban populations consist of sub-communities identified by a set of economic and other attributes which describe an individual's status or class. This study of Kuwait suggests that, while similar sub-communities exist in non-Western cities, the bases for identification are not those referred to above. In many oriental situations, ties of birth and kin outweigh other sorts of association in importance. Such ties often transcend what in the West are called class boundaries, resulting in a division of the inhabitants of non-Western cities into groups on the basis of other attributes, such as tribal affiliation, ethnic origin or nationality.

For several special reasons, national origins in Kuwait assume particular importance, but despite these peculiarities of the Kuwait situation, it is felt that more research in oriental cities will confirm rather than refute the conclusions arrived at here. Overall, the spatial effects of an explicit policy of discrimination on the basis of citizenship are wide ranging for not only has the policy created a highly segregated city structured in a form quite novel in Arabia, but it has also brought about contrasts in the patterns of movement of the various national groups comprising Kuwait's total population.

ACKNOWLEDGEMENTS

This work was undertaken with the financial support of a Hayter Middle East Studies scholarship held at the University of Durham. Grateful thanks are due to the University of Kuwait, to several government departments and to other organizations in Kuwait who provided invaluable assistance in the field. The author is indebted to Mrs M. Stone, Dr J. K. A. Thomaneck, Mrs A. Naylor and Miss S. V. Spilsbury for translation of the abstract and captions. Thanks are due to Hunting Surveys Ltd. for permission to reproduce Figures 3 and 4 and to the Kuwait Oil Company for Figures 8 and 9. A grant from the Carnegie Trust for the Universities of Scotland towards the cost of illustrations is gratefully acknowledged.

NOTES

1. F. W. BOAL, 'Territoriality on the Shankill-Falls divide, Belfast', *Irish Geogr.* 6, 1 (1969), 30–50
2. G. SJOBERG, *The pre-industrial city* (1965), especially chapters 4 and 5
3. See the conclusions drawn by D. T. HERBERT, 'Principal Components Analysis and urban social structure: a study of Cardiff and Swansea' in H. CARTER and W. K. D. DAVIES (eds), *Urban essays* (1970), 79–100
4. I. M. LAPIDUS, 'Muslim cities and Islamic societies' in I. M. LAPIDUS (ed), *Middle Eastern cities* (1969), provides a well-documented statement of this argument.
5. A. T. WILSON, *The Persian Gulf* (1959), 25–109
6. G. BIBBY, *Looking for Dilmum* (1969) See also 'Arabian Gulf archaeology', *Kuml* (1964), 86–111
7. Reprinted in 1970 with original pagination by Gregg International Publishers and the Irish Universities Press
8. J. G. LORIMER, *Gazateer of the Persian Gulf, Oman and Central Arabia* (1870), II B, 1050
9. Ibid., 1051
10. For a fuller analysis, see A. G. HILL, 'Aspects of the urban development of Kuwait', unpubl. Ph.D. thesis, Univ. of Durham (1969)
11. £1 sterling was worth 0·857 Kuwaiti dinars in 1972.
12. Fertility of non-Kuwaiti women was marginally above that of Kuwaiti women in 1965. See G. E. FFRENCH and A. G. HILL, *Kuwait—urban and medical ecology* (1971), chapter V
13. Further details of the whole re-development programme are available in A. G. HILL, op. cit. (1969), and in the annual reports of Kuwait municipality (Arabic only).
14. *Central Directorate of Statistics, Population Census* (1965), Table 32 (Arabic)
15. The threatened invasion of Kuwait by Iraq in 1961 is just one example of the risks involved in relying on foreign labour. At that time, there were officially 27 148 Iraqis in Kuwait and probably several thousand more unrecorded entrants.
16. *Planning Board, Family Budget Survey* (1968), Table 9 (Arabic)
17. The terms are taken from A. BOSERUP and C. IVERSEN, 'Rank analysis of a polarized community: a case study from Northern Ireland', *Peace Res. Soc. (Int.) Pap.* 7 (1967), 59–76
18. The programme was written by J. E. KLOVAN, *Q-mode factor analysis program in Fortran IV for small computers* (1967), Kansas State Geological Survey, Lawrence, Kansas. For a discussion of the varimax rotation, see W. K. D. DAVIES, 'Varimax and the destruction of generality: a methodological note', *Area* 3, 2 (1971), 112–8
19. Important comparative work is available on Cairo—J. ABU-LUGHOD, 'Varieties of urban experience: contrast coexistence and coalescence in Cairo' in I. M. LAPIDUS, op. cit., and J. ABU-LUGHOD, 'The ecology of Cairo, Egypt: a comparative study using factor analysis', unpubl. Ph.D. thesis, Univ. of Massachusetts (1966)
20. Most of the new suburbs built to house Kuwaitis contained a neighbourhood shopping centre. There were no co-operatively operated supermarkets outside these centres.

RÉSUMÉ. *La ségrégation au Koweit.* Il se produit au Koweit une ségrégation résidentielle marquée entre citoyens et immigrants et c'est un fait particulièrement marqué à Koweit-Cité. Vue la pression constante sur les excellents services sanitaires et sociaux et sur l'éducation, le gouvernement a été forcé de donner préférence aux citoyens (les Koweitis) par opposition aux non-Koweitis (les immigrants). De plus, les lois sur l'emploi forcent les employeurs de façon explicite à donner préférence à la population indigène à tous les niveaux de l'emploi. Les Koweitis, quoique minoritaires, restent cependant la force dominante du gouvernement et de l'administration. Ils disposent de salaires et de traitements plus élevés et ils se réservé l'exclusivité de certains quartiers de la ville pour en faire leur zônes résidentielles. Ils se distinguent par le processus de leurs déplacements quotidiens et par leurs caractéristiques socio-démographiques qui sont en contraste très net avec ceux de la population immigrante. Les non-Koweitis ne sont pas un groupe homogène mais viennent de nationalités diverses ayant des attributs socio-économiques et démographiques dont on peut se servir pour diviser le groupe en sous-classes par l'analyse factorielle. Certains résultats d'une étude originale des trajets d'approvisionnement parmi les sous-groupes montrent comment les communautés vivent en cellules semi-indépendantes à l'intérieur de l'ensemble de la structure urbaine. On a dressé des parallèles entre ségrégation résidence et activité au Koweit, d'une part, et d'autres zones ou il a été observé des dichotomies semblables, d'autre part. On a émis la suggestion qu'un accroissement rapide de la population puisse être un facteur important pour empêcher l'absorption d'un sous-groupe en communauté par un autre.

FIG. 1. Composition par âges de la population, Koweitis et non-Koweitis en 1957 et 1965. Les parties complètement noires indiquent l'endroit où le chiffre des pourcentages de 1957 était plus important que celui de 1965. La pyramide de 1957 pour les Koweitis fournit une preuve évidente de l'enregistrement eronné de l'âge dans le groupe des gens âgés de plus de 70 ans.

FIG. 2. Distribution de la population du Koweit en 1970. On définit Koweit-Cité, avec une population de 456 562, comme l'étendue continue de constructions comprises à l'intérieur de la 4ᵉ rocade. La capitale du gouvernement comme circonscription administrative n'est pas une division satisfaisante du point de vue géographique car elle exclut, par example, les faubourgs de Hawalli et de Salimiya et elle comprend des centres éloignés comme Jahra et Dawha.

FIG. 3. Cette perspective aérienne de la Vieille Ville en 1951 nous offre un portrait de la cité qui n'est guère différent de celui que nous en a fait Lorimer au début du siècle. Le palais du souverain, donnant sur la mer, domine les grandes jetées. On peut distinguer la direction des passages couverts du *Suq* qui, en quittant le palais, s'éloignent de la mer pour déboucher sur la petite place en ovale—la place Safat. Seuls les cimetières rompent la structure cellulaire, étroitement serrée, de la cité à l'intérieur du mur d'enceinte.

FIG. 4. La Vieille Ville en 1967 a été transformée par la construction de larges routes à deux chaussées et de hauts bâtiments municipaux qui ont remplacé les maisons sans étage. De nouveaux centres commerciaux ont été introduits entre le vieux *Suq* et le port des dhaws; à l'ouest de la place Safat les additions les plus importantes sont le parc municipal, situé sur l'emplacement d'un ancien cimetière, et le «cañon» de hauts immeubles et magasins de la rue Fahad as-Salim.

FIG. 5. Distribution du facteur 1

FIG. 6. Distribution du facteur 2

FIG. 7. Distribution du facteur 3

FIG. 8. On voit ici la rue Fahad as-Salim qui va dans la direction nord-est vers le *Suq*. Cette rue a été construite surtout pour donner un air de modernité à la Vieille Ville. Ses magasins, bien qu'ils se louent à meilleur marché que certains établissements fort estimés au *Suq*, vendent pour la plupart des objets de luxe comme, par exemple, des appareils électriques, des accessoires photographiques et des vêtements coûteux.

FIG. 9. Le *Suq* reste toujours le centre du petit commerce de Koweït. Les produits qui s'y vendent et la disposition des magasins visent un marché «traditionnel». La plupart des femmes qui font leur marché au *Suq* portent toujours le voile.

ZUSAMMENFASSUNG. *Bevölkerungstrennung in Kuwait.* In Kuwait besteht eine klare Trennung der Wohngebiete der eingeborenen Bevölkerung und der Einwanderer, und dies zeigt sich besonders deutlich in Kuwait-Stadt. Die ständig zunehmende Belastung der ausgezeichneten Gesundheits- Wohlfahrts- und Erziehungseinrichtungen zwangen die Regierung, der eingeborenen Bevölkerung (Kuwaitis) grössere Vorzüge einzuräumen als den Nicht-Kuwaitis (Einwanderern). Zusätzlich zwingen die Arbeitsgesetzen die Arbeitgeber ausdrücklich, die eingeborene Bevölkerung auf allen Beschäftigungsstufen zu bevorzugen. Die Kuwaitis bleiben auch weiterhin, obwohl sie in der Minderheit sind, die herrschende Macht in der Regierung und Verwaltung. Sie beziehen höhere Gehälter und Löhne und haben bestimmte, für sie freigemachte Viertel der Stadt als exklusive Wohngebiete. Die Orte, zwischen denen sie täglich verkehren und ihre sozio-demograpischen Kennzeichen sind eindeutig festgelegt und unterscheiden sich grundsätzlich von denen der eingewanderten Bevölkerung. Die Nicht-Kuwaitis sind keine einheitliche Gruppe, sondern bestehen aus einer Vielzahl von Nationalitäten, deren sozio-wirtschaftliche demographische Eigenschaften dazu dienen können, um die Gruppe in Untergruppen mittels der Faktoranalyse einzuteilen. Einige Ergebnisse einer ursprünglichen Untersuchung von Einkaufsgewohnheiten der Untergruppen zeigen, dass diese Gemeinden als zum Teil unabhängige Zellen innerhalb der städtischen Gesamtstruktur funktionieren. Es werden Parallelen gezogen zwischen der Trennung der Wohngebiete und alltäglicher Tätigkeiten in Kuwait und anderen Gebieten, wo eine ähnliche Dichotomie beobachtet wurde. Es wird die These aufgestellt, dass der rapide Bevölkerungszuwachs eine wichtiger Faktor ist, der das Aufgehen einer Untergruppe oder Gemeinde in der anderen verhindert.

ABB. 1. Bevölkerungspyramiden für Kuwaitis und Nicht-Kuwaitis 1957 und 1965. Die völlig schwarzen Teile zeigen, wo die Prozentzahl für 1957 grösser war als für 1965. Die Kuwaiti Pyramide von 1957 zeigt ganz klar, dass Alter in der Gruppe der Über-Siebzig-Jährigen falsch aufgezeichnet wurde.

ABB. 2. Die Verteilung der Bevölkerung von Kuwait 1970. Kuwait-Stadt, mit einer Bevölkerung von 456 562, wird als kontinuierlich bebautes Gelände innerhalb der vierten Ringstrasse definiert. Die Einteilung in Verwaltungsbezirke durch die Zentralregierung ist für geographische Zwecke nicht befriedigend, denn sie schliesst zum Beispiel die Vorstädte Hawalli und Salimiya aus und umfasst Aussenbezirke wie Jahra und Dawha.

ABB. 3. Dieses Luftbild der Altstadt im Jahre 1951 zeigt die Stadt so wie sie Lorimer zu Beginn dieses Jahrhunderts beschrieb. Der Fürstenpalast liegt am Wasser mit dem Blick auf die vorspringenden Landungsstege; und die überdachten Gassen des *Suq* lassen sich vom Palast bis zu der kleineren ovalen offenen Fläche verfolgen, die der Safat Platz ist. Nur die offenen Flächen der Friedhöfe durchbrechen die dicht gedrängte zellenartige Struktur der Stadt innerhalb der einschliessenden Mauer.

ABB. 4. Im Jahre 1967 war die Altstadt verändert durch den Bau von breiten zweibahnigen Schnellstrassen und dem Verschwinden von einstöckigen Häusern zugunsten von höheren öffentlichen Gebäuden. Neue Geschäftszentren sind zwischen dem alten *Suq* und dem Dauhafen entstanden, während westlich des Safat Platzes die hervorragendsten Veränderungen der öffentliche Park, der einen älteren Friedhof verdrängte, und die Flucht von hohen Apartment-häusern und Geschäften, die Fahad as- Salim Strasse sind.

ABB. 5. Die Verteilung des ersten Faktors

ABB. 6. Die Verteilung von Faktor 2

ABB. 7. Die Verteilung von Faktor 3

ABB. 8. Die Fahad as- Salim Strasse hier mit dem Blick nordöstlich nach dem *Suq* wurde bewusst angelegt, um das Bild der Altstadt zu modernisieren. Ihre Geschäfte verkaufen, obwohl ihre Mieten nicht so hoch wie einige teure Positionen im *Suq* sind, zum grössten Teil Luxusartikel wie elektrische Geräte, photographisches Zubehör und teure Kleidung.

ABB. 9. Der *Suq* ist das Zentrum des Kleinhandels von Kuwait geblieben. Seine Verkaufsartikel und die Art der Geschäfte halten sich an die Formen des traditionellen Marktes. Die meisten weiblichen Kunden des *Suq* tragen den Schleier.

Residential differentiation in major New Zealand urban areas: a comparative factorial ecology

R. J. JOHNSTON

Reader in Geography, University of Canterbury, Christchurch, New Zealand

Revised MS received 12 May 1972

ABSTRACT. Factorial ecologies, usually principal components analyses of large data matrices, have been extensively used in recent years to test Shevky and Bell's deductive model of residential differentiation within cities. Few detailed comparative studies of different urban areas, however, have been conducted. This paper uses a comparative methodology for the factorial ecologies of the four main urban areas in New Zealand. Analyses are conducted for the total data matrix and also for separate matrices representing the separate dimensions of the Shevky-Bell model. In general, the main dimensions are as hypothesized, except for considerable variations between places in the distributions of various ethnic minorities. Certain sub-dimensions of the two major axes of differentiation were identifiable.

SOCIAL area analysis (E. Shevky and M. Williams, 1949; Shevky and W. Bell, 1955) was initially devised as a model of social change with relevance to the patterns of differentiation in the population characteristics of urban neighbourhoods. It postulated three separate dimensions to these patterns: one of social rank (or economic status), by which people were spatially segregated according to occupation, income and education (the three usual indices of socio-economic status); one of urbanization (or family status), which produced spatial clustering of groups who had chosen certain life styles; and one of segregation (or ethnic status), which suggested that members of certain minority groups tend to live apart from their host society. The relationships between the theory of social change and residential patterns have been the subject of considerable debate,[1] though links between the two have been suggested by F. L. Jones (1968) and D. W. G. Timms (1971) among others (for a review, see R. J. Johnston, 1971a). However, the empirical validity of the scheme has been demonstrated for many cities throughout the 'developed' world (Jones, 1969; reviews are given in J. L. Abu-Lughod, 1969 and P. H. Rees, 1971). Dimensions, generally termed socio-economic status, family status and, where relevant, ethnic status, have been reported from most studies of this phenomenon of intra-urban areal differentiation of population and housing characteristics, though little has been done in the way of truly comparative inter-urban studies.

Much of the empirical testing of Shevky and Bell's initial model has been carried out with the family of techniques generally known as factor analysis. This has led to the term 'factorial ecology' (F. L. Sweetser, 1965) replacing the original 'social area analysis', though Rees (1971) has given the new methodology a broader definition. Recently, B. J. L. Berry and Rees (1969) have suggested that there are two ways in which factorial ecology may be used to test the postulates of social area analysis: the first (*sensu stricto*) analyses

143

a data matrix whose variables conform very closely to the six or seven used in the studies by Shevky and his associates;[2] the second (*sensu lato*) factor analyses a data matrix containing a much wider range of variables relating to neighbourhood population and dwelling characteristics. This latter method has the advantage over the former in that it does not *assume* that three dimensions are sufficient to describe the patterns of residential differentiation in an urban area: instead it *tests* whether this is in fact so. (Indeed, the first factorial ecology of this latter type (T. R. Anderson and L. L. Bean, 1961) suggested that the family status dimension should be split into two sub-dimensions.)

The techniques used in factorial ecology permit a wide range of approaches, some of which are reflected in the literature (see A. A. Hunter, 1972). For example, Bell (1955) employed the hypothesis-testing methods (see also D. W. G. Timms, 1970), but most works in recent years have preferred the less demanding principal components and principal factor methods (despite the usual problem of assuming that the dimensions are both separate and statistically independent: see Johnston, 1971b).[3] Methods are also available for comparing the dimensional patterns in different places, but have not been much used. Most investigators prefer 'eyeball' comparisons, even between the results of ten factorial ecologies (M. D. van Arsdol Jr., S. F. Camilleri and C. F. Schmid, 1958). Both Sweetser (1969) and Timms (1970) have used congruence coefficients to compare pairs of factors between places, but no comparisons of total structures have been reported.[4]

The aim of the present paper is to provide comparative analyses of the dimensions of residential patterns in New Zealand's four major urban areas. Factorial ecology *sensu lato* is employed, so that this report complements that by Timms (1970) which discussed factorial ecologies *sensu stricto* for the same places.[5] The approach used here is preferred because there is evidence that the three Shevky-Bell dimensions are often insufficient to describe all of the residential differentiation, and that rather than being statistically independent, these dimensions are more likely to be complexly inter-related (Johnston, 1971b). Factorial ecology *sensu lato* better allows exploration of these possibilities. In detail, a methodology pioneered by Jones (1969) is employed, in which the data matrix is disaggregated according to the Shevky-Bell model as well as being looked at in total. This allows hypotheses to be posed in the form of the following questions:

(1) Are the factorial ecologies of the main urban areas of New Zealand comparable?

(2) Are there the same single dimensions of socio-economic, family, and minority group status within each urban area?

(3) Is a similar typology of residential districts produced from these dimensions for each place?

As Jones has pointed out, 'There is no suggestion that social reality is uniquely and exhaustively explained by these three dimensions above' (1969, 25), though the accumulation of completed studies on this topic allows a general assumption that they should exist. A major problem in testing the three-dimensional model, however, has always been that it is difficult to obtain measures, or indicants, which adequately represent the theoretical constructs of socio-economic, family, and ethnic status (Timms, 1971). The *sensu stricto* approach of the social area analysts uses a small number of variables, which may not exhaustively cover all aspects of areal differentiation in residential patterns. Alternatively, the large data matrices used, for example, by R. A. Murdie (1969) often create many problems of interpretation. By splitting the data matrix into various sections, *as well as* looking at the total matrix, it is easier to investigate whether the expected pattern of one single axis of differentiation representing each of the postulated dimensions is indeed valid. The succeeding analyses of the total data matrix then allow the inter-dependencies among these dimensions in the total residential structure to be studied separately.

THE NEW ZEALAND URBAN SCENE

New Zealand's welfare state system is well known and the egalitarian nature of its society is often remarked upon. Indeed, income differentials are relatively slight (C. Vellekoop, 1969), though expanding. But there is, nevertheless, a social stratification, reflected in occupational, educational and income differences, as in most countries; in turn this stratification is reflected in patterns of residential differentiation. Elite neighbourhoods are clearly recognizable (A. Aburn, 1971; Johnston, 1969; T. G. McGee, 1969), and there are low income areas of several types; inner city 'near-slums'; State housing areas, provided for families earning less than a certain income;[6] and low-cost private developments financed by cheap government loans to people with low incomes (Johnston, 1972). Between these extremes are the middle income suburbs of various prestige levels (Johnston, 1971c). As well as clear residential differences in socio–economic status, there are also patterns which apparently conform to the Shevky-Bell family status dimension. Family-centred living is generally associated with home ownership and low density housing, so that households practising this style of life tend to live in different areas from the flat-renting, non-family oriented groups. Age-groups, too, are considerably separated (P. H. Curson, 1967) because of the State's encouragement of young families to build new homes. There is also some difficulty of transferring State mortgages, so that suburban households (especially those in the middle income brackets and below) tend to be relatively immobile, often building extra rooms on to their existing homes rather than moving to larger ones (Johnston, 1972).[7]

Apart from these two major dimensions of the Shevky and Bell model, the minority group component is also applicable to New Zealand. Although not as much a 'melting-pot' for many cultures as its Australian neighbour (S. Lieberson, 1963; Jones, 1967), New Zealand has been the destination for several migration streams from Europe (K. Thomson and A. D. Trlin, 1970 gives a good introduction). Members of these streams have often formed very tight clusters within the urban areas (I. H. Burnley, 1972). In addition, there has been a massive movement of the indigenous Maori to the cities in recent decades (M. F. Poulsen and Johnston, 1972; D. T. Rowland, 1971, 1972), and considerable migration of Polynesian islanders to the country's cities, especially to Auckland (Curson, 1970).

SOURCES OF DATA

The New Zealand urban scene therefore offers a satisfactory laboratory for testing the Shevky-Bell model via comparative factorial ecologies. Unfortunately, no data are available for the very small census districts (usually termed census tracts) which are common in many other countries but, for several decades, data have been published for a series of sub-divisions of local government areas in the main centres. Thus Auckland City and Mt Eden, Mt Roskill and Mt Wellington Boroughs are subdivided for the Auckland Urban Area: in the other four—Wellington, Hutt, Christchurch, and Dunedin—the major city only is subdivided. These districts contain only 39·7 per cent of Auckland's

TABLE I

Characteristics of New Zealand's four main urban areas

	Auckland	Wellington-Hutt	Christchurch	Dunedin
Population 1966	548 293	282 487	247 248	108 734
No. of districts in study	61	59	38	27
Size range of districts	650 to 23 098	282 to 22 190	1105 to 17 812	234 to 8997
Population excluded from study	102 690	5354	50 539	5832
Number of Maoris	33 926	10 500	2837	647
Number of Polynesians	16 057	4262	848	212

total population (Table I), 69·5 per cent of Dunedin's, 65·3 per cent of Christchurch's, and 62·7 per cent of Wellington-Hutt's (the two latter areas adjoin each other and function as a single unit, so they have been combined here). But, in addition, because of the fragmented local government framework in New Zealand, it is possible to get almost complete coverage by small areal units for the remainder of Dunedin and Wellington-Hutt. Both Auckland and Christchurch contain large counties which are not subdivided, however, and these have been omitted to avoid bias;[8] this should not detract too much from the findings since residential differentiation patterns ought not to be significantly affected by the omission of parts of the city. (Sweetser's (1969) factorial ecologies of the various zones and sectors of Boston and Helsinki support this argument.)

Apart from this question of coverage, the nature of the areal units is not ideal. They vary considerably in size (Table I), and were not designed to conform to the social realities of the cities. Nevertheless, a pattern of residential differentiation should emerge, as factorial ecologies by Timms (1970) and R. A. Bowman and P. L. Hosking (1971) have shown, which is sufficient for answering the questions posed here.

The 1966 census data for these districts cover age, sex, marital status, race, religion, occupational status, occupation, industry, income, house type, house tenure and household amenities, with the first three cross-classified. From these, eighty-two variables have been selected. Some of them are virtually duplicates of others; some have little direct relevance to the Shevky-Bell model, and are introduced largely for exploratory purposes. Such an approach is valid on the grounds that we still lack indicants which are unequivocally related to the constructs, so the use of many variables can assist the search for 'ideal' representatives (which probably will be specific to each cultural situation). Use of duplicate variables will not influence the type of analysis attempted here, which is focused on the nature of the dimensions and their comparability over four places. No attempt is made to order components in terms of their importance, since this clearly is strongly influenced by the selection of variables, nor is the size of the components, as indicated by eigenvalues, a salient element in determining how many dimensions to extract.

The eighty-two variables have been placed in the following four groups for separate study (see Appendix I for the full list):

(1) Socio-economic status. Separate occupational status, occupation, and income data for males and females give many of the usual measures of this concept.

(2) Family status. Most of the thirty-three in this group are directly relevant to the Shevky and Bell construct, having been used in other studies, and cover age, sex, marital status, and work force participation among the population, plus housing type and tenure.

(3) Migrants and minority groups. Only the census data on race give direct information for this concept, and these refer to Maoris, Polynesians, Indians and Chinese. Since minority groups are often associated with certain religions, however (O. D. Duncan, 1959; R. A. Murdie, 1969), membership figures for the main denominations have also been included in this group.

(4) Housing conditions. Eight variables are in this group. Cases could be made for their inclusion in either of the first two groups—the higher a household's income the better its housing is likely to be—but, because of the State housing policy, young families are also likely to live in new, good-standard homes. Hence these variables are separately analysed in the first part of the study.

Following many other factorial ecologies *sensu lato*, principal components analysis has been applied to each of the five data matrices for each urban area (R. J. Rummel, 1967, provides a lucid introduction to the method). In the decision on how many components to extract, the major criterion was interpretability of the patterns of loadings after rotation (using the varimax criterion). This procedure was adopted rather than more usual methods, such as R. B. Cattell's (1966) scree test, because of the inclusion of duplicate variables. No component whose squared loadings summed to less than 1·0 was extracted, since this would indicate a dimension accounting for less of the total variation in the spatial pattern than did one variable in the original data matrix.

Testing whether single dimensions occur in each of the four disaggregated data matrices simply involves the percentage of the total variation subsumed by the first component. Following this, since in virtually every matrix (with the exception of the housing conditions set) it was clear that a single dimension did not exist, the component structures were rotated by the varimax criterion to provide a better fit to the 'groups' of variables in the component space and thereby aid interpretation. No single general dimension was expected in the total data matrix.

After the extraction, rotation and identification of each set of components,[9] two sets of comparative statistics were obtained. The first were used to investigate whether dimensions of the same size existed in each matrix in each of the four places. These were the *sums of squared component loadings* for every component, which are the equivalents of the eigenvalues for the unrotated components. If the patterns are the same in each place, then each should have a similar set of summed loadings.

The second set of statistics is used to compare the size of the individual loadings in the relevant analyses for each place, one pair of places at a time. Two approaches are used. In the first, individual components are compared using a coefficient of congruence (H. H. Harman, 1966), a method also employed by Sweetser (1969) and Timms (1970). This coefficient takes into account both absolute and relative sizes of the loadings for each of the variables. Components are studied in isolation from the total factorial structures of which they are part, so that one might compare the loadings of each variable on a socio-economic status component for Christchurch, for example, with loadings for the same variables on a similar component for Dunedin, irrespective of their loadings on other components.

In the second method, developed by H. F. Kaiser and outlined by D. J. Veldman (1967), the complete factorial structures are compared. One set of components (say for socio-economic status in Dunedin) is rotated to its best-fitting position with another set (for socio-economic status in Christchurch, perhaps), and the new component loadings ('new Dunedin') are compared with those for the same variables on the other (Christchurch). Two elements of the output are relevant: (1) a matrix of cosines among components in the two structures, which indicate the degree of similarity between them prior to rotation; the larger the cosine, the smaller the angle, and so the closer the fit. The whole matrix of cosines shows the total fit, within the constraints of orthogonality. (2) A vector of test correlations comparing the loadings of each variable across all components in the two matrices (Christchurch and 'new' Dunedin). The larger the correlation, the closer the fit, so low correlations indicate variables with different patterns of loadings in the two places.

Output from these analyses is considerable, so most of it is only summarized here. Coefficients have been categorized into four groups: greater than 0·9 (very close fits); between 0·7 and 0·9 (close fits); between 0·5 and 0·7 (poor fits); and less than 0·5 (no fit).

Finally, the third question formulated in the introduction referred to types of neighbourhood, suggesting that similar typological bases should apply in each place. Typologies were produced for each place in the following way. Orthogonal component scores for the various observations were computed from the factorial ecologies using the total data matrices. The similarity between each pair of areas was then computed using Pythagoras's theorem in the *n*-dimensional space (where *n* equals the number of components). Classification was achieved through applying McQuitty's iterative inter-columnar correlational analysis algorithm (L. L. McQuitty and J. A. Clark, 1968; Johnston, 1971c gives a brief description of this technique).

THE PARTIAL FACTORIAL STRUCTURES

Socio-economic status

Initial analyses indicated that the hypothesis of a single socio-economic status dimension in each place was clearly invalid, since the first component never accounted for more than 41 per cent of the variation in the spatial patterns of the thirty-three variables (Table II). After experimentation, five components were then extracted for rotation: the sizes of the components were generally comparable between the four places, except in the case of Wellington-Hutt.

These data suggest that there is no single component of socio-economic status in the residential patterns in each place, but rather a more complex pattern of neighbourhood differentiation. As in Jones's (1969) analysis of Melbourne, however, identification of the components indicates that the minor dimensions do not in fact contradict the generally held view of a single socio-economic structure. The first component in each place clearly reflects this construct, loading strongly on the high income, professional and administrative occupations (variables 1, 2, 9, 10, 11, 27 and 28: see Appendix for full identification of variables).

The brief descriptions of the other components in Table III suggest similar patterns in each place. In three of them, there is an urban fringe component, identifying areas with high proportions of farmers, and resulting from the interdigitation of urban and rural land within the defined urban areas. Clearly, this results from a feature of the data source and should not be used to invalidate the hypothesis.

A further minor component, identified in all centres, has been named 'unemployment'; it has its highest loadings on the unemployment males and male low-income variables. This suggests that unemployment and low incomes are not related to the socio-economic

TABLE II
Component sizes (sums of squared rotated component loadings)[1]

Socio-economic status—thirty-three variables

Component	I	II	III	IV	V	
Auckland	11·9	7·1	3·2	2·3	2·0	(39)
Wellington-Hutt	7·7	5·9	5·7	2·7	1·9	(31)
Christchurch	11·8	6·4	3·8	2·5	2·2	(37)
Dunedin	11·4	6·2	2·9	2·9	2·8	(35)

Family status—thirty-three variables

Component	I	II	III	IV	V	
Auckland	13·8	6·2	3·8	1·4	1·4	(56)
Wellington-Hutt	11·0	5·2	4·9	2·9	2·6	(50)
Christchurch	12·8	5·7	4·1	1·9	1·8	(50)
Dunedin	9·0	5·9	5·4	5·0	2·2	(51)

Migrants and minority groups—eight variables

Component	I	II	III	
Auckland	4·2	1·1	1·1	(54)
Wellington-Hutt	2·5	1·9	1·4	(46)
Christchurch	2·3	1·8	1·7	(39)
Dunedin	2·5	1·7	1·6	(36)

Housing conditions—eight variables

Component	I	II	
Auckland	5·8	1·4	(80)
Wellington-Hutt	4·8	1·4	(65)
Christchurch	5·7	1·4	(76)
Dunedin	6·0	1·2	(74)

All variables—eighty-two variables

Component	I	II	III	IV	
Auckland	28·8	17·9	7·2	5·9	(39)
Wellington-Hutt	24·7	13·1	8·1	6·6	(31)
Christchurch	29·8	16·0	9·1	5·6	(37)
Dunedin	24·9	15·9	12·9	5·6	(35)

[1] Figures in parentheses indicate the percentage of the total variation accounted for by the first, *unrotated*, component.

status construct. Maps of the component scores indicated otherwise, however, since the areas with high unemployment rates virtually all fell in the central parts of the cities, where socio-economic levels are generally low. This suggests a non-linear relationship between the socio-economic status and unemployment constructs (Johnston, 1970, terms these 'triangular relationships'); this has the form that all high unemployment areas are low socio-economic status areas, but all low socio-economic status areas do not have high unemployment levels, unemployment being low in the suburban low status districts. The unemployment dimension can thus be interpreted as a sub-dimension of socio-economic status (Johnston, 1971b).

Most of the other minor components can also be interpreted as sub-dimensions rather than as independent constructs. Some, such as the female professional components identified in all four centres and the unemployed females component in Christchurch (Table III), might be more meaningfully interpreted as sub-dimensions of a general family status construct. This would take the following form: (1) All districts with high pro-

TABLE III
Brief component identifications

	Auckland	Wellington-Hutt	Christchurch	Dunedin
Partial factorial structures				
Socio-economic status				
I General S.E.S.	General S.E.S.	General S.E.S.	General S.E.S.
II Urban fringe	Female professionals	Urban fringe	Urban fringe
III Unemployment	Unemployment	Unemployment	Unemployment
IV Female professionals	Upper middle class	Female professionals	Female professionals
V Female middle class	Female lower class	Unemployed females	Female middle class
Family status				
I Non-familism	Non-familism	Non-familism	Non-familism
II Old and young	Old and young	Old and young	Older families
III Older families	Older families	Sex ratios	Old and young
IV Sex ratios	Sex ratios	Fertility	Sex ratios
V Fertility	Rental areas	Student flats	Fertility
Migrants and minority groups				
I Maoris-Polynesians-Indians	Polynesians	Maoris-R.C.	Maoris-Chinese
II Methodists	Chinese	Chinese	Maoris-Polynesians
III Chinese	Maoris-R.C.	Polynesians	Indians
Housing conditions				
I General	General	General	General
II Sanitary conditions	Sanitary conditions	Sanitary conditions	Sanitary conditions
Total factorial structures				
I Non-familism	Non-familism	Non-familism	Non-familism
II General S.E.S.	General S.E.S.	General S.E.S.	General S.E.S.
III Urban fringe	Old-young	Old-young	Minorities
IV Old-young	Sex ratios	Minorities	Old-young

portions of employed females in professional occupations also have high rates of female participation in the workforce. But (2), all districts with such high rates of female participation do not also have high proportions in professional occupations. Hence the female professional construct is a sub-dimension of a general urbanization construct (as is also the female unemployment dimension in Christchurch).

Apart from the major socio-economic status dimension, therefore, each of the four main centres in New Zealand also contained several sub-dimensions related to this general construct in its residential patterns. This is, to a considerable extent, a function of the use of a much wider number of variables than in the factorial ecologies *sensu stricto*. The results of studies which employ the *sensu lato* approach often suggest a complex pattern of *independent* dimensions to researchers. Closer investigation, however, suggests that the true situation is of several sub-dimensions related to the major construct, and the use of techniques which allow identification of this pattern gives a fuller picture of the social patterning of the city than does the more restricted approach using fewer variables.[10]

In comparing the four factorial structures, considerable conformity was suggested. Matching one five-component structure with another gives a matrix of twenty-five coefficients: if the structures are very similar, five of these twenty-five should indicate good

TABLE IV
Comparative partial factorial structures: congruence coefficients

Size of coefficient	Comparison					
	A-WH	A-C	A-D	WH-C	WH-D	C-D
Socio-economic status—five components						
>0.9		1	1		1	
0.7—0.89	3	2	2	2		2
0.5—0.69	1	1	1	3	3	1
<0.5	21	21	21	21	21	22
Family status—five components						
>0.9	1	1	1	3	2	2
0.7—0.89	4	4	3	1	2	1
0.5—0.69	2	1	6	3	7	7
<0.5	18	19	15	18	14	15
Migrants and minority groups—three components						
>0.9				1		
0.7—0.89	3	2	2	1	1	2
0.5—0.69		2	3	3	3	1
<0.5	6	5	4	4	5	6
Housing conditions—two components						
>0.9	2	2	1	1	2	1
0.7—0.89			1	1		1
0.5—0.69	2	2	1	2		
<0.5			1		2	2

Key to centres: A—Auckland; WH—Wellington-Hutt; C—Christchurch; D—Dunedin

fits, and the other twenty coefficients should be very small. The congruence coefficient matrices, comparing one pair of components at a time, came fairly close to this ideal state (Table IV), although in no comparison were there five coefficients of 0·7 or greater, and in only one were there five greater than 0·5. This suggests considerable concordance on the major dimension, and perhaps some of the others, but minor dimensions were more place-particular. Comparisons of the total factorial structures using the Kaiser-Veldman method confirm this, especially those involving Dunedin (Table V). Some total fits were very good, producing high cosine values and high test correlations for most variables (note especially Auckland/Wellington-Hutt and Auckland/Christchurch), but in others (for example, Wellington-Hutt/Dunedin) the overall fit was clearly not very good. Table VIA, which shows the values of the test correlations for each variable over the six comparisons, indicates that the bad fits were largely related to the minor dimensions: low correlations were most frequent for variables 21 (female transport workers), 2 (self-employed males), 23 (female service workers) and 5 (female employers), none of which had high loadings on any of the principal, general socio-economic status, components.

Family status

Principal components analyses of the four data matrices containing this group of thirty-three variables again suggested the absence of any single dimension with about 50 per cent

TABLE V

Comparative partial factorial structures: rotation analyses

| | Comparison | | | | | | | | | | |
Size of Coefficient	A-WH (A)	(B)	A-C (A)	(B)	A-D (A)	(B)	WH-C (A)	(B)	WH-D (A)	(B)	C-D (A)	(B)
Socio-economic status—five components—thirty-three variables												
>0·9	1	16	3	16	1	17		7		5	1	12
0·7—0·89	4	12	2	11	1	7	4	11	4	18	1	13
0·5—0·69		4		4	8	7	4	11	2	4	6	2
<0·5	20	1	20	2	15	6	17	4	19	6	17	6
Family status—five components—thirty-three variables												
>0·9	1	26	2	23	1	17	1	16	1	15	3	15
0·7—0·89	3	4	3	4	2	10	2	9	2	11	1	13
0·5—0·69	3	1	3	6	5	4	1	4	6	3	3	2
<0·5	18	2	17		17	2	21	4	16	4	18	3
Migrants and minority groups—three components—eight variables												
>0·9		4	3	4	3	3	2			2		3
0·7—0·89	2	3		3	2	3		4	2	2	2	3
0·5—0·69	3	1		1	5			2	5	3	3	1
<0·5	4			6	2	2		6	2	1	4	1
Housing conditions—two components—eight variables												
>0·9	2	8	2	8	2	6	2	7	2	7	2	8
0·7—0·89						2		1		1		
0·5—0·69												
<0·5	2		2		2		2		2		2	

Column (A) gives the values of the rotation cosines, (B) gives the sizes of the variable fits.

of the total variation subsumed by the first, unrotated, component (Table II). Five rotated components were identified.

Several other factorial ecologies (Anderson and Bean, 1961; Sweetser, 1969; Jones, 1969; see also Berry and Rees, 1969) have suggested that the family status dimension might be split into two parts, one of which represents the Shevky-Bell urbanization construct (the familism/non-familism life style dichotomy), whereas the other usually has high loadings on certain age groups or on a fertility measure (Sweetser, 1969, termed such a component 'progeniture'). Again it might be suggested that these are two separate, but not independent, dimensions of the residential pattern. All districts with high fertility, for example, would be in the familism life style parts of the city, but not all districts with high familism need have high fertility rates (since fertility is usually measured by an age-specific ratio, such as the children 0–4/women 15–44 ratio used here (M.G.A. Wilson, 1971), and the average New Zealand housewife has had her last child by the time she is 29 (M. Gilson, 1970).

Table III shows that two of the five components identified in the New Zealand cities refer to these related dimensions. In all cases the largest conforms to the Shevky-Bell construct, with high positive loadings on the proportions of working females, of single adults, of separated and divorced persons, of persons aged 21–24, of flats and of rented dwellings, and high negative loadings on the proportions of children, of owner-occupied

TABLE VIa
Comparative partial factorial ecologies : variable fits A

Variable	Size of coefficient				Variable	Size of coefficient			
	>0·9	0·7—0·89	0·5—0·69	<0·5		>0·9	0·7—0·89	0·5—0·69	<0·5
Socio-economic status									
1	5	1			18	1	2	2	1
2			4	2	19	1	4		1
3	2	4			20	2	1	2	1
4	2	2	1	1	21		1		5
5	1	2		3	22	2	1	2	1
6	1	3	2		23		1	3	2
7	1	5			24	3	2	1	
8		2	4		25	4	2		
9	6				26	4	2		
10	5	1			27	3	3		
11	2	3	4		28	4	2		
12	3	1	2		29		3	3	
13		3	1	2	30		4	1	1
14	1	3	1	1	31	3	2	1	
15	6				32	6			
16		5	1		33	3	3		
17	3	3							
Migrants and minority groups									
1	1	4	1		5	1	2		3
2	3	1	2		6	2	2	2	
3	1	3	1	1	7	4	2		
4	3	3			8	3	1	1	1

homes, and of dependants. (It is the larger, of course, only as a result of the configuration of input variables.) The other, the second component in all but Dunedin, where it was third, contrasted areas with different age structures, having high positive loadings for children, young adults and the holding of mortgages, and high negative loadings for the proportions of old people.

As with the previous group of variables, it can be suggested that most of the minor dimensions are in fact sub-dimensions of one of the first two, for the same reason (triangular relationships). For example, the third component in Auckland and Wellington-Hutt and the second in Dunedin was identified as 'older families'. Its highest loadings were for the 5-14, 35-44 and 45-54 age-groups, and inspection of the component scores showed the highest were identifying the older districts (mostly developed during the 1950s) within the larger suburban matrix of areas with high familism scores. Similarly, the sex ratio components suggest 'Skid-Row' type districts within the city centre; the rental areas component in Wellington-Hutt identifies areas of State Housing.[11] Note that the fertility in Christchurch had its highest scores in some of the lowest socio-economic status districts (but not all; hence the absence of a high loading for the fertility variables on the general socio-economic status component in the total factorial structure).

The comparative statistics indicate considerable similarity between the four places, except that Dunedin is a relative deviant. In five of the six comparisons, at least four congruence coefficients were greater than 0·7 (Table IV). Similarly in the rotation analyses, there were many large cosines (Table V) and close fits for most variables: only variables

TABLE VIb

Comparative partial factorial structures: variable fits B

Variable	Size of coefficient				Variable	Size of coefficient			
	>0.9	0.7—0.89	0.5—0.69	<0.5		>0.9	0.7—0.89	0.5—0.69	<0.5
	Family status								
1	6				17	2	1	2	1
2	6				18	6			
3	2	3		1	19	5	1		
4	1	2	2	1	20			2	4
5	2	4			21			3	3
6	4	2			22		4	2	
7	1	5			23	4	2		
8	1	2	3		24	6			
9	6				25	5	1		
10		6			26	5	1		
11	3		1	2	27	5	1		
12	3	3			28	4	1	1	
13		2	2	2	29	6			
14	2		2	1	30	2	4		
15	6				31	3	3		
16	4	2			32	6			
					33	6			
	Housing conditions								
1	6				5	6			
2	5	1			6	3	3		
3	6				7	6			
4	6				8	6			

20 (males of all widowed persons) and 21 (fertility) generally recorded either poor or no fit (Table VIb), though 13 and 14 (persons in the 21–24 and 25–34 age groups who were male), 17 (widowed persons) and 4 (persons aged 65+) recorded poor fits or worse in half of the comparisons. Of these, only the fertility measure is generally associated with the Shevky–Bell family status construct, and so the general conclusion of this section is of a high level of concordance between the four places on this set of variables.

Migrants and minority groups

In all four places, the first component in the unrotated solution for this eight-variable matrix accounted for a relatively small portion of the total variation. Only in Auckland was there evidence of a general minorities dimension, which also stands out in the rotated solution (Table II). The other three places had three separately identifiable components.

Identification of the rotated components also indicated considerable differences between the urban areas (Table III: in this Table, racial groups are mostly used to identify the components). In Auckland, for example, the first component represented a general racial dimension, with high positive loadings for Maoris, Polynesians and Indians, and also for Roman Catholics, and high negative loadings for Church of England adherents and Presbyterians. The other two components had single high loadings, for Methodists on II, and for Chinese on III.[12] The other three centres all had a component on which Maoris and Roman Catholics had high loadings in the same direction: in Wellington-Hutt and Christchurch these were contrasted with a high loading in the other direction for the proportion of Church of England adherents, but in Dunedin the contrast was with the proportion of Presbyterians (thereby reflecting the peculiar religious composition of the southern city, based on its Scottish origins (L. D. B. Heenan, 1967), and the probable relationship between this and the class structure). In Christchurch, Indians and Chinese loaded highly on the same component, contrasted with Presbyterians; in Wellington-Hutt, Indians and Polynesians were contrasted against Presbyterians and Roman Catholics on the one component; in Dunedin, Indians and Church of England adherents had high positive loadings on a third component which had no high negative loadings.

These interpretative differences are borne out by the comparative statistics. The congruence coefficients (Table IV) include only one close fit, while the considerable number of poor fits suggests much variation. The rotation cosines, too, were all relatively low (Table V), and there were few close fits among the test correlations for individual variables. Of the eight measures used, the proportion of Roman Catholics displayed the most consistent pattern of loadings (Table VIA), whereas the Church of England, Methodist and Indian measures were least stable.

The clearest conclusion to be drawn from this is that each of the four places has a virtually unique residential · pattern of racial and religious groups, the only common feature being the spatial associations between Maoris and Roman Catholics. Much of this must result from the varying sizes of the racial groups among the urban places (Table I). Auckland has by far the largest Maori and Polynesian populations (it has the largest Polynesian population of any city in the world), whereas Dunedin has few representatives of any of the four groups. The spatial association of three of the four groups in Auckland, however, should not be interpreted as definite evidence of a single racial dimension, because of the broad categories which have had to be employed and the relatively coarse areal units employed. Within the Polynesian population there is considerable separation of the various island communities (Curson, 1970); there is also separation between each of these groups and the indigenous Maori, and even among the various Maori caste (*sic*) groups (Trlin, 1971).

Housing conditions

Not surprisingly, there was much more indication of close spatial association among the members of this data matrix. The high percentages of variation accounted for by the first, unrotated components clearly suggest a single major dimension of housing conditions, except in Wellington-Hutt. However, in both unrotated and rotated solutions a second component was clearly identifiable, so two were extracted for each place. The first, general housing conditions, had high loadings for seven of the eight variables; the other had a single high loading, for the proportion of homes with exclusive use of a flush toilet, in each place.

Maps of the scores for each district on the first components indicated patterns whose dominant elements were an improvement in housing conditions away from the city centre. Similar maps for scores on the second components had their lowest values both in central city districts and in suburban areas with high proportions of State houses.[13] The comparative statistics (Table IV, V, VIA and VIB) all show good fits, except in two comparisons involving Dunedin and one for Christchurch; in each the variable involved was the proportion of homes with television.

Summary

With regard to these partial factorial structures, the answers to the first two questions formulated in the introduction to this paper are not unequivocal. It could be reasonably concluded there there is a single major socio-economic status component in every city, with all four of these very similar to each other, but each place has a number of sub-dimensions of the general construct, some of which are somewhat unlike those existing elsewhere. One component is much larger than any other in the family status matrices, though again there are several relevant, interpretable sub-dimensions: in this case, however, similarity between the four places is very high overall. For migrants and minority groups, patterns are much more varied and place-particular, but with housing conditions there is a simple pattern common to all four places.

In comparing the structures among the four places, the general impression is that Dunedin is relatively unlike the other three. In many cases, it was most like Christchurch, and since this latter place was quite often considerably different from Wellington-Hutt, this suggests a North Island-South Island dichotomy in factorial structures. (This is in line with Timms's finding (1970, p. 462), relating to socio-economic and family status only in the total ecological structure). In general terms, the degrees of association can be related to the nature of the places: Auckland is the largest city and the most cosmopolitan; Wellington-Hutt is both the political capital and an industrial centre; Christchurch is a large provincial city with considerable industry; Dunedin is a regional centre only, with a much narrower economic base. The farther apart two places are on this simple continuum, the more unlike are their factorial structures.

THE TOTAL FACTORIAL STRUCTURES

Considerable experimentation was carried out in exploring the total factorial ecology of each place. One method which provided interesting results involved the use of the findings from the partial factorial ecologies. The inputs for this were the orthogonal scores for the districts on each of the fifteen components identified in the previous analyses (five socio-economic status, five family status, three migrants and minority groups, and two housing conditions). Six components were extracted from each 15×15 matrix correlating these scores, and these accounted for 80 per cent of the variation in the Auckland matrix, 82 per cent for Christchurch, 90 per cent for Dunedin, and 78 per cent for Wellington-Hutt. Since the five socio-economic status components were completely unrelated to each other, as also was the case among the five family status components, these results suggest considerable association between components from the separate analyses. The 'new' component loadings confirmed this: each of the original components had a loading of at least 0·5 on one of the six components extracted in these second order analyses. Indeed of the sixty 'old' components (fifteen in each of the four places), forty-nine had 'new' loadings exceeding 0·7, and thirteen exceed 0·9.

In all four places, the original general socio-economic status and the Maori-Polynesian components loaded strongly on the same dimension, indicating that the low income earners and the ethnic minorities tend to concentrate in the same residential areas. Also loading highly on that dimension was the non-familism component, indicating that low socio-economic status and minorities were associated with rental housing areas that contain above-average proportions of unmarried young adults and working females.[14] No further general patterns could be discerned, however, as the search was hindered by the different identifications of the minor components in each place.

Description of the total structures

Since the input data were not strictly comparable, being based on separate factorial ecologies, it was not possible to compare the results of the above second-order analyses among the four places. Hence, further investigation was based on analyses of the full 82-variable data matrices. From these, a few components accounted for a large proportion of the variation: in each place, after rotation, the first encompassed 30–36 per cent of the total, and the second 16–22 per cent (Table II). The first four in Auckland, Christchurch and Dunedin accounted for just under 75 per cent, but in Wellington-Hutt for only two thirds.

After scrutiny of various solutions, it was decided to focus on only the first four principal components, thereby concentrating attention on the main elements of the residential patterns. This approach was supported by the earlier analyses of the disaggregated data matrices, which suggested that the Shevky-Bell model was largely validated with regard to the socio-economic and family status dimensions, though not the migrants and minorities. (It was expected that the housing conditions variables would be related to the other dimensions in a general analysis.) Various sub-dimensions of the socio-economic and family status axes of residential differentiation were identified in those analyses, but it must be stressed that almost certainly these were *sub-dimensions* and not completely independent axes. Hence it was decided to look only at the major patterns in the total data matrix, to inquire whether in fact the various theoretical dimensions are independent of each other in New Zealand's main urban areas.

Of the four components extracted, the first two were very similar in each place, with the partial exception of Dunedin. They were identified as follows:

(I) A bi-polar component with high loadings at one extreme on the proportions of children, dependants, young adults, mortgaged homes, household amenities (except flush toilets), males earning $2000–2999 a year, and females in clerical occupations. At the other extreme were high loadings on the proportions of flats, rented dwellings, unmarried persons, persons in their late 'teens and early 'twenties, and males earning low incomes. (Note that the former group of loadings were positive in Auckland and Dunedin, but negative in Christchurch and Wellington-Hutt; hence the signs on the coefficients in Tables VII and VIII.) This suggests a *non-familism, middle income* component, which clearly differentiates areas of non-family living in the central residential districts from the young, middle-income, family-oriented suburbs whose womenfolk work in offices.

(II) A further bi-polar component, identified as one of *general socio-economic status*. Its large positive loadings were for the higher status male occupations (9, 10 and 11: Appendix I), for high incomes, and for Church of England adherence. High negative loadings were recorded for low incomes and for low status occupations, excluding employment in service occupations and also unemployment, both of which variables had their highest loadings on the first components. In addition, there were high negative loadings on the proportions of Maoris and Polynesians in the Auckland and Wellington-Hutt matrices, indicating a relationship between socio-economic status and the residential patterns of minority groups in these places, but not the other two. Timms (1970, p. 459)

TABLE VII
Total factorial structures: congruence coefficients

Auckland	Wellington-Hutt				Auckland	Christchurch			
	I	II	III	IV		I	II	III	IV
I	−0·96	0·24	−0·12	−0·07	I	−0·97	−0·02	0·25	0·03
II	−0·22	0·93	0·35	−0·12	II	−0·21	0·89	−0·27	0·45
III	0·22	−0·26	0·40	0·52	III	0·31	0·05	0·04	0·44
IV	−0·41	−0·33	−0·55	0·24	IV	−0·29	−0·28	0·87	0·38

Auckland	Dunedin				Wellington-Hutt	Christchurch			
	I	II	III	IV		I	II	III	IV
I	0·84	−0·08	−0·72	0·19	I	0·94	0·01	−0·32	−0·07
II	0·13	0·74	−0·28	0·18	II	−0·24	0·78	−0·25	−0·51
III	−0·26	−0·19	0·23	0·29	III	0·18	0·49	−0·60	−0·16
IV	0·49	−0·37	−0·17	−0·43	IV	0·05	−0·05	0·09	0·43

Wellington-Hutt	Dunedin				Christchurch	Dunedin			
	I	II	III	IV		I	II	III	IV
I	−0·82	0·12	0·70	−0·17	I	−0·84	0·11	0·73	−0·18
II	0·15	0·74	−0·33	0·13	II	−0·11	0·74	−0·09	0·13
III	−0·35	0·27	0·07	0·58	III	0·48	−0·26	−0·18	−0·44
IV	−0·06	−0·38	0·08	0·29	IV	0·06	−0·57	0·10	−0·09

reached a similar conclusion from his multiple-group factorial ecologies. Correlations between the socio-economic and ethnic status factors were −0·703 in Auckland and Wellington, but only −0·510 in Christchurch and −0·263 in Dunedin. Timms (1970, p. 460) wrote that 'Given the greater numbers of Maoris and other Polynesians living in Auckland and Wellington, it might have been anticipated that it would be in these cities that ethnicity would form an independent axis of differentiation. The data, however, suggest otherwise'. An alternative interpretation could be based on the triangular relationship concept. Auckland and Wellington-Hutt have sufficient Maoris and Polynesians for these persons to be spread throughout the low socio-economic status areas: hence the absence of a separate minorities dimension. In Christchurch and Dunedin the groups are smaller, both relatively and absolutely, and concentrate in only some of the low socio-economic status districts.

Thus there is no strong correlation between the two as there is in the larger centres, because whereas all districts with high proportions of Maoris and Polynesians are all of low socio-economic status in Christchurch and Dunedin, not all of the lower status areas contain many Maoris or Polynesians. Hence, in these two centres, ethnic status is only a sub-dimension of socio-economic status.

The third and fourth components in each place did not conform as closely to those in the other three (Tables VII and VIII), though a second family-status dimension, which compared with the *young and old* components extracted in the partial analyses, was identified in each. In Christchurch, for example, this component had substantial positive loadings on the proportions of persons aged 0–4, 5–14 and 25–34, of properties being purchased on table mortgages,[15] and of persons per unit; substantial negative loadings were for proportions of persons aged 45–54 and 55–64, for the proportions of widowed persons, of owner-occupied properties, and of homes with exclusive use of flush toilets. Clearly, this component identifies suburbs of various ages, contrasting the older districts where

TABLE VIII
Total factorial structures: rotation analyses

Auckland	Wellington-Hutt I	II	III	IV	Auckland	Christchurch I	II	III	IV
I	−0·99	0·01	0·10	−0·06	I	−0·98	−0·11	−0·04	0·13
II	0·00	0·98	0·14	0·14	II	−0·13	0·96	−0·04	−0·25
III	0·01	−0·20	0·61	0·76	III	0·10	0·26	−0·10	0·95
IV	−0·12	0·02	−0·77	0·63	IV	−0·03	0·06	0·99	0·10

Auckland	Dunedin I	II	III	IV	Wellington-Hutt	Christchurch I	II	III	IV
I	0·69	−0·18	−0·64	0·28	I	0·99	0·10	0·00	−0·11
II	0·22	0·97	0·01	0·11	II	−0·14	0·90	0·14	−0·39
III	0·12	−0·13	0·53	0·83	III	0·01	0·27	−0·92	0·28
IV	0·68	−0·11	0·55	−0·47	IV	0·06	0·33	0·37	0·87

Wellington-Hutt	Dunedin I	II	III	IV	Christchurch	Dunedin I	II	III	IV
I	−0·71	0·18	0·66	−0·12	I	−0·71	0·08	0·08	−0·50
II	0·08	0·91	−0·14	0·00	II	0·18	0·91	0·10	−0·17
III	0·08	0·10	0·19	0·69	III	0·66	−0·14	0·19	−0·34
IV	−0·50	−0·17	−0·34	0·53	IV	−0·12	0·00	0·69	0·53

late-middle-aged households own their own homes with the newer neighbourhoods of large, young families.

The final component in each centre (the third in Auckland and Dunedin and the fourth in Wellington-Hutt and Christchurch) was more place-particular. In both Christchurch and Dunedin it has been identified by high positive loadings on the proportions of Maoris and Polynesians. There were few other large loadings in the former centre, but in Dunedin there were many, associating the minority group districts with those of social disorganization (high positive loadings on socio-economic status variables 8 and 16 and family status variables 16,17,18,19, 25 and 26). The Wellington component has high positive loadings on the proportions of males in the unmarried young adult age-groups, suggesting the rooming-house, areas of flats in student residential districts: according to the other loadings, such districts also have above-average proportions of working females who are employers, and below-average proportions of female wage and salary earners. This pattern is suggestive of a sub-dimension of the non-familism element of urban residential patterns. The final Auckland component had a high positive loading for the proportion of farmers—and its highest positive scores were for outer suburban areas too, hence its identification: it also had similar loadings for the high status female variables (5,6 and 18).

Inspection of the next three dimensions in a seven-component solution for each place showed these all to be place-particular. In Auckland, the extra three components represented female professionals, a separate Polynesian dimension, and owner-occupied homes with few residents; in Wellington-Hutt they were identified as middle age, Maori, and low income constructs; the identifications in Christchurch were unemployment, fertility, and white-collar workers; and finally, in Dunedin the nominations were urban fringe, Indians, and female professionals. Since there were few similarities between these, it can be concluded that, while the four places were very similar in the major elements of their residential patterns, they were quite dissimilar in their minor components. Comparative analyses confirmed this for in the 7×7 matrices of congruence coefficients the total number of close and very close fits was as follows:

Auckland/Wellington-Hutt	3
Auckland/Christchurch	3
Auckland/Dunedin	4 (no very close fits)
Wellington-Hutt/Christchurch	3
Wellington-Hutt/Dunedin	3 (no very close fits)
Christchurch/Dunedin	4 (no very close fits)

Comparative total factorial structures

Two major conclusions can be drawn from these analyses. The first is that, although the different major dimensions have been interpreted as representing socio-economic or family status axes of residential differentiation, in fact there were several important 'cross-loadings'. This is particularly clear with the first component in each place—'non-familism, middle-income'—which suggests clear socio-economic status connotations to the pattern of surburban development. In a precise sense, therefore, the Shevky-Bell model is only generally confirmed, and residential patterns in New Zealand are determined according to several amalgams of, rather than the additive, independent effects of, socio-economic and family status. Secondly, as the comparative statistics discussed in this section confirm, the basic patterns were similar in each place.

The six matrices of congruence coefficients show close fits between all pairs of first and second components (Table VII); four of the twelve indicate very close fits, and the lowest coefficients are 0.74 (the reasons for negative coefficients in four of the matrices were outlined above). Only four other coefficients indicate close fits, however. Three of these relate first components in the other places to the third in Dunedin, demonstrating negative correlations between the Maori/Polynesian/social disorganization component in the latter place, and the middle-income familism dimension of Auckland, Wellington-Hutt and Christchurch (this appears as a positive correlation in the last two comparisons of Table VII because of the sign of the loadings on the first component in Wellington-Hutt and Christchurch).

This division of the major family status component in Dunedin into a dimension and sub-dimension is also illustrated by the lower coefficients for first component correlations involving that city (average 0.84, compared with 0.96 for those involving the other three centres only: Table VII). Few other comparisons indicate other than poor fits, the main exceptions being those involving the 'young and old' components in Auckland, Wellington-Hutt and Christchurch.

The rotation analyses add to these interpretations. The cosines are all high, except in the comparisons including Dunedin, indicating great overall similarity (note, in particular, the Auckland/Christchurch and Wellington-Hutt/Christchurch matrices: Table VIII). The variables with poor fits were also few (an average of twelve out of the eighty-two), again excepting the Dunedin comparisons (Table IX), and not many of them referred to what could be termed 'key' variables in the Shevky-Bell model (and subsequent factorial ecologies): even in the comparison with the worst overall fit—Wellington-Hutt/Dunedin socio-economic status variables—none of the income measures came into this category. Clearly, however, the residential patterning of migrant and minority groups in Dunedin (where they are few in number) is different from that in the other centres.

TABLE IX
Total factorial structures: variable fits

	Variable group			
Comparison	Socio-economic status	Family status	Migrant and minority groups	Housing conditions
Auckland/ Wellington-Hutt	2,3,8,21	6,8,13,14,21	8	
Auckland/ Christchurch	2,13,20,21	8,13,15		
Auckland/ Dunedin	2,3,4,5,8,18	4,6,14,17,20,33	1,3,4,5,6,7,8	1
Wellington-Hutt/ Christchurch	2,3,8,11,13,19,20 21,23,24	8,13,14,21,33	2,5,8	2
Wellington-Hutt/ Dunedin	2,3,4,5,8,11,12,14, 16,18,19,20,21,22,23	13,14,16,19,21,33	1,2,3,5,7,8	1,2,8
Christchurch/ Dunedin	2,3,5,7,11,12,13, 18,20,21	3,8,13,14,17,20, 32,33	3,4,6,8	

The variables listed are those for which the test correlations were lower than 0·7.

NEIGHBOURHOOD TYPOLOGIES

The final question posed in this paper asks whether a similar typology of districts occurs in each of the four centres. Typologies were produced according to the methodology outlined earlier, using the standardized orthogonal component scores from the total factorial structures just discussed.

The algorithm employed is a divisive one, and in each place it produced three major groups. Each of these was then sub-divided into minor groups, ranging from two to five in number. As with many grouping procedures, there was no clear indication where the process should be halted. Subjective interpretation of the means and standard deviations for the various component scores for each group was used, the grouping being considered complete when the variation was low.

There were considerable similarities among the four urban areas in the general features of the neighbourhood types (Table X). One type in each place, for example, was characterized by its young populations and high family status ratings (Types I in Auckland and Christchurch and III in Wellington-Hutt and Dunedin): the Wellington-Hutt pattern was not as clear, however, and two of the sub-types had below-average scores on the young-old component. Most of these sub-types also had below-average socio-economic status and suburban locations, so in general the type represents lower-middle class, outer suburbs with young populations, with occasional nodes of State housing (as for Christchurch type I, sub-type 2). The one exception to this was sub-type 1 for Christchurch type I, which comprised one central city district housing large proportions of young flat dwellers.

A second major type (II in Auckland and Christchurch, I in Wellington-Hutt and Dunedin) is characterized by its generally low scores for both socio-economic and family status. In Auckland and Christchurch, too, most districts contained relatively old populations, while in Christchurch and Dunedin (the only two centres with separate minority group components), above-average proportions of minority group members were usual

TABLE X
Characteristics of neighbourhood types and sub-types
(Average component scores)

Auckland

Main type		I				II				III		
Components	FS	SES	OY	UF	FS	SES	OY	UF	FS	SES	OY	UF
Sub-types 1	++	−	+	++	−−	−−	−	−	−−	+	+	−
2	++	−	+	+	+	−	−	−	−	++	−	−−
3	+	+	+	−	−	−	−−	−	+	+	−	−
4	+	−	++	−−								

Wellington-Hutt

Main type		I				II				III		
Components	FS	SES	OY	M	FS	SES	OY	M	FS	SES	OY	M
Sub-types 1	−	−−	+	−	+	+	+	−	++	−	−	+
2	−	−−	+	−	+	−	−	−	+	−	+	−
3	−−	+	+	+	+	++	−−	+	+	−−	+	−
4	−−	−−	++	++	−	++	+	−	+	−	+	−
5									−	−	−−	++

Christchurch

Main type		I				II				III		
Components	FS	SES	OY	MG	FS	SES	OY	MG	FS	SES	OY	MG
Sub-types 1	−	+	++	−−	−	−−	−−	+	+	+	−	−−
2	+	−−	++	++	−−	−	+	+	+	+	−−	−−
3	++	−	++	−	+	−	−	+	+	++	−	−

Dunedin

Main type		I				II				III		
Components	FS	SES	OY	MG	FS	SES	OY	MG	FS	SES	OY	MG
Sub-types 1	−−	−−	+	−−	+	++	−	−	++	−−	++	−−
2	−−	+	+	+	+	−	−	−	+	−	+	−
3	−	−	−−	++								

Key to Components and symbols:

	Average component score		
	++(+1·0 or greater) +(+0·1 − 1·0) −(−0·1 − 1·0) −−(−1·0 or greater)		
SES—Socio-economic status	High S.E.S.		Low S.E.S.
FS —Family status	Family-centred		Non-family centred
OY —Old-young	Young families		Older families
VF —Urban fringe	Farming areas		Non-farming areas
M —Sex ratios	High % males		Low % males
MG—Minority groups	High % minorities		Low % minorities

(Table X). These, then, are the poorer, older districts of the central city and inner sub-urban areas. The apparently deviant, above-average family status scores for two of the Auckland sub-types can probably be accounted for by the large band of low prestige inner suburbs in that city, and also the wider distribution of young minority group families in Auckland in contrast to the other centres; the above-average socio-economic status for one sub-type in each of Wellington-Hutt and Dunedin can probably be associated with areas of student flats.

The third major types encompass most of the districts with above-average socio-economic status (III in Auckland and Christchurch, II in Wellington-Hutt and Dunedin), which are also characterized by older populations but above-average family status. Auckland contains some exceptions to the overall pattern, two of its three sub-types having below-average family status: note also that two of the four Wellington sub-types had younger populations than average. Dunedin is the major exception, however: its first sub-type contains all of the city's fashionable neighbourhoods, but the second sub-type comprises three below-average status districts with older populations, two of them being spatially separated from the main body of the urban area. In general, these types contain the 'better' suburbs. The sub-types with highest socio-economic status are the élite suburbs which share common locational patterns: a cluster of fashionable districts close to the city centre (east in Auckland and Hutt, west in Wellington and Dunedin, north-west in Christchurch), plus isolated exclusive nodes in certain topographically attractive, outer suburban districts. The other sub-types represent the middle class districts which occupy those parts of the urban periphery not occupied by the lower-middle class and State housing suburbs.

As the component scores were standardized, each component was given equal weight in the grouping process. Nevertheless, the major lineaments of the four typologies were very similar and the fourth, place-particular components were not the bases of separate neighbourhood types. In Auckland, for example, most sub-types had below-average urban fringe scores, not surprisingly. In the first type, the two sub-types which contained farming areas had very high family status scores, and the two with low proportions of farmers also had lower family status than the first two sub-types: this suggests that the urban fringe component was a sub-dimension of the family status, with interdigitation of rural and urban a feature of only some of the new housing areas. In Christchurch and, to a lesser extent, Dunedin the dimension/sub-dimension relationship between the socio-economic status and minority group components appears. Finally, in Wellington-Hutt the sex ratio component had no apparent relationship to any of the three main types.

CONCLUSIONS

This paper has outlined a methodology for comparing the *sensu lato* factorial ecologies of several urban areas, and has reported on one such comparative study for New Zealand's four largest centres. Three questions were formulated for such a study, enquiring whether the major dimensions of the social area analysis model could be represented by single components from factorial ecologies, whether these dimensions and the total factorial structures were similar in each place, and whether similar neighbourhood typologies existed in each place.

There is no simple answer to the first question. Although the same socio-economic status dimension is extracted in each place, other sub-dimensions of this component exist in the occupational and income residential patterning of the cities. Similarly with the matrices of family status variables, no one component dominates the results: instead two major and several minor dimensions are identified. As with the socio-economic status patterns, the major patterns are very similar in all four places, but some of the minor, sub-dimensions are peculiar to one or two centres. Dimensions of housing conditions are highly comparable, but place-particular factorial structures are the main feature of the principal components analyses of the migrant and minority group variables.

Detailed interpretation of these partial factorial structures confirms an earlier suggestion (Johnston, 1971b) that, rather than a few independent dimensions as hypothesized in Shevky and Bell's social area analysis and forming the basis of interpretations of factorial ecologies, urban residential patterns comprise a few major dimensions, each with several sub-dimensions. This is so in the total factorial structures also. The major dimensions are the same in all four places, but minor dimensions are more specific to each place: for example, Christchurch and Dunedin have minority group sub-dimensions of the socio-economic component, but in Auckland and Wellington-Hutt these two constructs are part of the same dimension. Although these major elements in the residential patterns are close to the original Shevky-Bell constructs, it should be noted that New Zealand's family status dimension also has loadings on certain socio-economic status measures, making it a middle class suburban component.

New Zealand's four main urban areas have similar broad neighbourhood structures, therefore, which are somewhat akin to the patterns generally associated with North American cities. Socio-economic status divisions, differences of life style and population age structures are major discriminants between the various districts of the cities. In also identifying such patterns, Timms (1970, p. 466) has claimed that 'the demonstration that there are consistent patterns in the factorial invariance of cities in different parts of the world poses a major challenge to urban theory. The task of accounting for the patterns has hardly begun . . . As yet it may be doubtful whether urban theory has caught up with the truths which factorial ecology can produce.' But in addition to the main dimensions, the use of factorial ecologies *sensu lato*, rather than Timms's *sensu stricto* approach, and analysis of partial as well as total structures, has unveiled a range of minor dimensions, some of them general, some place-specific, which suggest a more complex system of residential patterns. The challenge to urban theory of these empirical patterns is even greater than may have been anticipated.

NOTES

1. Key elements in this debate are the paper by A. H. Hawley and O. D. Duncan (1957), and those by M. Dl van Arsdol, S. F. Camilleri and C. F. Schmid (1961), on one side, and by W. Bell and C. C. Moskos (1964) and Bel. and S. Greer (1962) on the other.

2. The variables used by Shevky and Bell (1955) were: social rank (per cent in low status occupations, and per cent adults with no more than grade school education); urbanization (fertility ratio (children 0–4/females 15–44), per cent women aged $14+$ in the labour force, and per cent of single-family dwelling units); segregation (per cent of persons in a number of racial and birthplace categories). Bell (1955) used average per capita rent as a further social rank variable.

3. Much doubt centres around the assumptions regarding the separate nature of these dimensions. Bell (1955) used the term *discrete* to describe their inter-relationships, but B. J. L. Berry (1965) has claimed that the three dimensions are independent and additive. The early studies by Bell and by van Arsdol *et al.* indeed indicated that, while the three dimensions were statistically separate and necessary for accounting for all of the variation in residential differentiation patterns, they were certainly not independent of each other. Recent studies have tended to assume independence, however (except D. W. G. Timms, 1970).

4. D. T. Herbert (1968) makes an 'eyeball' comparison of total structures.

5. There are also some slight differences in the data and areal units employed.

6. In 1971 the income limit was a maximum weekly total income of \$42 for the head of the household.

7. Note, however, that whereas in 1902 the average married couple spent $7\frac{1}{2}$ of their $45\frac{1}{2}$ years of married life without any children at home, in 1962 they spent 23 of their $53\frac{1}{2}$ years living alone (M. Gilson, 1970). This has had important recent repercussions on housing patterns. Large suburban homes are not needed for much of married life for many couples, but instead of moving into flats they occupy ownership units, which are usually blocks of two to four semi-detached bungalows built on single residential sections. These are being constructed in most suburbs, as renewal, and on newly-developed sections.

8. Timms (1970) did include these areas.

9. Note that this use of the separate data matrices referring to the groups of variables means that the number of variables is sometimes almost as large as the number of observations. In the case of the full set of eighty-two variables, this is always the case, since the largest of the urban areas, Auckland, contains only sixty-one districts. Some factor analysis texts suggest that there should be at least twice as many observations as variables, but J. Galtung (1967, p. 308) implies that this is not the case when one is dealing with populations (as in this case) and not samples: all New Zealand census data refer to the total population.

10. In Johnston (1971b) several ways of testing for the nature of these sub-dimensions were suggested. Because of the small number of districts in each place, however, such testing was not possible in this study, although the neighbourhood typologies reported later give some lead: interpretation was therefore subjective.

11. The very large State Housing areas in Auckland are in the excluded Manukau County: hence the absence there of such a component. Such extensive State Housing areas are not a major feature of either Christchurch or Dunedin.

12. The Chinese would not group with the others on a completely general racial dimension because many of them lived or were employed on suburban market gardens.

13. Note, however, that in the district with the lowest score on this component in Christchurch, 88 per cent of homes had exclusive use of a flush toilet.

14. This may seem surprising, but much Polynesian migration has been of the 'classical' young single male to the central city rooming-houses variety. Family Maori migration is mainly to Auckland's outer suburbs (D. T. Rowland, 1971, 1972), which are excluded from this study.

15. The loading on this component for table mortgages (interest paid on the principal still outstanding) but not for flat mortgages (interest paid on the size of the original principal), which loaded on the first component with the non-familism variables, presumably indicates that different types of mortgages are given on dwellings of different ages.

REFERENCES

ABU-LUGHOD, J. L. (1969) 'Testing the theory of social area analysis: the ecology of Cairo, Egypt', *Am. sociol. Rev.* 34, 198–212
ABURN, A. A. (1971) 'The high status residential areas of Dunedin', *Proc. 6th N.Z. Geogr. Conf.* 227–33
ANDERSON, T. R. and L. L. BEAN (1961) 'The Shevky-Bell social areas: confirmation of results and a reinterpretation', *Soc. Forces* 40, 119–24
BELL, W. (1955) 'Economic, family, and ethnic status: an empirical test', *Am. sociol. Rev.* 20, 45–52
BELL, W. and S. GREER, (1962) 'Social area analysis and its critics', *Pacif. sociol. Rev.* 5, 3–9
BELL, W. and C. C. MOSKOS (1964) 'A comment on Udry's "Increasing scale and spatial differentiation"', *Soc. Forces* 42, 414–7
BERRY, B. J. L. (1965) 'Internal structure of the city', *Law Contemp. Probls* 30, 111–19
BERRY, B. J. L. and P. H. REES (1969) 'The factorial ecology of Calcutta', *Am. J. Sociol.* 74, 445–91
BOWMAN, R. A. and P. L. HOSKING (1971) 'A factorial ecology of Auckland', *Proc. 6th N.Z. Geogr. Conf.* 273–80
BURNLEY, I. H. (1972) 'Ethnic settlement formation in a New Zealand city', *N.Z. Geogr.* 28
CATTELL, R. B. (1966) 'The meaning and strategic use of factor analysis' in R. B. CATTELL (ed.) *Handbook of multivariate experimental psychology* (Chicago), 174–243
CURSON, P. H. (1967) 'Age-sex analysis within Auckland', *Pacif. View.* 8, 181–5
CURSON, P. H. (1970) 'Polynesians and residence in Auckland', *N.Z. Geogr.* 26, 162–73
DUNCAN, O. D. (1959) 'Residential segregation and social differentiation', *Proc. int. Population Conf., Vienna*
GALTUNG, J. (1967) *Theory and methods of social research*
GILSON, M. (1970) 'The changing New Zealand family: a demographic analysis' in S. HOUSTON (ed.) *Marriage and the family in New Zealand* (Wellington), 41–65
HARMAN, H. H. (1966) *Modern factor analysis*
HAWLEY, A. H. and O. D. DUNCAN (1957) 'Social area analysis: a critical appraisal', *Land Econ.* 33, 337–45
HEENAN, L. D. B. (1967) 'Rural-urban distribution of fertility in South Island, New Zealand', *Ann. Ass. Am. Geogr.* 57, 713–35
HERBERT, D. T. (1968) 'Principal components analysis and British studies of urban-social structure', *Prof. Geogr.* 20, 280–3
HUNTER, A. A. (1972) 'Factorial ecology: a critique and some suggestions', *Demography* 9, 107–18
JOHNSTON, R. J. (1969) 'Processes of change in the high status residential districts of Christchurch, 1951–1964' *N.Z. Geogr.* 25, 1–15
JOHNSTON, R. J. (1970) 'Components analysis in geographical research', *Area* 2 (4), 68–71
JOHNSTON, R. J. (1971a) *Urban residential patterns: an introductory review*
JOHNSTON, R. J. (1971b) 'Some limitations of factorial ecologies and social area analysis', *Econ. Geogr.* 47, 314–23
JOHNSTON, R. J. (1971c) 'Mental maps of the city: suburban preference patterns', *Environment Plann.* 3, 63–71
JOHNSTON, R. J. (1972) 'Towards a general model of intra-urban residential patterns: some cross-cultural observations', *Progr. Geogr.* 4, 83–124
JONES, F. L. (1967) 'Ethnic concentration and assimilation: an Australian case study', *Soc. Forces* 45, 412–23
JONES, F. L. (1968) 'Social area analysis: some theoretical and methodological comments illustrated with Australian data', *Br. J. Sociol.* 19, 424–44
JONES, F. L. (1969) *Dimensions of urban social structure: the social areas of Melbourne, Australia* (Canberra)
LIEBERSON, S. (1963) 'The old-new distinction and immigrants in Australia', *Am. sociol. Rev.* 28, 550–65

McQuitty, L. L. and J. A. Clark (1968) 'Clusters from iterative, intercolumnar correlational analysis', *Educ. Psych. Meas.* 28, 211–38

McGee, T. G. (1969) 'The social ecology of New Zealand cities: a preliminary investigation' in J. Forster (ed.) *Social process in New Zealand* (Auckland), 144–83

Murdie, R. A. (1969) 'Factorial ecology of metropolitan Toronto, 1951–1961', Univ. of Chicago, Dept. of Geography Res. Pap. 116

Poulsen, M. F. and R. J. Johnston (1972) 'Patterns of Maori migration' in R. J. Johnston (ed.) *Urbanization in New Zealand; geographical essays* (Wellington)

Rees, P. H. (1971) 'Factorial ecology: an extended definition, survey and critique of the field', *Econ. Geogr.* 47, 220–33

Rowland, D. T. (1971) 'Maori migration to Auckland', *N.Z. Geogr.* 27, 21–37

Rowland, D. T. (1972) 'Processes of Maori urbanization', *N.Z. Geogr.* 28, 1–22

Rummel, R. J. (1967) 'Understanding factor analysis', *J. Conflict Resolution* 40, 440–80

Shevky, E. and W. Bell (1955) *Social area analysis* (Stanford)

Shevky, E. and M. Williams (1949) *The social areas of Los Angeles* (Los Angeles)

Sweetser, F. L. (1965) 'Factorial ecology: Helsinki, 1960', *Demography* 2, 372–85

Sweetser, F. L. (1969) 'Ecological factors in metropolitan zones and sectors' in M. Dogan and S. Rokkan (eds.) *Quantitative ecological analysis in the social sciences* (Cambridge, Mass.), 413–56

Thomson, K. W. and A. D. Trlin (1970) *Immigrants in New Zealand* (Palmerston North)

Timms, D. W. G. (1970) 'Comparative factorial ecology: some New Zealand examples', *Environment Plann.* 2, 455–68

Timms, D. W. G. (1971) *The urban mosaic: towards a theory of residential differentiation* (Cambridge)

Trlin, A. D. (1971) 'Residential patterns and segregation of racial groups in the Auckland, Wellington and Hutt urban areas', *Proc. 6th N.Z. Geogr. Conf.*, 244–51

Van Arsdol, M. D., S. F. Camilleri, and C. F. Schmid (1958) 'The generality of urban social area indexes', *Am. sociol. Rev.* 23, 277–84

Van Arsdol, M. D., S. F. Camilleri, and C. F. Schmid (1961) 'An investigation of the utility of urban typology', *Pacif. sociol. Rev.* 4, 26–32

Veldman, D. J. (1967) *Fortran programming for the behavioural sciences*

Vellekoop, C. (1969) 'Social strata in New Zealand' in J. Forster (ed.) *Social process in New Zealand* (Auckland), 233–71

Wilson, M. G. A. (1971) 'Alternate measures of human reproduction—some geographic implications', *N.Z. Geogr.* 27, 185–96

Résumé. *Différentiation résidentielle des principales régions urbaines en Nouvelle Zélande: une écologie factorielle comparative*. Des écologies factorielles, normalement des analyses de composantes principales de grandes matrices de données, ont été utilisées souvent au cours des dernières années pour éprouver le model déductif de Shevky et Bell de la différentiation résidentielle dans des villes. Peu d'études comparatives détaillées de différentes régions urbaines ont cependant été menées. Ce travail applique une méthodologie comparative pour l'écologie factorielle de quatre principales régions urbaines en Nouvelle Zélande. Des analyses furent entreprises pour la matrice entière des données ainsi que pour des matrices séparées représentant des dimensions séparées du model Shevky-Bell. En général, les dimensions les plus importantes correspondent aux hypothèses, à part des variations considérables d'endroits dans la distribution de différentes minorités ethniques. Cependant, certains sub-dimensions des deux axes différentielles furent identifiées.

Zusammenfassung. *Differenzierung von Wohnzonen in den wichtigsten Stadtgebieten Neuseelands: eine vergleichende faktorielle Ökologie*. Faktorielle Ökologien, üblicherweise die wichtigsten Komponentenanalysen von grossen Datenmatrizen, wurden in den letzten Jahren oft dazu verwendet, die Anwendung des deduktiven Modells von Shevky und Bell über die Differenzierung von Wohnzonen in Städten zu untersuchen. Es wurden jedoch nur wenige vergleichende Studien von verschiedenen Stadtgebieten durchgeführt. Diese Arbeit verwendet eine vergeichende Methodologie für die faktoriellen Ökologien der vier wichtigsten Stadtgebieten Neuseelands. Untersuchungen wurden für die gesamte Datenmatrix durchgeführt, sowie für einzelne Matrien, die gesonderte Dimensionen des Shevky-Bell-Modells vertreten. Im allgemeinen entsprachen die einzelnen Dimensionen den Hypothesen, mit Ausnahme von beträchtlichen Unterschieden zwischen Orten in der Verteilung ethnischer Minderheiten. Allerdings wurde eine Anzahl von Subdimensionen der beiden wichtigsten Differentiationsachsen identifiziert.

Group 1. Socio-economic status
Proportion of
1. MALES in the workforce who are employers
2. ,, in the workforce who are self-employed
3. ,, in the workforce who are wage/salary earners
4. ,, in the workforce who are unemployed
5. FEMALES in the workforce who are employers
6. ,, in the workforce who are self-employed
7. ,, in the workforce who are wage/salary earners
8. ,, in the workforce who are unemployed
9. MALES in the workforce in the professions
10. ,, in the workforce in administrative jobs
11. ,, in the workforce in clerical jobs
12. ,, in the workforce in sales jobs
13. ,, in the workforce who are farmers
14. ,, in the workforce who are transport workers
15. ,, in the workforce who are craftsmen
16. ,, in the workforce who are service workers
Proportion of
17. FEMALES in the workforce in the professions
18. ,, in the workforce in administrative jobs
19. ,, in the workforce in clerical jobs
20. ,, in the workforce in sales jobs
21. ,, in the workforce who are transport workers
22. ,, in the workforce who are craftsmen
23. ,, in the workforce who are service workers
24. Income-earning males earning < $1000
25. Income-earning males earning $1000–2199
26. Income-earning males earning $2200–2999
27. Income-earning males earning $3000–3999
28. Income-earning males earning > $4000
29. Income-earning females earning < $1000
30. Income-earning females earning $1000–2199
31. Income-earning females earning $2200–2999
32. Income-earning females earning $3000–3999
33. Income-earning females earning > $4000

Group 2. Family status
Proportion of
1. Persons aged 0–4
2. Persons aged 5–14
3. Persons aged 15–20
4. Persons aged 65+
5. Persons aged 21–24
6. Persons aged 25–34
7. Persons aged 35–44
8. Persons aged 45–54

9. Persons aged 55–64
10. Unmarried persons in 21–24 age group
11. Unmarried persons in 25–34 age group
12. Unmarried persons in 35–54 age group
13. Males in 21–24 unmarried group
14. Males in 25–34 unmarried group
15. Unmarried persons aged over 15
16. Legally separated persons of all married persons
17. Widowed persons of all aged over 15
Proportion of
18. Divorced persons of all married persons
19. Males of all divorced persons
20. Males of all widowed persons
21. Children 0–4 per 1000 females 15–44 (Fertility)
22. Dependants (aged under 16 or over 64)
23. Not economically active persons
24. Not income earners
25. Flats of all housing units
26. Properties rented
27. Properties being purchased on table mortgages
28. Properties being purchased on flat mortgages
29. Properties being purchased on either mortgages
30. Properties owner-occupied
31. Non-private properties
32. Females aged 15–64 working
33. Persons per unit

Group 3. Migrants and minority groups
Proportion of
1. Maoris
2. Polynesians
3. Indians
4. Chinese
5. Members of the Church of England
6. Members of the Presbyterian Church
7. Members of the Roman Catholic Church
8. Members of the Methodist Church

Group 4. Housing conditions
Proportion of
1. Homes with exclusive use of a bath
2. Homes with exclusive use of a flush toilet
3. Homes with a refrigerator
4. Homes with a telephone
Proportion of
5. Homes with a washing machine
6. Homes with a T.V.
7. Homes with a radio
8. Homes with a vacuum cleaner

M

Residential patterns in an emerging industrial town

A. M. WARNES

Lecturer in Geography, University of Salford

Revised MS received 27 September 1972

ABSTRACT. The paper takes as its starting point current axioms about residential spatial structures and the lack of progress towards an evolutionary model of these structures. By using two sources of data relating to Chorley, Lancashire, in the early nineteenth century, it is shown that this deficiency can be remedied. The sources are a Vestry Committee Survey of the town in 1816 and the enumerators' books of the 1851 census. In the first decades of the nineteenth century the dominant determinant of residential location was the location of employment: socio-economic status was expressed in the residential pattern only when it paralleled differences in employment location. By 1851, however, a socio-economic status component was clearly identified although it was not entirely independent of occupation. The distribution of social classes did not conform to any existing model. It is concluded that the relationship alters in response to changing industrial organization, size of employing units, hours of work, wealth, family structure, and transport technology. Urban geographers should draw on the considerable work in this field by economic and social historians to develop improved models of the evolution of residential areas within towns.

THIS paper is intended as a contribution to the study of urban residential structure. Like many recent studies in this field, it analyses a wide range of variables referring to small areas of a city, and uses a multivariate statistical technique to summarize this information and to identify major patterns of spatial variation within the urban area. Inferences are then made about the organizing principles behind these patterns. Unlike most recent studies, however, it concentrates upon the applicability of recent general findings to a British nineteenth-century town, taking as its subject the small, rapidly growing and industrializing township of Chorley in Lancashire.

Although there used to be confusing tendencies to elevate spatial models of specific elements of the city into comprehensive or holistic models, and then to treat them as competing alternatives, recent investigations have sought a more sensitive appreciation of the applicability of different spatial structures. The search has already had some success; from many studies of individual cities have come some consistent results which have been valuable additions to our knowledge, and, less happily, some premature and over-confident conclusions. This paper does not repeat the task of reviewing recent contributions to urban ecology, as this has been done thoroughly elsewhere (J. Abu-Lughod, 1969; H. Carter, 1972; F. L. Jones, 1968; R. A. Murdie, 1969; B. T. Robson, 1968 and 1969; D. W. G. Timms, 1970 and 1971.). Instead, it takes as its starting point the reviewers' conclusions about recent research. In particular, this paper looks critically at two sets of results about which there is a growing consensus of opinion.

THE AXIOMS TO BE EXAMINED

The first concerns the components or independent contributors to the total spatial pattern of residential variation. As Timms (1971, p. 84) has put it, 'at least in the urban–industrial cities of North America, Western Europe and Australasia, much of the detailed variation in the population characteristics of different parts of the community may be accounted for in terms of the underlying variation along three or four basic differentiating factors'. Alone, this result is inevitable from the factorial techniques commonly employed, but this is not true of the important rider that the components tend to be stable from city to city and are readily and intuitively understood. The now well-known view of Shevky, Williams and Bell (E. Shevky and M. Williams, 1949; Shevky and W. Bell, 1955) that social rank, familism and ethnicity are the independent factors that together explain a large part of the variation in the modern city has been substantially upheld. 'Not only is a socio-economic factor always isolated, but it is frequently the factor that accounts for the largest proportion of the variance in the correlation matrix' (Abu-Lughod, 1969, p. 202). A familism or urbanization component is also frequently found but its chief elements, fertility and economically active females, are not always independent of socio-economic rank. Ethnicity is rarer, and Abu-Lughod found that it had never been replicated outside the United States, even when it was consciously sought. On the other hand, a wide range of other components has been found, partly because of the various combinations of variables used by investigators, and partly because of real differences in the structure of urban areas in different parts of the world. For example, a first or second component strongly related to housing conditions has been found in some studies of contemporary British cities (D. T. Herbert, 1968 and 1970; Robson, 1969, pp. 162–4).

There is a growing feeling that the complete independence of the socio-economic rank and familism components is only reached in the most modern societies. This idea has had a lengthy evolution, being an explicit feature of the urbanization concept of the social area analysts, who in turn were adopting the ideas of L. Wirth (1938) about the decreasing importance of primary contacts and the decreasing role of the family as a social unit in modern cities. It is now receiving some empirical support from studies of cities in non-western areas, but because there is hardly any sufficiently detailed evidence of the evolution of even a western urban area over more than a few decades, it is too early to incorporate these notions into evolutionary models. Indeed, the evidence from the only comparable study of a western city in the past contests the hypothesis, because it was found that in 1870 'economic status, family status, and segregation of locally identifiable minority groups were distinctive features of Toronto's social scene. Furthermore, these dimensions were independent in a statistical sense' (P. G. Goheen, 1970, p. 219). Clearly, the expectation of B. J. L. Berry and P. H. Rees (1969, p. 491) that 'differing urban ecologies relating to differing factor combinations can be arranged along a scale of urban development from pre- to post-industrial forms' must, as they stress, be subjected to systematic testing.

This study contributes towards such testing by providing evidence from a town which was neither modern nor pre-industrial, but which by 1851 had experienced half a century of industrialization and which might be described as an emerging industrial town. One focus of this paper is therefore to test the axiom that the components of residential variation in Chorley in 1851 cannot be adequately described under the headings of socio-economic status, family status and ethnicity.

The second set of results of particular interest are those relating to the spatial patterning of these independent components. Berry (1965, p. 115) claimed that socio-economic rank varies axially, family structure varies concentrically and that particular ethnic groups are locally segregated in a pattern analogous to the multiple-nuclei distribution. His conclusion was based partly on J. A. Egeland and T. R. Anderson's (1961) study of four medium-sized North American cities, and has since been supported by studies of Calcutta, Toronto, Chicago and New Zealand cities (Berry and Rees, 1969; Murdie, 1969; Rees, 1968; Timms, 1970 and 1971). Rees, from a comparison of his work with similar studies of smaller cities, has suggested that the smaller the city, the closer it approximates to the integrated spatial model built from the three classical designs.

It cannot yet be claimed, however, that the generality through time and space of these distinctive spatial patterns has been established. It is true, of course, that in a limited field, that of the distribution of socio-economic rank within the city, more cross-cultural and cross-temporal studies have been made. G. Sjoberg (1960, pp. 95–6) has made three general-izations for non-industrial cities, the first of which is that there is a 'pre-eminence of the "central" area over the periphery, especially as portrayed in the distribution of social classes'. Sjoberg was concerned mainly with the feudal city which, he emphasizes, was generally small: 'even pre-industrial centres with populations between 25 000 and 100 000 have been relatively uncommon' (ibid., p. 83). His generalizations have been applied, how-ever, to later and even contemporary cities of all sizes and in all parts of the world. Whereas the empirical validity of an inverted distribution of social classes in non-western cities has been demonstrated many times, for example, in studies of Indian and Nigerian towns (Rees, 1968 (reprinted 1970, p. 292); A. L. Mabogunje, 1968, p. 177), firm evidence of Sjoberg's generalization holding for western cities before they were industrialized has not been produced. Yet it has frequently been applied to early nineteenth-century European and North American cities, even if only implicitly. This extension of the generalization follows easily when one of its conditions specified by Sjoberg, the low level of spatial mobility, is emphasized. This was done explicitly by F. W. Boal (1968) exploring the relationship between transport technology and urban form in the most highly developed countries.

From the point of view of extending and refining our present knowledge of spatial patterns within urban areas of different types, therefore, there are three questions which can most usefully be asked about Chorley in the mid-nineteenth century: (1) What were the spatial patterns of socio-economic status, family status and ethnic groups, whether or not they were distinguished as components of the total variance? (2) What are the spatial patterns of the principal components of residential variation? (3) Is there evidence from this example of an emerging industrial town of a distribution of the higher social classes transitional between those characteristic of pre-industrial cities and those character-istic of modern western cities? By considering these questions, and the first problem of identifying the components of residential structure in the town, it is hoped that the investigation of Chorley will have more than local interest and significance. Before examin-ing the results, it is necessary, however, to describe and evaluate the data which differ from those used in studies of contemporary towns.

EVIDENCE

A necessary condition of progress towards understanding the internal structure of towns is that sufficiently detailed data are available. It is not surprising, therefore, that the release of enumeration district data for British towns in 1961 and 1966 has been followed by new insights into the spatial organization of these towns, nor that cross-cultural and cross-temporal comparisons of this organization have relied on studies of the largest and most 'modernized' settlements. It is this bias which undermines confidence in the generality of the results.

For this study, in addition to standard sources such as contemporary maps, directories, census figures, rateable values and travellers' accounts, which are described and assessed elsewhere (Warnes, 1969 and 1970), two particularly detailed and relevant sources have been exploited. The first is a Vestry Committee Survey of the town in 1816 which is recorded in *Chorley Town's Book, 1781–1818*, a manuscript copy of which is preserved in the Borough Library. It is particularly valuable because the Committee divided the town into eight districts consisting of named streets. With this information, and with the aid of the first commercial directory specific to Chorley (T. Rogerson, 1818) and Greenwood's excellent map of Lancashire surveyed in 1818, it is possible to define these districts with precision (Fig. 1). The results of the survey were reported to the Committee on 13 September 1816, and at least some of these were recorded in the minutes. They are reproduced in Table I.

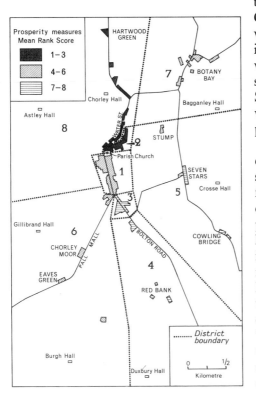

FIGURE I. Vestry Committee Survey districts in 1816, and the mean 'prosperity' ranking

Whether the surveyors collected additional information, as the Committee resolved, is not known, but no document giving fuller details survives. The 3307 people recorded were only about half of the total population indicated by the census. The most likely explanation for this under-enumeration is that the survey dealt only with families and not with lodgers, servants or childless households, although there is some suggestion in the Town Book that children under 5 years of age were not counted. Although the 'prosperity' and occupational information of the survey was poorly defined, it can be accepted as giving a broad indication of the economic status of the various districts of the town. It also represents the earliest quantitative record of the distribution of population in the town.

The second and most important source is the enumerators' books of the census. This source has become increasingly well known since the detailed descriptions by A. J. Taylor (1951), M. Beresford (1963), H. J. Dyos and A. B. M. Baker (1968) and W. A. Armstrong (1966 and 1968), and their pioneer use for geographical purposes by R. Lawton (1955). The enumerators made the first transcriptions of the original household schedules in these books which are kept in the Public Record Office, and which became available as historical documents on their centenary. In the important field of recording occupations, as in many others, the 1841 census took a major step forward in that 'for the first time, all the principal occupations in the country are recorded, and the whole population is brought

TABLE I

The Vestry Committee Survey of Chorley, 1816

| | Districts | | | | | | | | |
	1	*2*	*3*	*4*	*5*	*6*	*7*	*8*	*Total*
Families	103	87	110	100	36	88	67	82	673
Heads of families (parents)	201	171	213	195	68	162	126	164	1300
Those well off	17	28	—	19	4	14	30	13	125
Those meddling	42	24	57	26	12	41	22	22	246
Those very poor	46	35	53	55	20	31	15	47	302
Males, children	144	113	185	163	66	140	89	102	1002
Females, children	134	112	195	177	67	104	102	114	1005
Looms	33	82	117	190	67	89	89	53	720
Unemployed	16	4	28	53	5	10	20	4	140

'Making a total of 3307 souls'

directly into the tables of enumeration' (C. Booth, 1886, p. 315). The full benefit of these changes came with the following census which was better executed, required new precision in the recording of birthplaces and ages, and introduced new questions about marital condition and the relation of each individual to the head of the household. For these reasons the 1851 books are held to be the most useful of the available collections, particularly as the 1861 volumes are generally in poorer condition.

In some respects, superior statistics can be produced from the enumerators' books than from modern small-scale data. First, the items from individual households can be aggregated into any geographical unit, and secondly, the investigator does not have to rely upon inferences from a 10 per cent sample of households. On the other hand, the quality of the responses from the less literate population, and the conscientiousness of the enumerators, probably did not match current standards. When assembling the data from the books, the fullest possible detail was preserved by classifying the statistics by streets, the smallest possible units which could be precisely located. From this collection, a data matrix consisting of nineteen variables and fifty-eight areas was constructed for this paper. It was supplemented by two other variables, 20 and 21, the first being measured from the Ordnance Survey 1:10 560 'Record' map surveyed in 1844–47, the second being derived from the roll of rateable values for 1848 which is preserved in Chorley Town Hall. A complete list of the variables is given in Table III.

The derivation of the majority of the variables was quite straightforward and needs no explanation. Two definitions should perhaps be made clear: any person with a recorded gainful occupation was regarded as economically active, and cotton-spinning workers were those entered as reelers, winders, piecers and spinners. Some explanation of the method of classification of occupations into social classes is also required. This is a difficult and inevitably partially subjective procedure even for the present day, but for the mid-nineteenth century the difficulties are compounded. It was decided to follow closely W. A. Armstrong's scheme which is described in detail in his thesis (1967, Appendix A) and elsewhere (1966). It is based largely on the occupational 'status' classification of the General Register Office published in 1950, but some attention is given to the assessed skill of an occupation, and to distinctions between employers and employed. Not surprisingly, this scheme has stimulated much controversy, as evidenced in Armstrong (1968a) and a terse debate in the *Economic History Review* (R. C. Floud and R. S. Schofield, 1968; W. A. Armstrong, 1968b). As the usefulness of the scheme has been demonstrated by several historians, and it was judged to be sufficiently accurate and detailed, it was adopted with minor modifications.[1]

RESIDENTIAL DISTRIBUTIONS IN EARLY NINETEENTH-
CENTURY CHORLEY

The components of residential differentiation

Although there is insufficient information for a multivariate statistical analysis of Chorley's residential structure before 1851, enough can be established about its physical form, employment structure, employment location, and the residential location of its high-status groups, for confident inferences to be made about the factors that were influencing its residential patterns. Despite the inherent limitations of such inferences, they form a useful account of earlier conditions to set beside the more detailed evidence from 1851.

The earliest picture of the internal geography of the town is given by William Yates' map of Lancashire, published in 1786 but surveyed some 6 years earlier. This demonstrates that 'the settlement pattern in 1780 consisted of two main elements; a fairly even scatter of isolated houses; and superimposed on this, a single, discrete and nucleated town' (Warnes, 1970). These elements can be related to the small-holding economy of cloth manufacture and agriculture, and to the service functions of the town. The only other noticeable element consisted of a few estates of the nobility and gentry scattered around the township. Most of these survived into the mid-nineteenth century and are located on the Record map. By 1816, the distribution of settlement had changed. In the intervening period the growth of factories and other non-domestic employing units together with clusters of houses about them had created another element in the settlement pattern. This is clearly shown on Greenwood's map and on Figure 1.

Of the developing clusters, Botany Bay (district 7) had grown around the wharves of the Lancaster Canal, Red Bank and Chorley Moor were closely associated with coal mines, and Cowling Bridge and Seven Stars with cotton factories. These associations are obvious from all the sources, but the Vestry Committee Survey and the commercial directories provide additional evidence of the distribution of employment in 1816. The survey indicates that the ratio of looms per head varied from 0·07 to 0·36 among the eight districts (Table II.) Low ratios were found mainly where there were alternative forms of employment, as in the core (district 1) with nearly all the town's retailing and commercial premises, in the Water St district (8) with a large proportion of the town's cotton factories, and in district 6 with coal mining. Only the Hollingshead St—Bengall St area (district 2) had a ratio less than the town average but no evident alternative employment. The available evidence strongly suggests therefore that the majority of the inhabitants of each cluster and of each Vestry Committee district worked in their home areas (Warnes, 1970). It follows that the fundamental principle organizing the residential pattern in 1816 was the location of employment. To what extent socio-economic status operated as an independent factor in decisions on residential location is more difficult to ascertain from the data. It is possible, however, to calculate the over- or under-representation of 'well-off', 'meddling' and 'very poor' families in each district and to summarize this information in a single measure which may be compared with the unemployment and age-structure statistics.

TABLE II
Prosperity and occupational measures from the 1816 Vestry Committee Survey

					Districts				
	1	*2*	*3*	*4*	*5*	*6*	*7*	*8*	*Chorley*
1. Looms per person	0·07	0·21	0·20	0·36	0·33	0·22	0·28	0·14	0·22
Ranking	8	5	6	1	2	4	3	7	
2. Percentage distribution of prosperity groups									
Well off	13·6	22·4	—	15·2	3·2	11·2	24·0	10·4	100
Meddling	17·1	9·7	23·2	10·6	4·9	16·7	8·9	8·9	100
Very poor	15·2	11·6	17·5	18·2	6·6	10·2	5·0	15·6	100
Population	14·5	12·0	17·9	16·1	6·1	12·3	9·6	11·5	100
3. Over- or under-representation of prosperity groups									
Well off a	0·94	1·87	—	0·94	0·52	0·91	2·50	0·90	1·00
Meddling b	1·18	0·81	1·30	0·66	0·80	1·36	0·72	0·77	1·00
Very poor c	1·05	0·97	0·98	1·13	1·08	0·83	0·40	1·36	1·00
(3a+2b+c)/6	1·04	1·35	0·60	0·88	0·71	1·05	1·56	0·93	1·00
4. Percentage distribution and index of unemployment									
Percentage of unemployed	11·4	2·9	20·0	37·9	3·6	7·1	14·3	2·9	100
do. : population percentage	0·79	0·24	1·12	2·35	0·59	0·58	1·49	0·25	1·00
5. Percentage distribution of children									
Percentage of children	13·9	11·2	19·0	16·9	6·6	12·2	9·5	10·8	100·1
do. : population percentage	0·95	0·93	1·01	1·05	1·09	0·99	0·97	0·94	1·00
6. Aggregate prosperity ranking of districts									
Prosperity categories	4	2	8	6	7	3	1	5	
Unemployment	5	1	6	8	3	4	7	2	
Children	3	1	6	7	8	5	4	2	
Mean ranking	4	1·3	6·6	7	6	4	4	3	

The figures are reproduced in Table II and the mean rankings of the districts are mapped on Figure 1.

In general, the prosperity of the districts accords with the varying status of their prominent occupations; the hand-loom weaving and cotton-factory districts are relatively depressed and the market core and Botany Bay appear relatively prosperous. The only evidence for the independence of social class as a factor in residential location comes from districts 2 and 3. The former is consistently rated as a very prosperous area. Rogerson's directory shows that its principal street, Hollinshead or New St, was a popular residential area for the town's gentry and clergy, and that it may be regarded as the first sign of a specialized high-class residential area in the town. The latter district around Bolton St is consistently poorly rated, and being spatially associated not with a single place of employment but with foundries, mills and other low-skilled employers such as brickworks, it is the first sign of the emergence of a residential area which is relatively homogeneous in its class composition, but diverse in its occupational composition.

During the following 35 years, the population of the town increased from less than 7000 to over 12 000. By 1851 there were nearly 1500 separate dwellings in the town, and the built-up area had considerably expanded (Fig. 2). Although the outlying nuclei had continued to grow and proliferate, the intervening period had seen the central nucleus

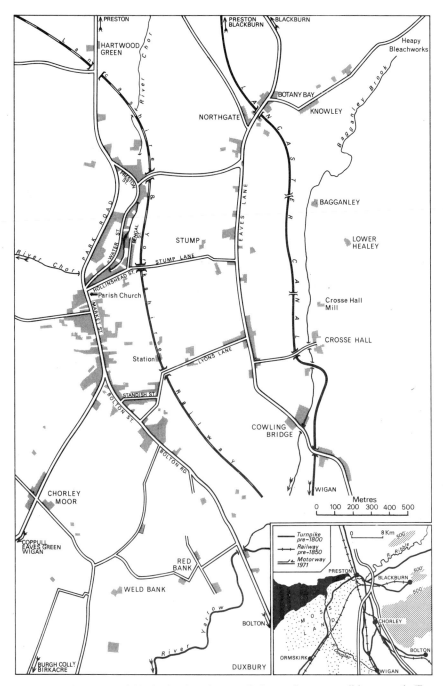

FIGURE 2. The built-up area of Chorley in 1851. *Sources:* Ordnance Survey 1st edition 1:10 560 'Record' map surveyed 1844–47, modified from the details in the 1851 census enumerators' books. The map locates place and street names used in the text. *Inset:* the situation of Chorley

TABLE III

Loadings of the original variables on the first five principal components

Variable	Trans-formation	Loadings on components				
		I	*2*	*3*	*4*	*5*
1. Economically active[1]	0	0·679	−0·138	0·068	−0·313	·0·139
2. Social class I and II[2]	I	−0·709	−0·026	−0·349	−0·150	−0·151
3. Social class III[2]	0	0·634	−0·127	−0·625	0·229	0·189
4. Social class IV and V[2]	0	−0·371	0·160	0·837	−0·173	−0·106
5. House servants[2]	I	−0·865	−0·153	−0·228	0·137	−0·011
6. Hand-loom weavers[2]	I	0·843	−0·131	−0·036	0·007	−0·133
7. Agricultural workers[2]	I	−0·188	0·610	−0·303	−0·465	0·029
8. Coal mining workers[2]	I	0·300	0·135	−0·129	0·350	0·025
9. Retailing workers[2]	I	−0·346	−0·456	0·190	0·259	0·374
10. Cotton spinning workers[2]	I	0·179	−0·117	0·620	−0·103	−0·480
11. Born in Chorley[1]	0	0·551	−0·492	0·065	0·013	0·011
12. Born in Ireland[1]	I	−0·017	0·057	0·559	0·104	0·458
13. Less than 15 yrs old[1]	0	−0·046	0·703	0·384	0·284	0·164
14. 60 yrs old or more[1]	I	0·120	−0·514	−0·089	−0·502	0·146
15. Scholars under 15 yrs[3]	I	−0·819	−0·240	−0·203	0·091	0·029
16. Farm workers 15–60[4]	0	−0·485	0·435	−0·433	−0·047	0·122
17. Children: women ratio[5]	0	0·228	0·623	0·078	0·518	−0·001
18. Population per house	0	−0·052	−0·079	−0·009	0·486	−0·641
19. Male:female ratio	0	0·563	0·253	−0·290	0·177	0·078
20. Distance from centre	2	0·215	0·470	−0·183	−0·383	−0·592
21. Mean rateable value[6]	2	−0·206	−0·589	−0·095	0·321	−0·393

Notes: Variables: 1—as a percentage of the population, 2—as a percentage of the economically active population, 3—as a percentage of the population under 15 years old, 4—as a percentage of the female population aged 15 to 60 years, 5—under 15 years as a ratio of the female population 15 to 44 years old, 6—the average rateable value of residential units.

Transformations: 0—no transformation, 1—square root, 2—logarithm to base 10

increase its relative importance; in 1851, it held three-quarters of the total number of dwellings. The residential structure of the town had also increased in complexity, but because the sources for 1851 are far more detailed and reliable than those for 1816, it is possible to describe and analyse the later situation with much more confidence.

As a basis for the analysis, the data matrix constructed from the enumerators' books was standardized and converted into its principal components. The loadings, or correlations with the original variables, of the first seven components are given in Table IV, and a summary of other results is presented in Table V. In comparison with most applications of this technique to modern western cities, fewer variables have been entered in the analysis. Although demographic, ethnic, social status, occupation and valuation variables are represented, including approximations to the social area analysis measures (variables 2 to 5, 12, and 15 to 17), their specification differs from modern counterparts. Overall there is a relative abundance of occupational variables at the expense of demographic and housing measures. The results therefore will not be directly comparable with those from other applications. The size of areal units also differs in this study. There were only ten enumeration districts in the town in 1851 and they were even less homogeneous than those of today. Smaller units had therefore to be used; although in many ways this is an advantage, different results from studies using different areal units may be attributable to the change of scale.

TABLE IV

Summary of results of the principal components analysis

Component	1	2	3	4	5	6	7	8
Eigenvalue	4·93	2·99	2·67	1·78	1·68	1·23	1·03	0·82
Percentage explanation	23·5	14·2	12·7	8·5	8·0	5·8	4·9	3·9
Cumulative explanation	23·5	37·7	50·4	58·9	66·8	72·7	77·6	81·5

Despite the fact that the variables were weakly correlated with each other, only two pairs, scholars and servants (0·958), and social class III and social classes IV and V (−0·912) had coefficients greater than 0·7; the analysis was successful in summarizing much of the total variance into a few components. In general, as may be seen by reference to Table III, the components reveal the lack of independence of status, occupational, demographic and ethnic variables, and show that the last—the distribution of Irish born—was of only minor significance in determining the components' compositions. Component 1 accounted for more than one-fifth of the variance, and the first three for more than one-half. Seven components had eigenvalues greater than one.

The first component is undoubtedly a measure of socio-economic status, specifically referring to the presence or absence of social classes I and II in contrast to the absence or presence of numerous hand-loom weavers. This is made clear when the five original variables making the strongest contributions to component 1 are identified. This has been done in Figure 3 which, by representing all the correlation bonds between the original variables with a modulus greater than 0·5, demonstrates the polarization between the areas of the highest social groups with high proportions of scholars and servants, and the areas of high proportions of economically active and of weavers. Bearing in mind the economic development of the town during the generation prior to 1851, the component can be associated with a traditional division among its population, established before the factory system and the widespread application of mechanical power by early 'domestic' industrialization.

Component 2 has a more complex and less easily interpreted composition. Its strongest associations are with the proportion of the population under 15 years old, the ratio of children to females, and with agricultural workers, all of which have positive loadings greater than 0·6; and with the average rateable value of residential units, the proportion of the population over 60 years old, and the percentage born in Chorley, each with inverse loadings stronger than −0·49. It is, therefore, predominantly a demographic measure which scales each small area of Chorley according to the youthfulness or age of its population. Although agricultural workers formed only 4·9 per cent of the town's active population, they are associated with areas scoring highly on component 2.

The third principal component has a clearer structure, and is another measure of social class, being built around the strongest individual correlation between the original variables (Fig. 3). In order of importance, the four strongest variables contributing to the component are: social classes IV and V, social class III which has an inverse association, cotton spinners and the percentage of the population born in Ireland. It therefore separates those areas with concentrations of the unskilled occupations, commonly associated with cotton-spinning factories and with concentrations of the Irish born, from those areas with

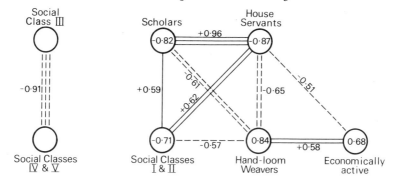

FIGURE 3. Correlations among the 1851 variables of over +0·5 or under −0·5. The numbers in the circles refer to the loadings of the variables on component one.

a more highly skilled working population, occupied very probably in more traditional crafts and industries. Although full details of the loadings on the first five components are given in Table III, no attempt has been made to interpret the structure of the third and subsequent components because they are not strongly related to any of the original variables.

The analysis has demonstrated that, by 1851, individual occupations were not the most important determinants of residential differentiation. Instead, generalized groupings of occupations on the basis of status and skill had become pre-eminent, although they were still not entirely divorced from individual occupations and industries. In this respect, the Chorley evidence adds weight to the claim that only in the most modernized societies are the socio-economic, familism, and ethnic components independent. Such a conclusion from the evidence is indisputable but negative and potentially less valuable than a hypothesis from a more liberal interpretation; that a significant change in the nineteenth century was the declining importance of occupation in determining, or at least indicating, demographic patterns and residential location. In Chorley, this process was in part a result of the increasing variety of occupations, as new factory trades were superimposed on a well-established pattern of domestic crafts, commerce and agriculture. These new employment opportunities were inevitably accentuating the divorce of homes from workplaces and thereby creating the conditions in which other factors could influence decisions about residential location. This change was therefore an important aspect of the 'modernization' process, and the creation of large-scale employing units a necessary, if not sufficient, condition for the emergence of residential areas distinguished by their concentration of status groups or population cohorts.

Spatial patterns

As already shown, occupation was the only effective influence on residential location in Chorley in the early nineteenth century and before. Comments about the locations of occupational or status groups at that time must therefore be based on understanding the locational requirements of the relevant economic activities. In Chorley, as in most towns, this would require careful inspection of the distributions of cultivable land, mineral resources, stream power, transport facilities and accessibility. Realistic generalizations about these distributions and therefore about residential distribution in the emerging industrial town are difficult to make, but even the few that follow are more helpful to understanding

TABLE V
Residential structure of the emerging industrial city

	Centre	Adjacent to centre	Intermediate	Periphery
Lower floors	Professional classes Shop and inn keepers	Non-landed gentry Town houses in larger towns and cities	Unskilled and semi-skilled workers in domestic or non-domestic employment. Mobile population, with recent immigrants. Typical employers: workshops factories, foundries, gasworks, rope works and timber yards	Landed nobility and gentry Smallholders, domestic manufacturers
	Consumer-goods manufacturers, e.g. bakers, tailors, cordwainers			Workers at water-powered factories Mineral workers, e.g. brickmakers, miners, quarrymen
Upper floors, cellars, yards, back premises	House, shop and office servants	House servants		House servants
Institutions	Religious and educational establishments	Religious and educational establishments	Old and destitute in workhouse and almshouses	

TABLE VI

*Product-moment correlation coefficients between the
variables and distance from the Market Place*

Three highest

7	Retailing workers	−0·50
5	Agricultural workers	0·41
18	Born in Ireland	−0·36

Others

21	Children:women ratio	0·07
20	Women in the labour force	0·07
17	Social class I and II	0·01
16	Social class III	0·05
19	Social class IV and V	−0·06

the subject than an exclusive pre-occupation with the distribution of the upper classes. The landed nobility and gentry established their fortunes by agriculture and commonly added to them in the eighteenth century by exploiting their mineral resources. Except in the larger towns of political, religious, mercantile or social significance where they established their town houses, they lived on their land outside the towns. Lesser non-landed gentry, including professional people, lived near the centre of towns along with shop-keepers and workers, publicans, and small manufacturers of consumer goods, all attracted by the point of most profitable exchange. Smallholders, who formed a large proportion of domestic manufacturers, were necessarily more predominant on the less built-up periphery of the town, as would be those groups working the mineral resources of the area, such as miners and brick-makers. Water-powered factories, and their workers, were also scattered because of the limited number of suitable stream-side sites, but when powered by steam they were attracted to the source of fuel, whether mine or, more often, transport terminal. They were therefore more clustered and often nearer to the centre of the urban area. These generalizations agree with those made by a contemporary geographer, J. G. Kohl (1841; see Berry and Rees, 1969) who, justifiably emphasizing the vertical distribution of social classes, recognized 'arches' of homogeneous social structure through the town. Both sets of observations are summarized in Table V.

It is clear from this summary that the changing structure of employment characteristic of the early nineteenth century resulted in a changed distribution of settlement. As domestic manufacturing and water power declined in relative importance and were replaced by ever-larger employment units and steam power, so growth at the centre, and the extent of the continuously built-up area, were bound to increase. This was one factor in encouraging the relatively fortunate to dissociate their homes from their work and therefore to introduce social class as a new criterion of residential location.

This had happened in Chorley by 1851, but only in a small way, and had not yet created a new spatial order in the residential pattern. The chaotic shape of the built-up area (Fig. 2) reflects the transitional state of the town, in which new single-class residential streets were being added to the earlier clusters of houses about centres of employment. The shape is so convuluted and disjointed to make an analysis by zones and sectors impossible, but the possibility of there having been an ordered relationship between the variables

TABLE VII

Summary of results of one-way analysis of variance by zones

| | Zones | | | | | | |
	1	*2*	*3*	*4*	*5*	*6*	*F ratio*
Number of areas	11	9	9	11	9	9	—
Population	1895	1760	3218	2018	1953	1243	—
Mean distance from market place (km)	0·18	0·36	0·51	0·70	1·05	1·63	—
Zone means of variables							
Social class I & II %	7·3	1·7	3·7	5·9	6·6	7·6	1·39
Social class III %	52·3	49·1	44·1	63·2	47·5	49·1	1·98
Social class IV & V %	40·2	49·1	50·9	30·8	45·8	43·8	3·05[1]
Women in labour force	22·3	20·8	17·7	20·6	21·0	25·3	1·74
Children:women	1·54	1·79	1·55	1·67	1·61	1·63	0·49
Irish born %	7·5	15·6	13·1	12·2	11·7	7·3	2·70[1]
Zone means of components							
First	−0·71	−0·34	−0·03	0·54	0·78	−0·24	2·24
Second	−0·79	−0·20	−0·50	0·12	0·37	0·76	3·99[2]
Third	−0·13	0·50	0·77	−0·55	1·02	−0·55	3·28[1]

Notes: Degrees of freedom: between zones, 5; within zones, 52

1. Significantly different from H_0 at $P = 0·05$
2. Significantly different from H_0 at $P = 0·01$

and distance from the centre of the town was investigated. This was done first by calculating simple correlation coefficients, some of which are reproduced in Table VI.

Table VI shows that the two highest but nevertheless unimpressive correlations are with occupations that have an obvious zonal variation, and that neither of the familism variables nor any of the measures of social class had a simple linear relationship with distance from the centre. In order to determine whether there were other 'wave' relationships, geometrically irregular zones were defined by ranking the fifty-eight areas in order of distance from the centre and separating them into sextiles, and an analysis of the variance between and within zones was carried out. The results are given in Table VII.

None of the variance ratios of the variables is significant at the 1 per cent level, and only those of the distribution of social classes IV and V and of the Irish born are significant at the 5 per cent level. The zone means of the variables reveal that the innermost and outermost zones have the highest proportions in social classes I and II. The proportion drops sharply from the centre to a minimum in the second area but then rises steadily until the sixth zone. It can also be seen that there are similarities between the distributions of social classes IV and V and the Irish born. Both had relatively low densities in the innermost and outermost zones and relatively high densities in the zones adjacent to the centre. The distribution of the percentage of Irish born had a particularly regular and positively skewed distribution away from the centre of the town.

As far as can be ascertained from this analysis and from visual inspection of the distributions, the answer to the first question posed on page 171 is therefore that socioeconomic status, family status and ethnicity were distributed fairly evenly through the town. Marked variations in these characteristics were extremely local—at the scale of the street or part of a street, and there was in 1851 little sign of distinctive status, demographic

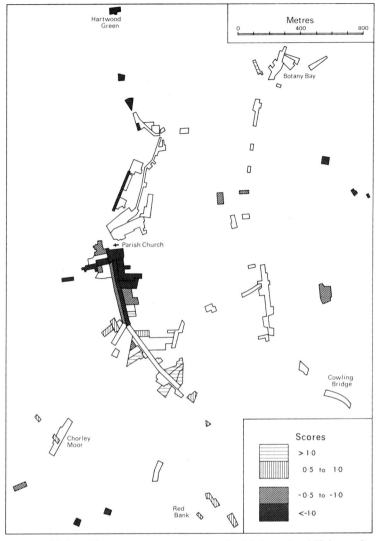

FIGURE 4. High and low scores on component one (social classes I and II, inverted)

or immigrant areas having been created. The exceptions to this generalization are that the central area was distinguished by relatively high numbers of the upper three status groups and an unusually low density of the unskilled and the Irish born. To a lesser extent, the areas adjacent to the centre were distinguished by the inverse of the central area's characteristics.

In order to answer the second question raised on page 171, the districts with high positive and negative scores on the first three components have been mapped on Figures 4–6. As expected from the distribution of the highest social classes, low scores on component 1 were heavily concentrated in the central area and are also found occasionally around the periphery of the township. Fewer districts had unusually high scores, but these tend to be

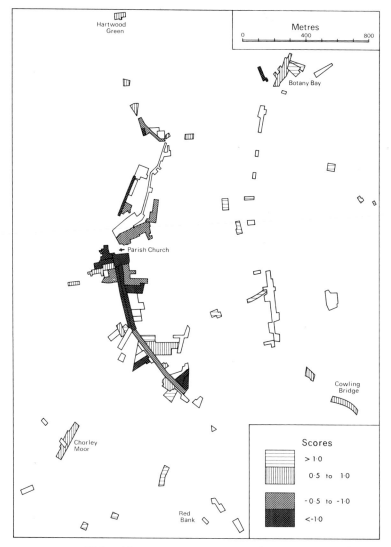

FIGURE 5. High and low scores on component two (young age structure)

concentrated in the southern half of the central nucleus, where there were many hand-loom weavers.

The distribution of scores on component 2 (Fig. 5) was more complex, with high and low scores in juxtaposition. Although only one district outside the central nucleus had a score of under −0·5, within that area both high- and low-status districts had both high and low scores. In other words, an elderly population was found in some commercial streets, some weavers' districts, as well as in most of the highest-status residential districts. This diversity is not surprising in view of the fact that a high average age could be the result of one or more of the following: unusually low fertility or unusual longevity, immigration of single adult workers, including servants and apprentices, and a concentration of people

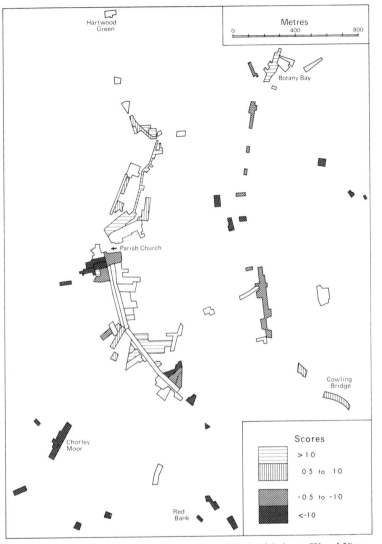

FIGURE 6. High and low scores on component three (social classes IV and V)

working in a declining industry, such as domestic weaving. Whatever the significant process in each case, Figure 5 provides no evidence of any overall spatial sorting of component 2 scores, or therefore of the town's population by age.

The distribution of component 3 scores shown on Figure 6 highlights the component's item structure. The highest scores are found close to the largest cotton factories, in Water, Preston and Standish Streets, and at Cowling Bridge. The lowest scores are found in all other parts of the town except the commercial core. They include the southern coal-mining districts, but elsewhere are clearly associated with weaving districts.

It is apparent from the maps of the component scores that only the distribution of the first 'high socio-economic status' component forms any neat geometrical pattern which

N*

might be related to simple models of urban structure. Component 2 scores have a seemingly haphazard distribution, while the scores on the third component are clearly influenced by idiographic features of the town and, in particular, by the location of cotton-factory employment. The common element in the three distributions is once again the proximity of homes and workplaces. This evidence therefore adds weight to the claim that, even though individual occupations were declining in importance as determinants of residential location by 1851, their role was still strong and pervasive.

CONCLUSIONS

All the evidence reported in this paper suggests strongly that hypotheses about 'pre-industrial' cities cannot be simply transferred to early nineteenth-century cities in western society. The fact that in certain cities, 'the traditional élite are found close to the centre of the city in locations which help to minimise the effort of getting about the city' (Mabogunje, 1968) has its counterpart in Chorley and possibly in other emerging industrial towns, in that the higher socio-economic groups live in the central areas for one simple reason, namely, to live close to their employment. This follows from the low degree of spatial mobility characteristic of all cities prior to the advent of modern transport. By no means all cities in the nineteenth century had the strong religious or governmental functions that sustained the élite in the feudal city, but most had several growing industrial functions, each with its own characteristic locations.

The evidence also makes it clear that the role of changing spatial mobility in transforming the residential structure of towns should not be overemphasized. At least as important in Chorley was the changing organization and scale of employment during the first half of the nineteenth century. As the prevalence of domestic occupations ended and the size and range of other employing units increased, adjustments to the residential structure of the town were taking place. These adjustments owed nothing to improvements in internal mobility. A more intensive study of the relationships between residence and workplace might therefore improve our understanding of western cities in the past. J. E. Vance (1960, 1966, 1967 and 1971) has already shown the value of this approach; it is the empirical studies that are missing.

Present knowledge about evolving urban structures, as this study has demonstrated, consists of as many tentative hypotheses as well-founded axioms. While we have improved our understanding of the modern city, and owe to Sjoberg detailed knowledge about some aspects of the medieval city, the suggestion of a continuous evolution from one to the other is too simple. It has been based on insufficient evidence about the spatial patterns and the processes that create them in urban areas at different dates and in different geographical environments. Although it will be particularly difficult to identify processes in the past, and in many instances there will be little option but to undertake the hazardous procedure of making inferences from spatial patterns, only when this is done will it be possible to define clearly and to calibrate the scales of change associated with evolving urban structures.

This paper has attempted to identify the dominant factors of residential location and the dominant residential patterns in one town in the early nineteenth century, and to isolate the factors and patterns particular to this town. The remaining features, thought likely to be generally characteristic of British towns in the early nineteenth century, have been incorporated in a simple model of the residential structure of an emerging industrial town. Although social class divisions do appear in the model, the greatest weight is placed on the characteristic locations within the urban area of different types of occupation. On this basis it is argued that a profitable line of inquiry in historical urban and social geography would be to establish the changing relationship between workplace and residence.

ACKNOWLEDGEMENTS

The author thanks Mr R. Oliver who drew the illustrations to this paper, and the University of Salford for making a grant towards the cost of the illustrations. The Editor of the *Transactions of the Historical Society of Lancashire and Cheshire* has kindly given permission for Figures 1 and 2 to be reproduced in modified form from illustrations appearing in volume 122 (1970) of that Journal.

NOTE

1. Full details of the modifications to Armstrong's scheme, and a lengthier discussion of the problems of classifying nineteenth-century occupations, appear in Appendix 1 and Chapter 9 of Warnes (1969).

REFERENCES

ABU-LUGHOD, J. (1969) 'Testing the theory of social area analysis: the ecology of Cairo, Egypt', *Am. sociol. Rev.* 34, 198–212

ARMSTRONG, W. A. (1969) 'Social structure from the early census returns' in E. A. WRIGLEY (ed.) *An introduction to historical demography*, 209–234

ARMSTRONG, W. A. (1967) 'The social structure of York, 1841–51: an essay in quantitative history', unpubl. Ph.D. thesis, Univ. of Nottingham

ARMSTRONG, W. A. (1968a) 'The interpretation of the census enumerators books for Victorian towns' in H. J. DYOS (ed.), *The study of urban history*, 67–86.

ARMSTRONG, W. A. (1968b) 'Rejoinder', *Econ. Hist. Rev.* (2nd ser.) 21, 609

BERESFORD, M. (1963) 'The unprinted census returns of 1841, 1851 and 1861 for England and Wales', *Amateur Hist.* 5, 260–7

BERRY, B. J. L. (1965) 'The internal structure of the city', *Law Contemp. Probls* 30, 111–19

BERRY, B. J. L. and P. H. REES (1969) 'The factorial ecology of Calcutta', *Am. J. Sociol.* 74, 447–91

BOAL, F. W. (1968) 'Technology and urban form', *J. Geogr.* 67, 229–36

BOOTH, C. (1886) 'Occupations of the people of the United Kingdom, 1801–81', *J. R. statist. Soc.* 49, 314–435

CARTER, H. (1972) *The study of urban geography*, 257–87

CHORLEY PUBLIC LIBRARY, *Chorley town's book, 1781–1818*, MS copy, n.d.

DYOS, H. J. and A. B. M. BAKER (1968) 'The possibilities of computerising census data' in H. J. DYOS (ed.) *The study of urban history*, 87–112

EGELAND, J. A. and T. R. ANDERSON (1961) 'Spatial aspects of social area analysis', *Am. sociol. Rev.* 26, 392–8

FLOUD, R. C. and R. S. SCHOFIELD (1968) 'Social structure from the early census returns', *Econ. Hist. Rev.* (2nd ser.) 21, 607–9

GOHEEN, P. G. (1970) 'Victorian Toronto, 1850 to 1900: pattern and process of growth', Univ. of Chicago, Dept. of Geogr. Res. Pap. No. 127

HERBERT, D. T. (1968) 'Principal components analysis and British studies of urban-social structure', *Prof. Geogr.* 20, 280–3

HERBERT, D. T. (1970) 'Principal components analysis and urban social structure: a study of Cardiff and Swansea' in H. CARTER and W. K. D. DAVIES (eds.) *Urban essays: studies in the geography of Wales*, 79–100

JONES, F. L. (1968) 'Social area analysis: some theoretical and methodological comments illustrated with Australian data', *Br. J. Sociol.* 19, 424–44

LAWTON, R. (1955) 'The population of Liverpool in the mid-nineteenth century', *Trans. Lancs. Ches. hist. Soc.* 107, 89-120.

MABOGUNJE, A. L. (1968) *Urbanisation in Nigeria*

MURDIE, R. A. (1969) 'Factorial ecology of metropolitan Toronto, 1951–1961: an essay on the social geography of the city' Univ. of Chicago, Dept. of Geogr. Res. Pap. No. 116

REES, P. H. (1968) 'The factorial ecology of metropolitan Chicago', unpubl. M.S. thesis, Univ. of Chicago (adapted and reprinted in B. J. L. BERRY and F. E. HORTON (eds.) (1970) *Geographic perspectives on urban systems*)

ROBSON, B. T. (1968) 'New techniques in urban analysis' in H. CARTER *et al.* (eds.) *Geography at Aberystwyth*, 235–52

ROBSON, B. T. (1969) *Urban analysis: a study of city structure with special reference to Sunderland*

ROGERSON, T. (1818) *Lancashire General Directory* (Manchester)

SHEVKY, E. and W. BELL (1955) *Social area analysis: theory, illustrative application and computational procedures* (Stanford)

SHEVKY, E. and M. WILLIAMS (1949) *The social areas of Los Angeles* (Berkeley)

SJOBERG, G. (1960) *The pre-industrial city: past and present*

TAYLOR, A. J. (1951) 'The taking of the census: 1801–1951' *Br. medic. J.* 4709 (7 April), 715–20

TIMMS, D. W. G. (1970) 'Comparative factorial ecology: some New Zealand examples', *Environment Plann.* 2, 455–67

TIMMS, D. W. G. (1971) *The urban mosaic: towards a theory of residential differentiation*

VANCE, J. E. (1960) 'Labour-shed, employment field and dynamic analysis in urban geography', *Econ. Geogr.* 36, 189–220

VANCE, J. E. (1966) 'Housing the worker: the employment linkage as a force in urban structure', *Econ. Geogr.* 42, 294–325

VANCE, J. E. (1967) 'Housing the worker: determinative and contingent ties in nineteenth century Birmingham', *Econ. Geogr.* 43, 95–127

VANCE, J. E. (1971) 'Land assignment in the pre-capitalist, capitalist and post-capitalist city', *Econ. Geogr.* 47, 101–20

WARNES, A. M. (1969) 'The increase of journey to work and its consequences for the residential structure of towns', unpubl. Ph.D. thesis, Univ. of Salford

WARNES, A. M. (1970) 'Early separation of homes from workplaces and the urban structure of Chorley', *Trans. Lancs. Ches. hist. Soc.* 122, 105–35

WIRTH, L. (1938) 'Urbanism as a way of life', *Am. J. Sociol.* 44, 1–24

RÉSUMÉ. *L'habitat dans une nouvelle ville industrielle.* Cette étude prend comme point de départ, des axiomes courants sur les structures de l'habitat et le manque de progrès dans la connaissance du mode d'évolution de ces structures. En utilisant deux points de comparaison pour Chorley, dans le Lancashire au début du dix-neuvième siècle, il apparait que l'en peut remédier à ce défaut. Les sources utilisées viennent d'un inventaire de la ville par le comité paroissial en 1816 et des livres tenus par les enquêteurs du recensement de 1851. On découvre que dans les premières décennies du siècle, le facteur qui déterminait le lieu de résidence était le lieu de travail; le rang socio-économique ne se révélait dans l'habitat qu'en fonction des différents lieux de travail. Pourtant vers 1851, le facteur socio-économique était clairement mis en évidence, bien qu'il ne fut pas entièrement indépendant de l'emploi. La répartition des classes sociales ne relevait d'aucun mode connu. On en conclut que le rapport entre résidence et lieu de travail est un facteur déterminant de la structure de l'habitat. Le rapport se modifie tandis que l'organisation industrielle change, que la dimension des sociétés d'emploi varie, ainsi qu'en fonction des heures de travail, du niveau de vie, de la cohésion de la famille et de la technologie des transports. Les urbanistes devraient tires profit du travail considérable fourni dans ce domaine par les spécialistes de l'histoire économique et sociable pour améliorer les modes d'évolution de l'habitat dans les zones urbaines.

FIG. 1. Secteurs délimités par le «Relevé du Conseil Paroissial» de 1816 et l'indice de prosperité moyen

FIG. 2. L'agglomération de Chorley en 1851. *Sources:* Service topographique 1ere édition 1/10 560, établie entre 1844 et 1847, modifiée selon les détails contenus dans les livres des agents recenseurs en 1851. La carte porte les noms des lieux-dits et des rues mentionnés dans le texte. *Médaillon:* situation de Chorley

FIG. 3. Corrélations entre les variables de 1851 supérieurs à +0,5 et inferieurs à −0,5. Les nombres à l'intérieur des cercles se rapportent aux contenus des variables de la composante 1.

FIG. 4. Taux maximum et minimum de la composante 1 (classes sociales I et II, inversées)

FIG. 5. Taux maximum et minimum de la composante 2 (structure de la population jeune)

FIG. 6. Taux maximum et minimum de la composante 3 (classes sociales IV et V)

ZUSAMMENFASSUNG. *Wohnmodelle in einer allmählich entstehenden Industriestadt.* Ausgangspunkt dieses Referats sind die allgemein bekannten Grundsätze über Wohn- und Raumstrukturen und der mangelnde Fortschritt in Richtung eines evolutionären Modells dieser Strukturen. Anhand zweier verschiedener Datenquellen für die Stadt Chorley in Lancashire Anfang des 19. Jahrhunderts wird bewiesen, dass diese Lücke gefüllt werden kann. Bei den Quellen handelt es sich um den Bericht des Kirchengemeindevorstands der Stadt aus dem Jahre 1816 und die Bücher der Zählhelfer der Volkszählung von 1851. Dabei wird deutlich, dass in den ersten Jahrzehnten des 19. Jahrhunderts der Standort des Arbeitsplatzes bei der Wohnortwahl fast ausschliesslich entscheidend war; sozio-ökonomischer Status drückte sich nur dann in der Wohnstruktur aus, wenn es parallel dazu Unterschiede beim Standort des Arbeitsplatzes gab. 1851 kann man jedoch eindeutig eine neue Komponente, die des sozio-ökonomischen Status erkennen, obwohl auch hier Berufsstrukturen nicht völlig ausser Acht gelassen werden können. Die Verteilung der sozialen Schichten entsprach keinem bestehenden Modell. Daraus folgt, dass die Beziehung zwischen Wohnort und Arbeitsplatz eine entscheidende Determinante bei der Wohn- und Raumstruktur ist. Diese Beziehung wandelt sich mit den veränderten Bedingungen in der Industrie: Grösse der Arbeitseinheiten, Arbeitszeit, Wohlstand Zusammenhalt der Familie und Verkehrstechnologie. Stadtgeographen sollten sich auf die beachtliche Vorarbeit auf diesem Gebiet durch historische Untersuchungen wirtschaftlicher und soziologischer Probleme dieser Art stützen und anhand dieser Erkenntnisse verbesserte Modelle über die Evolution von Wohngebieten innerhalb von Stadtgebieten entwickeln.

ABB. 1. Bezirke des Vestry C.S. (Vermessung des Vestrykomittees) von 1816 und den Durchschnittswerten des Wohlstands

ABB. 2. Die verbaute Fläche von Chorley, 1951. *Quellen*: O.S. (Amtliche Landvermessung) 1. Ausgabe, 1:10 560. Vermessen 1844–47, abgeändert nach Angaben der Volks: zählungsbücher von 1851. Die Landkarte zeigt die Platz- und Strassennamen, die im Text erwähnt werden. *Kleines Bild*: die Lage von Chorley

ABB. 3. Wechselbeziehungen zwischen den Abweichungen von 1851 von über +0,5 oder unter −0,5. Die Zahlen in den Kreisen beziehen sich auf die Stärke der Abweichungen der ersten Komponente.

ABB. 4. Hohe und niedere Werte der ersten Komponente (Stand I und II, umgekehrt)

ABB. 5. Hohe und niedere Werte der zweiten Komponente (niedere Altersstruktur)

ABB. 6. Hohe und niedere Werte der dritten Komponente (Stand IV und V)

The Institute of British Geographers

Details of Membership are available from the Administrative Assistant, Institute of British Geographers, 1 Kensington Gore, London, SW7 2AR (tel. 01-584 6371).

Papers or monographs intended for publication must be sent in the first place to the Hon. Editor, Dr R. J. Price, Department of Geography, Glasgow University, Glasgow, G12 8QQ. Papers for reading at the Annual Conference (even if they are subsequently to be considered for publication) should, however, be sent to the Hon. Secretary, Professor R. Lawton, Department of Geography, University of Liverpool.

Requests for copies of publications should be made to the Administrative Assistant, who also has available 'Notes for the guidance of authors submitting papers for publication by the Institute.'

Publications in Print

These publications may be obtained from any bookseller at the prices quoted above. Members of the Institute may buy copies at two-thirds of these prices. Application for these should be made to the Administrative Assistant, Institute of British Geographers, 1 Kensington Gore, London, SW7 2AR.